AMERICAN INDIANS' KITCHEN-TABLE STORIES

AMERICAN INDIANS' KITCHEN-TABLE STORIES

CONTEMPORARY CONVERSATIONS WITH
CHEROKEE, SIOUX, HOPI, OSAGE, NAVAJO,
ZUNI, AND MEMBERS OF OTHER NATIONS

KEITH CUNNINGHAM

AMERICAN
FOLKLORE
SERIES

This volume is a part of
THE AMERICAN FOLKLORE SERIES
W.K. McNeil, *General Editor*

August House Publishers, Inc.
L I T T L E   R O C K

Published by August House, Inc.,
P.O. Box 3223, Little Rock, Arkansas, 72203,
501–372–5450.

Printed in the United States of America

10 9 8 7 6 5 4 3 2 1

LIBRARY OF CONGRESS CATALOGING-IN-PUBLICATION DATA

Cunningham, Keith, 1939–
American Indians' kitchen-table stories : contemporary conversations with Cherokee,
Sioux, Hopi, Osage, Navajo, Zuni, and members of other nations / Keith Cunningham.
— 1st ed.
p.   cm. — (The American Folklore Series)
Includes bibliographical references and indexes.
ISBN 0–87483–203–9 (hb : acid-free) : $25.95
ISBN 0–87483–202–0 (pb : acid-free) : $14.95
1. Indians of North America—Southwest, New—Folklore. 2. Indians of North
America—Southwest, New—Interviews. 3. Indians of North America—Southwest,
New—Social life and customs. I. Title. II. Series
E78.S7C84   1992
398.2'08997079—dc20   92-5266

First Edition, 1992

This volume is a part of the American Folklore Series
Series Editor: W.K. McNeil
Design director: Ted Parkhurst
Cover design: Harvill–Ross Studios, Inc.
Cover illustration: Kitty Harvill
Typography: Lettergraphics / Little Rock

This book is printed on archival-quality paper which meets the
guidelines for performance and durability of the Committee on
Production Guidelines for Book Longevity of the
Council on Library Resources.

AUGUST HOUSE, INC.   PUBLISHERS   LITTLE ROCK

*To Kuiceyetsa, to Clyde, to Helen, to Max,
to all the other American Indians who have shared
their stories, lives, and cultures with me.*

Acknowledgments

Portions of the basic fieldwork reported in this book were partially funded by the United States Department of Education, National Institute on Disability and Rehabilitation Research; American Indian Rehabilitation Research and Training Center; the Northern Arizona University Organized Research Committee; and the Center for Colorado Plateau Studies. Some of the ideas, stories, sentences, and paragraphs included in this book were first presented in papers at English or American folklore, popular culture, or literature conventions and published in article form in *AFFword, Folklore, Northwest Folklore, Southwest Folklore, Western Folklore,* and *The World and I* or as chapters in *Monsters with Iron Teeth: Perspectives on Contemporary Legend,* edited by Paul Smith and Gillian Bennett, Sheffield Academic Press, 1988; *The Questing Beast: Perspectives on Contemporary Legend,* edited by Paul Smith and Gillian Bennett, Sheffield Academic Press, 1989; and *Spoken in Jest,* edited by Gillian Bennett, Sheffield Academic Press, 1991.

I wish to thank the funding agencies for their support; my colleagues for their comments, questions, and suggestions; August House Publishers Ted and Liz Parkhurst and general editor of the August House American Folklore Series Bill McNeil for their assistance; and the various book and journal publishers and editors for allowing these fragments to become a whole. As always, I am particularly indebted to Kathy for her unequaled fieldwork and editing.

Keith Cunningham
NORTHERN ARIZONA UNIVERSITY
FLAGSTAFF, ARIZONA

Contents

An accumulation of minute details, however silly it may appear, is the only correct means to reach fundamental truths.
—LETTER OF A. F. BANDELIER TO L. H. MORGAN
February 28, 1874

Introduction

FOR ALMOST FIVE HUNDRED YEARS the traditional narratives of American Indians have been of interest to outsiders. Indeed, the first book on the subject, *On the Antiquities of the Indians* (1496), appeared just four years after Columbus's first voyage to the New World. Friar Ramon Pane, the work's author, came on Columbus's second trip to America in 1493 for the purpose of gathering all the data he could from natives concerning "their ceremonies and their antiquities."[1] His subsequent volume consisted of material collected over a two-year period from the Taino, a now long-extinct tribe living in what today is Haiti. A variety of legends and myths, as well as non-narrative materials like customs and beliefs, are presented in twenty-six brief chapters in which Pane carefully emphasizes that the Indian is quaint, curious, exotic, inferior, and—most important from his viewpoint—in great need of conversion to Christianity and thus, by implication, to civilization. For Pane, and those who followed him in recording American Indian folklore, the collecting of such material was important because it provided significant insights into the mental makeup of the natives who were the most unusual people the European-Americans had encountered.

During the first few centuries after Pane's book appeared, the collecting of American Indian narratives was concentrated in the Northeast and the Southeast, most of the work being done by travelers, traders, and soldiers. Although many items were recorded during the years prior to the American Revolution, it would be inaccurate to characterize the collecting done as intensive. The most noteworthy effort prior to the nineteenth century, John Adair's *The History of the American Indian* (1775), was based on material collected mainly from Southeastern tribes. Dealing, as the title suggests, with more than just narratives, this book was the first work by an American using Indian traditions to advance a theoretical viewpoint. Adair's thesis, not original with him, maintained that the Indians had descended from the Ten Lost Tribes of Israel, and he utilized various types of traditions to advance his position.[2]

Gradually the attention to narrative traditions among the Northeastern and Southeastern tribes began to wane, and collectors started looking elsewhere for such materials. One of the main reasons for this shift was that several of the tribes in both regions disappeared early in the era of European contact, or were so altered that by the time outsiders became interested in recording their traditional narratives there were few people left who could provide the information. But in the Southwest, many outsiders found the situation exactly the opposite, and it became an ideal place to record Indian myths, legends, and folktales.[3] During the late nineteenth century much of the substantive work on American Indian lore, not only in the Southwest but throughout the United States, was carried out under the auspices of the Bureau of American Ethnology.

Established in 1879 under the leadership of John Wesley Powell (1834-1902), the new bureau was intended by Congress mainly as a department to carry on research already begun. But Powell wanted the agency to be something more—the focal point for all American Indian studies. Toward this purpose he implemented a research program including detailed bibliographic compilations; new field studies and questionnaires; and new publications, in the form of *Annual Reports* and *Bulletins*, with material from these studies. The *Annual Reports* were initiated in 1881 and the *Bulletins* in 1887, and from 1881 to 1893 there was also a series titled *Contributions to North American Ethnology*. Although other matters than folklore were embraced in these works, a sizeable number of volumes were devoted to oral traditions, in particular myths. There was good reason for the emphasis on myths, for Powell himself considered it essential to record this aspect of American Indian tradition. Like many intellectuals of the day, he was enthralled with evolutionary ideas and thought society passed through various levels on its way to the highest stage of culture. In his view myth was merely a mistaken but necessary first step in the evolution of science. It was the philosophy of the lowest stages of undeveloped human culture. As an attempt to explain the mysteries of the universe, it was embryonic science, a level of error-filled childhood through which the mature adult—science—had to pass. Thus, myths were significant because they offered insights into the development of science.

The first planned series, and the one containing the most narratives, was the *Annual Reports*. Although later they became merely unread, and virtually unreadable, accounts of administrative accomplishments,[4] under Powell's leadership, and that of his immediate successors,[5] they were hefty tomes containing not only the director's report but also accompanying essays by staff members and collaborators on all topics falling within the scope of ethnology as interpreted by the Bureau. These publications became very popular with scholars, so much so that in 1882 the secretary of the Smithsonian Institution wrote Powell, "We are continually receiving applications for copies of the report of your Bureau."[6] Yet, important as these books are for anyone interested in Southwestern Indian culture, they are relatively silent on *folk narratives* from the region. Indeed, only three publications mainly devoted to the topic appeared in the *Annual Reports* and only one in the *Bulletins*. Of these four the earliest was by a man who was the most colorful personality associated with the Bureau in the nineteenth century.

Frank Hamilton Cushing (1857-1900) spent his entire life in fragile health. This native of Pennsylvania weighed only one and a half pounds at birth and received delicate treatment as he grew. His physical weakness prevented him from participating in the usual activities of young boys, and his cloistered life made him a loner. Unable to attend school, he designed his own education from his surroundings; roaming freely over his father's farm and the nearby woods and fields, he soon acquired a reputation for being "odd" because he talked to the trees and animals around him. He also collected a large cache of arrowheads and Indian artifacts that he stored in a wigwam he built on an unused section of the family homestead. His fascination with things aboriginal began when he was only nine years old, and shortly thereafter he developed a number of other intellectual passions that he pursued wholeheartedly. As a result, by age eighteen he had acquired a broader-ranging education than many others of his generation who were conventionally trained.

In 1875 Cushing enrolled in a natural sciences course at Cornell University—the only formal schooling he ever received. A year later, he obtained his first regular job as an interpreter of American Indian handicrafts for the Centennial Exposition in Philadelphia. Prior to this time he had sent an article on the antiquities of Orleans County, New York, to Spencer F. Baird, secretary of the Smithsonian Institution. This essay appeared in the Smithsonian *Report* for 1874 and eventually led to Cushing's employment by the Bureau of Ethnology. Cushing came to Washington, D.C., right after his job in Philadelphia ended, and seems to have considered himself "of the Smithsonian Institution" immediately. Officially his association began in August of 1879 when he was appointed to the first Bureau of Ethnology fieldwork expedition—a party assigned to study Indian ruins in New Mexico and Arizona and to collect pottery, stone implements, and other artifacts. This was Cushing's introduction to Zuni culture (and indeed to the living Indian), but his previous history suggests that he was more than eager for this contact. Although he was never entirely able to overcome his feeling that white culture represented a higher level along the road to civilization than Indian culture, he was immediately taken with Zuni society, an infatuation that lasted for the remainder of his life. The Zuni were equally fascinated with *him*. They accepted Cushing into several fraternities and bestowed the sacred name "Medicine-flower," which is assigned to one person in a generation, on him. He also was made second chief of the tribe and lived with the family of the governor. In short, Cushing came as close as an outsider possibly could to understanding what it is like to be an Indian.

Cushing went beyond merely identifying with the tribesmen; he came to think of himself as a full-blown Indian, and many of his colleagues came to regard him as a "character." Stories of his eccentricities abounded, and it was expected that he would do things such as showing up for meetings dressed in full Zuni attire or interrupting with loud Indian war whoops. As is usually the case with "characters," the yarns about Cushing often were embellished, making him seem even "odder" than he was. But there is no denying that Cushing was vastly different from—and more colorful than—most other collectors of Southwestern Indian folklore. Even so, much of his reputation as a "character" resulted because he considered himself an Indian and wanted others to think the same thing. He believed he could do anything the Indians could do and could do it better, a conviction that often led him into predicaments.[7]

During his stay of several years with the Zuni, Cushing undoubtedly gathered a great deal of material. Unfortunately, very little of his data was ever written down. He may have had too many ideas to put them all on paper, or maybe he was just incapable of organizing his material, or he may have been too much a perfectionist about writing to ever produce a large number of publications. A fourth possibility is that he became so much a part of tribal life that he was no longer objective and developed second thoughts about divulging the esoteric lore of the tribe.

Whatever the reasons, Cushing published but three essays in the Bureau's *Annual Reports,* of which only "Outlines of Zuni Creation Myths" (1896) dealt with traditional narratives.[8] A few other works were published outside the Bureau, of which the posthumous *Zuni Folk Tales* (1901), with an introduction by John Wesley Powell, is the most important. This book contains an account of one of the first folklore field experiments. An unintentional exercise, it began in the summer of 1886 while Cushing and three Zuni friends were at Manchester-by-the-Sea, England, entertaining a crowd by relating folktales. When Cushing's turn came he presented a European tale, "The Cock and the Mouse."[9] Several months later, in a storytelling session at Zuni, one of the Zunis narrated a version of the European tale he first heard from Cushing in England. However, the story had been drastically altered to conform to Zuni narrative patterns. What was in Cushing's telling a relatively short story had become a lengthy yarn full of terminal explanatory motifs and the four symbolism characteristic of American Indian traditional tales. It had been transformed to conform with Zuni environment and thought, and therefore served as an excellent example of the Zuni folk narrative tradition. Although Cushing failed to realize it, the tale also served as an index of acculturation. Had the Zunis been more "Americanized," they would have been less likely to shape the tale to fit their own patterns.[10]

Although many contemporaries found Cushing "a bit odd," most also considered him brilliant. Thus, he was characterized as "a man of genius,"[11] "one of the greatest mythologists of this country,"[12] "a man of rare intuition,"[13] and as a man whose "greatest enemy is his genius."[14] Yet at the same time they praised him, many scholars were aware that Cushing's work had deficiencies. While no one could impart the flavor of the Zuni atmosphere so adroitly as Cushing, his interpretations of myths and folktales often seemed to reflect his own mentality rather than that of the Indians. More than forty years later, while doing research among the same tribe, Ruth Bunzel came to regard Cushing's versions of narratives as highly suspect, noting that the "endless poetical and metaphysical glossing of the basic elements" probably "originated in Cushing's own mind."[15] It *is* hard to take Cushing's work seriously when he offers lines such as this one, supposedly from the lips of Zunis: "But most of the young and handsome suitors who worried her with their importunities would depart forthwith, crestfallen, loving the girl as they did, forsooth, much less than they feared the warriors of Zuni—so degenerate they had become, for shame!"[16] The Zunis in Cushing's texts often talk in unrealistic ways reflecting anything but Indian ideals and modes of speech. Worst of all, the tribesmen he presents frequently seem to be speaking from a stage.

John Peabody Harrington (1884-1961), the second collector to provide an article primarily concerned with Southwestern Indian folk narratives for a Bureau publication, was the principal linguist associated with the organization during the first half of the twentieth century. At least one writer has said that his career is "nearly as remarkable for eccentricity as for its productivity,"[17] but it is safe to say that he lagged far behind Cushing where eccentricity was concerned. Still, Harrington was also a "character" who was memorable for many things besides his intelligence. It is said of him that he would start off on trips of thousands of miles without any money. On one occasion he took a bus home from deep in Mexico while having a railway ticket in his pocket.[18]

Yet no one, not even those who found him extremely odd, questioned Harrington's intelligence and abilities. He had such skill with languages that within a week he could learn a new tongue well enough to correct an informant's errors in his own language. Harrington was constantly taking notes, but he was too disorganized even to remember where he had stored reams of them at various points across the continent. After his death four hundred large boxes containing his scattered notes were compiled, but most remain uncatalogued. These materials—possibly the largest body of American Indian lore ever assembled by one person—are not always useful in revealing Harrington's methods of research. A very private man almost indifferent to the needs of scholars, he never identified informants by name, but instead used abbreviations that he made up himself or merely referred to them as "inf."

Like Cushing before him, Harrington produced relatively few publications, and his most important work appeared posthumously. Unlike Cushing, Harrington's posthumous books, *December's Child* (1975) and *The Eye of the Flute* (1977), are outside the scope of the present discussion. During his thirty-nine years with the Bureau of American Ethnology Harrington produced only three articles, of which only "Picuris Children's Stories" (1928) deals with traditional narratives. This paper contains twenty-one narratives and eleven song texts collected from a single informant, with free translations and background commentary included.

Ruth Bunzel, the third and last person to write an article for the *Annual Reports* on Southwestern Indian folk narratives, concentrated, as did Cushing, on the Zuni. Her major work, however, was in material culture, the classic *The Pueblo Potter: A Study of Creative Imagination in Primitive Art* (1929) being the publication for which she will be remembered. Bunzel's interest in the Zuni came about accidentally in 1924, when, serving as an editorial assistant and secretary to Franz Boas, she decided that she should know how a field anthropologist works. Ruth Benedict was planning a trip to Zuni that summer, and Bunzel first proposed to accompany her as stenographer and typist.

Boas, however, persuaded Bunzel to take on a research project of her own: the relationship of the artist to his work and culture. She spent time in 1924 and 1925 in Zuni and gathered the material for her pottery book, returning later to collect data on Zuni ceremonialism, ritual poetry, kachinas, and myths. Most of this information was utilized in the 47th *Annual Report* (1932), although she used much of the narrative material in *Zuni Texts* (1933), published by the American Ethnological Society. "Zuni Origin Myths," a sixty-four-page article published in the *Annual Report*, contains two texts dealing with the origins of Zuni cults and rituals. English translations are provided for both texts—interlinear and free translations for the first and just the free translation for the second. Bunzel provides a brief discussion of similar texts collected by Cushing and others, criticizing their translations in particular. Unfortunately, Bunzel says relatively little about her own translation practices. In her later *Zuni Texts* she includes fifteen myths and folk tales along with twenty-five "ethnological texts" (such as descriptions of customs) and lists her eight informants by name, sex, age, and degree of knowledge of English. This volume, however, is flawed because it contains no comparative or contextual information.

The only other work dealing mainly with Southwestern Indian folk narratives published by the Bureau of American Ethnology is Matthew W. Stirling's *Origin Myth of Acoma and Other Records* (1942), which appeared as Bulletin 135. Stirling was head of the Bureau from 1928 to 1957, longer than anyone else, and was also the only one of the seven men who headed the organization to remain a prolific author during his term in office. He produced more than eighty publications during his twenty-nine-year tenure, most dealing with topics other than folklore. His sole Bureau publication on Southwestern folk narratives (material coming from interviews with residents of Acoma and Santa Ana who were visiting Washington in 1928) includes several hero and creation myths, as well as miscellaneous notes on customs. Explanatory notes are given for the texts, which appear only in English.

While few scholars produced publications for the Bureau focusing mainly on Southwestern folk narratives, a number did contribute manuscripts that gave some attention to the topic. One of the most important figures in this regard was a very opinionated woman who was, along with Frank Cushing, a most highly regarded Zuni expert of the nineteenth century. Matilda Coxe Stevenson (1849-1915) became connected with the Bureau of Ethnology through her husband James Stevenson (1840-1888), a geologist hired in 1879 to locate archaeological remains in the Southwest. While accompanying him on this expedition, she developed a lifelong interest in the Indian and eventually did fieldwork that resulted in her two best-known publications, *The Sia* (1894) and *The Zuni Indians* (1904).

While Stevenson did come to know the Zuni very well, she failed to gain the admiration of the tribesmen that Frank Cushing enjoyed. She was an extremely determined woman who sometimes gained esoteric information through the use of overbearing force. Consequently, many of the Zuni that she worked among viewed her not as a friend but, rather, as a silly old woman and an object of scorn.[19] Her interests were wide-ranging, including material culture, folk art, ethnobotany, games, and mythology; but her main concerns were religious ritual and ceremonies. She emphasized the latter in *The Sia,* but also summarized people's mythology and offered four freely translated myths. In *The Zuni Indians*—a large work mainly devoted to songs, prayers, and ceremonies—she also included several myth texts and paraphrases.[20]

Jesse Walter Fewkes (1850-1930), the fourth director of the Bureau gained a place in the history of folklore studies for being one of the first fieldworkers, if not the first, to use commercial recording technology to collect traditional songs. In 1890 he visited Hopi villages in northeastern Arizona and recorded songs on sixteen wax cylinders. His main interests were in the seemingly disparate fields of Hopi ceremonials and archaeological ruins, but he found a way of demonstrating that the two complemented each other. However, his method raised a controversial issue that still is debated, namely, the value of folk traditions as historical records.[21] Basically, Fewkes thought that legends and myths were important guides in charting the Indians' past because such narratives contained historical fact.[22] It is not surprising, then, that his articles "Tusayan Katcinas" and "Tusayan Snake Ceremonies" explore myths related to these topics.[23] Judging from the title, one might think his "Tusayan Migration Traditions" is concerned solely with narratives, but it actually is a study of clan movements based on a synthesis of fragments of Hopi legendary history.[24]

Two other early Bureau authors published their major works on folk narratives outside the Bureau. John Gregory Bourke (1843-1896) was a professional soldier who gained fame as an Indian fighter before he turned to studying tribal cultures. His initial collecting resulted from assignments by the War Department to examine the traditions of various tribes. On one of these research efforts Bourke spent three months investigating the customs and manners of the Pueblo, Apache, and Navajo Indians. The material he gathered was utilized in his most important work, *The Snake-Dance of the Moquis of Arizona, Being a Narrative of a Journey from Santa Fe, New Mexico, to the Villages of the Moqui Indians of Arizona, with a Description of the Manners and Customs of This Peculiar People, and Especially of the Revolting Religious Rite, The Snake-Dance* (1884), a book consisting of ceremonial descriptions and texts of myths and legends. It is noteworthy primarily for being very ethnocentric; and, ulimately, this and Bourke's other writings reveal more about him and his attitudes than they do about those people he studied. In his various publications narrative traditions usually are noted, but they always are ancillary to his major purpose of discussing ceremonial and religious behavior.

Washington Matthews (1843-1905), like Bourke, came to his interest in American Indian culture while serving in the United States Army. A medical doctor, Matthews served several years at military posts in the northern plains, during which time he collected myths, folktales, and linguistic materials. In 1877 he published his first folklore volume, *Ethnography and Philology of the Hidatsa Indians*. This book came to the attention of John Wesley Powell, who thought Matthews could be helpful to Bureau staff members working in Navajo territory. Powell succeeded in getting the young scholar transferred to Fort Wingate, New Mexico, for the years 1880-1884. Later, after a period spent back East, Matthews was reassigned to the Navajo country for another four years.

Washington Matthews was initially interested in material culture, and his first Bureau publications on weaving and silver work examined that aspect of Navajo life. As his Navajo researches continued, his interest in oral traditions increased, and for the Bureau's *Fifth Annual Report* he produced his first work solely devoted to that form of culture: *The Mountain Chant: A Navajo Ceremony* (1887). This eighty-eight-page article includes a description of the ceremony accompanied by texts of its origin myth, prayers, and songs. Ten years later, in 1897, Matthews produced his major work on narrative traditions, *Navaho Legends* (number 5 in the memoir series of the American Folklore Society). Despite the volume's title, the tales are mostly myths. Matthews selected this misleading name, he wrote, because "the tales contained herein, though mostly mythical, are not altogether such. In the Origin Legend, the last chapter, The Growth of the Navaho Nation, is in part traditional or historical, and it is even approximately correct in many of its dates."[25]

Navaho Legends was published to refute the commonly held view that the Navajos had no traditions or religion. Matthews countered that "these heathens, pronounced godless and legendless, possessed lengthy myths and traditions—so numerous that one can never hope to collect them all."[26] One of the book's merits is that Matthews treats the narratives as something worthy of respect in themselves, and not just as curious tales showing Indians on the bottom level of the evolutionary scale of culture. Indeed, he eschews theoretical statements altogether, confining his commentary to elucidating the cultural background and providing explanatory notes to the texts. Unfortunately, Matthews fails to include comparative annotations, even though he was well aware that the tales are not unique to the Navajos.[27] Slowed by various illnesses, Matthews saw his scholarly output dwindle by the late 1890s. He produced no more major works on narrative and only one significant publication on any subject.[28] But his place in the history of scholarship on Southwestern Indian folk narrative was secure because of *Navaho Legends*—a book that was lauded by no less than William Wells Newell, the leading figure behind the American Folklore Society during its first two decades, as "a model of the manner in which mythologic material ought to be edited."[29] Several decades would pass before anyone disputed Newell's assessment.

We now come to Franz Boas (1858-1942), a man more important in Southwestern studies for his influence than for his actual publications. For many years he had an honorary position in the Bureau and apparently even exercised some power regarding the organization's publications.[30] Arguably the leading figure in American anthropology during the first four decades of the twentieth century, he trained several of the persons doing fieldwork among Southwestern Indians prior to 1950.

Unlike some early collectors of folk narratives, Boas had a well-defined view of the value of folktales. His main thesis was that folktales are a "reflector of culture," since ultimately everything important in a tribe's daily life turns up in its folktales, whether incidentally or as the basis of a plot.[31] This concept led Boas to think of tales as a type of tribal autobiography, overlooking the possibility that an oral literature might not mirror all aspects of life equally. In various publications Boas catalogued technological and sociocultural aspects of Indian life referred to in folktales and listed features that recur in stories told by tribesmen.[32] But he showed little curiosity about these recurrences, failing to ask such elementary questions as why one item appeared and another didn't, or why some features turned up more frequently than others. He failed even to count recurrent features, thereby missing an opportunity to help determine their significance.

Boas did publish some works dealing with Navajo, Pueblo, and Zuni folk narratives, but his major emphasis was on Northwest coast tribes.[33] He is central to this discussion mostly because of the people he influenced. Among the many scholars he initiated into the study of American Indian culture, none was more important from a folklore standpoint than Elsie Clews Parsons (1874-1941). The daughter of a well-to-do New York family, Elsie Clews married Herbert Parsons, a prominent politician and scion of a wealthy family. Yet, well off though she was, Elsie was determined to do more with her life than just bask in her wealth.

In 1899 Parsons received a Ph.D. in sociology, and during the next decade and a half she published such books as *The Family* (1906), *The Old-Fashioned Woman: Primitive Fancies About the Sex* and *Religious Chastity* (both 1913), and *Fear and Conventionality* (1914). In 1915 she met Boas, who was looking for someone to collect black folklore, and two years later she published a pair of articles on Negro folktales in the British journal *Folk-Lore*.[34] These essays were her first folklore publications but were far from being her last. For the rest of her life she held an active interest in folklore and did fieldwork, primarily collecting narratives, folksongs, and beliefs in areas ranging from Haiti to New England, from Barbados to Arizona, and from both blacks and Indians. In 1918 her paper "Pueblo Indian Folk-Tales: Probably of Spanish Provenience" appeared in the *Journal of American Folklore*. It was her first publication dealing with Southwestern Indian folk narratives.

Parsons was a prolific scholar whom cynics would say was only able to do so much because of her money and freedom. It is important to keep in mind, though, that her wealth also made it possible for her to do nothing challenging. Parsons' decision to pursue scholarly interests benefited many folklorists active in the first half of the twentieth century. She held professional offices in the American Folklore Society—but more importantly, she was one of the group's main benefactors during the years before 1940. She personally financed several of the Society's publications, as well as books published outside the organization. Furthermore, she supported fieldwork projects and research expeditions from Nova Scotia to Brazil, including some in the American Southwest. Her numerous publications notwithstanding, Parson's most lasting contribution is the financial backing and encouragement she gave to other scholars.

Ruth Fulton Benedict (1887-1948) was one who benefited directly from Parsons in an academic sense. She was Parsons' student at the New School for Social Research, and Parsons introduced her to Franz Boas, who became her most influential mentor. From him she learned much about the discipline of anthropology and about scholarly discipline in general. In 1924 she made her first field trip to the Southwest, collecting from the Zuni Pueblo. In 1925 and 1927 she gathered further material from Zuni and Cochiti Pueblos and Pimas. From data recorded on these expeditions she produced *Tales of the Cochiti Indians* (1931) and *Zuni Mythology* (1935). The former, which appeared as Bulletin 98 of the Bureau of American Ethnology, offers 256 pages of myths, legends, and folktales with some commentary on cultural background. Like a true Boasian, Benedict emphasized that the "fundamental material in these tales and the fundamental factor in their formation is the daily life of the people."[35] She mostly ignored the performance of stories here but later came to realize that tone and gesture often are as important as the text in transmitting a narrative.[36] Like Boas, Benedict adopted a single-informant approach, but unlike him she sought to place narratives in context so as to outline a culture "personality."

It was the publication of *Zuni Mythology*, a two-volume work, that brought Benedict acclaim as one of the foremost twentieth-century students of Zuni. Despite its title, the book is not confined to sacred stories, Benedict's point being that religion permeates every aspect of Zuni life. She prefaces her texts with a lengthy discussion of the themes of Zuni oral literature and attempts to demonstrate their relationship to the rest of the tribal culture. In doing so, she argues that the Zunis adjusted to and altered conditions within their society by means of a psychological mechanism manifested in their choice of tales. Although Parsons and Boas criticized this interpretation,[37] *Zuni Mythology* was, and still is, a noteworthy achievement. Ironically, given Boas's response, the work is very Boasian in its attempts to use folk narratives to delineate Zuni character.

Gladys Reichard (1893-1955) became interested in American Indian culture after taking an anthropology course at Swarthmore College. So enthused was she that she resolved to study under Boas at Columbia University. Succeeding in this, she also became such good friends with Boas that she lived in his home while working as a student. Although her mentor had a strong scholarly and personal influence, it was another person, Pliny Earle Goddard, curator of anthropology for the American Museum of Natural History, who initially interested Reichard in working among the Navajo. She first visited this tribe in 1923 and joined Goddard in 1924 for six weeks of fieldwork among them, much of this research being funded by Elsie Clews Parsons.

Reichard returned again in 1930, by which time she had become interested in Navajo religion, and sought to synthesize the various elements of the culture's sacred beliefs. Ultimately, she produced two important works on this topic: *Prayer: The Compulsive Word* (1944) and *Navaho Religion: A Study of Symbolism* (1950). In the former she discusses verbalized prayer as an oral literary form, and in the latter she provides what is still the most thorough treatment of Navajo religion. The initial section on dogma includes a number of myths, with information on the purpose they serve in the Navajo belief system.

Gladys Reichard's one other important publication dealing with folk narrative is *Navajo Medicine Man: Sandpaintings and Legends of Miguelito* (1939). This eighty-three-page booklet is based on material collected in 1924 during the decoration of the El Navajo Hotel in Albuquerque, New Mexico. Artist Fred Geary was using sandpainting designs on the hotel walls, and an accomplished chanter, Miguelito, was brought in as a consultant. Miguelito not only directed the painting of the designs but also provided explanations of them, frequently in the form of oral narratives. This material became part of the collection of John Huckel, an executive with the Fred Harvey hotel chain, who was interested in using native designs in hotel decor. After Huckel's death, Reichard edited the collection and provided commentary concerning each item. This, and Reichard's other publications dealing with folk narrative, are important because, unlike many other scholars of her day, she presented not just texts but analysis, commentary, and often a context as well.

Alfred L. Kroeber (1876-1960) was one of Boas's first Ph.D. students and also one of the most prolific scholars of the twentieth century. He left a legacy of five hundred and fifty publications from 1898 to 1960—writings that covered a broad range of subjects including archaeology, psychology, art, history, aesthetics, linguistics, and folklore. Kroeber was particularly active in the latter field during the first decade of the twentieth century, publishing seventeen articles in the *Journal of American Folklore,* organizing the Berkeley Folklore Club and a California branch of the American Folklore Society, and in 1906 becoming the first of Boas's students to serve as president of the American Folklore Society. He also did a considerable amount of folklore fieldwork—mostly in California, but in the Southwest, too—between 1900 and 1910. Some of the results appeared in *Seven Mohave Myths* (1948) and the posthumous *More Mohave Myths* (1972).

These two works reveal that Kroeber followed the lead of his teacher, Boas, in several respects but broke with Boasian tradition in others. Among the former is his virtual lack of theorizing—the analysis in both works being confined to occasional ethnographic glosses. Kroeber, like Boas, tells very little about the actual recording sessions, and he treats texts as linguistic samples. But in going to several informants, providing lengthy biographies of the people, and giving extensive discussions of performance style Kroeber was parting with his teacher. To appreciate how far, one needs only to peruse the posthumous publications *Yurok Myths* (1976) and *Karok Myths* (1980), both based on his California researches.

Several other scholars and collectors who were not directly associated with the Bureau of American Ethnology or with Boas deserve brief mention here. One is Charles F. Lummis, who is noteworthy because his books were popular in the late nineteenth and early twentieth centuries, reaching audiences that most of the other authors mentioned here could never hope to reach. His writing is interesting, if idiosyncratic, but rarely as interesting as Lummis himself. Dogmatic and given to flamboyant escapades, such as a well-publicized 1884 walk across the United States, Lummis nonetheless knew several Southwestern Indian cultures at first hand. Yet he was best acquainted with the Pueblos. In *The Man Who Married the Moon and Other Pueblo Indian Folk-Stories* (1894) and *Pueblo Indian Folk-Stories* (1920), he presented several Pueblo myths and folktales without annotations—though the 1920 volume included an introductory discussion of Pueblo storytelling. Unfortunately, the texts in both books are rewritten in a style far more reflective of Lummis's cultural background than of Pueblo society.

Since Lummis's time there have been a number of popularizers, two of the best known being Frank F. Applegate and Frank Waters. Although the texts in their publications are rewritten, sometimes none too well, their books are not valueless. Applegate's *Indian Stories from the Pueblos* (1929) is his most famous book, but his *Native Tales of New Mexico* (1932) is in one respect a better work because it places the rewritten texts in performance contexts. In *Masked Gods: Navaho and Pueblo Ceremonialism* (1950) Waters provides rewritten myth texts for a book mainly concerned with drawing parallels between ceremonialism in the Southwest, Western rationalism, and Eastern mysticism. *Book of the Hopi* (1963) presents unannotated, rewritten myth and legend texts; while *Pumpkin Seed Point* (1969), which may be Waters's most controversial book because it is more aggressively Jungian than his other works, is an anecdotal account of the field research for *Book of the Hopi.* It includes a few myth texts, but most appear in the 1963 volume.

Among the academic collectors and scholars of Southwestern Indian folk narratives active during the first half of the twentieth century, Pliny Earle Goddard, longtime curator of anthropology for the American Museum of Natural History and author of *Indians of the Southwest* (1921), an excellent general work for its day, deserves mention for several collections of Apache and Navajo traditional narratives.[38] They are noteworthy because they include both myths and folktales, and because at least one contains information about the collecting situation.[39] Unfortunately, such details are rare in pre-World War II publications.

Berard Haile, a Catholic priest who did fieldwork among the Navajo in 1908 and remained active until the 1950s, was primarily interested in tribal beliefs and ceremonies, in connection with which he collected a number of myths. Haile published a few pamphlets on narrative, but much of the material he gathered ended up in archive folders. That his field texts were valuable is shown by the fact that they have figured in the work of later scholars, notably, Katherine Spencer's *Mythology and Values: An Analysis of Navajo Chantway Myths* (1957). This study, which examines published versions of origin myths and Haile's unpublished texts, attempts to demonstrate how Navajo myths reflect cultural values. In short, it is a very Boasian volume.

Karl W. Luckert has performed a real service to those interested in Southwestern Indian folk narratives by bringing texts collected by Haile into print, and by increasing their value with his own extensive commentary. In *The Navajo Hunter Tradition* (1975), he presents texts of hunter mythology collected by Haile in 1929 and, more recently, by the author himself. He also discusses the ritual procedure and underlying belief system, concluding with a thorough cross-cultural survey of related mythology. In *Love-Magic and Butterfly People: The Slim Curly Version of Ajitee and Mothway Myths* (1978), Luckert provides editorial comments on myth texts collected by Haile from 1930 to 1931.[40]

Luckert has also produced some volumes based largely on his own fieldwork. One of the most interesting is *Navajo Mountain and Rainbow Bridge Religion* (1977), a book that came into existence because of a local crisis in Navajo religion. In 1971 a number of tribesmen in the northwestern region of the Navajo Indian Reservation became concerned about the constantly rising waters of Lake Powell. They were afraid that Rainbow Bridge, a large natural sandstone arch in southern Utah that is of religious significance to the Navajo, would be destroyed. The Navajos sought assistance from a legal services office on the reservation, and eventually Luckert was asked to document the sacred significance of the Rainbow Bridge region. The resulting book includes eight Navajo interviews containing prayers, songs, and myths. Like Luckert's other publications, this work is notable for giving considerable attention to the informants themselves.

Four other scholars merit mention for important contributions to the literature on Southwestern Indian folk narratives. In four major publications Morris E. Opler, a specialist in both Asian studies and Southwestern Indian lore, offers several hundred myth, legend, and folktale texts, most with lengthy explanatory and comparative notes.[41] W.W. Hill and Dorothy W. Hill touch on the relatively unexplored topic of *Navaho Humor* in a twenty-eight-page booklet published in 1943.[42] And Margaret K. Brady's *"Some Kind of Power": Navajo Children's Skinwalker Narratives* (1984) is a key addition both to children's folklore studies and to American Indian folklore scholarship. Her book examines one hundred narratives about the skinwalker (a human witch that wears coyote skins and travels at night), exploring "the ways in which these stories operate both within Navajo traditional culture and within the culture of a specific group of Navajo children."[43] Brady uses comments of the tradition bearers themselves in examining the narratives. She offers ample evidence of articulate children using narratives to make sense of the cultural worlds around them, and through these tales she provides insights into the emotional concerns of their culture.

This introduction has by no means listed every worthwhile publication on Southwestern Indian folk narratives. (There is, for example, *Stories of Traditional Navajo Life and Culture* [1977], in some ways one of the most interesting of the published collections because it was compiled and printed by the staff of the Navajo Community College in Tsaile, Arizona, specifically for members of the Navajo tribe.) The aim of this survey has simply been to show the general trends in articles and books, and to point out some of the most important and influential works.

Of the numerous collections done thus far, only a few have been gathered by folklorists, and most have been recorded by people with only an ancillary interest in folk narrative. In fact, nearly all the work to date has centered on *myths* (narratives set in the prehistoric past and dealing with the actions of gods). Much less attention has been given to *folktales* (narratives set in the historic past but told primarily for entertainment— and thus not necessarily believed to have happened), and *legends* (narratives set in the historic past and calling for belief or disbelief).

Keith Cunningham's present work should help correct that imbalance. Some readers will undoubtedly be surprised to find one of America's greatest legends—"The Vanishing Hitchhiker"—told by Southwestern Indians. But it is here, along with many conversational stories from vital Indian (and Anglo-American) folk narrative traditions. And there is something else. One way to know about the special cultures and lives of American Indians, says Cunningham, is to listen carefully to people's everyday stories.

W.K. McNeil
THE OZARK FOLK CENTER
MOUNTAIN VIEW, ARKANSAS

NOTES

1. Edward Gaylord Bourne, "Columbus, Ramon Pane and the Beginnings of American Anthropology," *Proceedings of the American Antiquarian Society*, New Series, 17 (April 1906), 313.

2. For a more extensive discussion of Adair's work, see my introduction to George E. Lankford, *Native American Legends* (Little Rock: August House, 1987), 15-17.

3. Although in popular parlance the Southwest covers an area stretching from Oklahoma to California, for present purposes the term refers to the Southwestern culture area, meaning, as far as the United States is concerned, the states of Arizona and New Mexico. The tribes in this region include Pueblo (both Hopi and Zuni), Navajo, Apache, Mohave, and Yuma.

4. The first forty-eight volumes contain the informative essays, some of which are very lengthy. Beginning with volume 49 (1931-32), the *Annual Reports* became merely a formal statement of what the director and his staff accomplished during the year. These volumes were rarely more than twelve pages long.

5. After Powell's death the following men headed up the Bureau: William Henry Holmes (1902-1910), Frederick Webb Hodge (1910-1917), Jesse Walter Fewkes (1918-1928), Matthew W. Stirling (1928-1957), Frank H.H. Roberts, Jr. (1957-1964), and Henry B. Collins, Jr. (1964).

6. Quoted in Neil M. Judd, *The Bureau of American Ethnology: A Partial History* (Norman: University of Oklahoma Press, 1967), 78. It should be pointed out here that the original name of the organization was Bureau of Ethnology. The word "American" was added in 1894.

7. Judd, *Bureau of American Ethnology*, 62.

8. The other two essays are "Zuni Fetiches" in the *Second Annual Report* (1883) and "A Study of Pueblo Pottery as Illustrative of Zuni Culture Growth" in the *Fourth Annual Report* (1886).

9. Cushing may have known the tale from Thomas Frederick Crane's *Italian Popular Tales* (1885), a widely read contemporary work on the folktale. The tale is Aarne-Thompson Type 2032, "The Cock's Whiskers."

10. The section of *Zuni Folk Tales* containing an account of the unintentional experiment is reprinted in Alan Dundes, *The Study of Folklore* (Englewood Cliffs, New Jersey: Prentice-Hall, Inc., 1964), 269-76.

11. By John Wesley Powell, in Frank Hamilton Cushing's *Zuni Breadstuff* (New York: Museum of the American Indian; Heye Foundation, 1920), 13.

12. By John Napoleon Brinton Hewitt, quoted in Judd, *Bureau of American Ethnology*, 62.

13. By Washington Matthews, in "Frank Hamilton Cushing," *American Anthropologist*, New Series, 2 (1900): 372

14. By Franz Boas, quoted in Judd, *Bureau of American Ethnology*, 62-63.

15. Ruth L. Bunzel, "Zuni Origin Myths," in *Forty-seventh Annual Report of the Bureau of American Ethnology*, 1929-30 (Washington: Government Printing Office, 1932), 547.

16. Frank Hamilton Cushing, *Zuni Folk Tales* (New York: G.P. Putnam's Sons, 1901), 186.

17. Thomas C. Blackburn, *December's Child: A Book of Chumash Oral Narratives Collected by J.P. Harrington* (Berkeley: University of California Press, 1975), 5.

18. Judd, *Bureau of American Ethnology*, 46.

19. A widely told anecdote concerning Mrs. Stevenson is the "Little Flower" story recounted in June Helm, ed., *Pioneers of American Anthropology* (Seattle: University of Washington Press, 1966), 64. In her article on women pioneers of anthropology, Nancy Oestreich Lurie quotes from a letter by A.V. Kidder, Sr.:

> I never cottoned much to her nor did the Indians at the pueblo, I think. Anyhow, she once told me that they called her "Little Flower" and when I passed that on to the linguist, John P. Harrington, he asked one of his San Ildefonso informants about her, telling him of the name she had been given. The Indian laughed and John asked why. He said, "That word doesn't mean 'Little Flower.' It means 'Big Bottom!'"

20. Stevenson touched on the topic of mythology in two other publications. In "Zuni Ancestral Gods and Masks," *American Anthropologist*, New Series, 2 (1898): 33-40, she summarizes several creation myths. In "Ethnobotany of the Zuni Indians," in *Thirtieth Annual Report of the Bureau of American Ethnology*, 1908-09 (Washington: Government Printing Office, 1915), 31-102, she gives some data on plants in mythology.

21. For a survey of this long-standing argument, see Richard M. Dorson, "The Debate Over the Trustworthiness of Oral Traditional History," in Fritz Harkort, et al., eds., *Volksüberlieferung* (Gottingen: O. Schwartz & Co., 1968), 19.

22. In "Tusayan Migration Traditions," in *Nineteenth Annual Report of the Bureau of American Ethnology,* Part 2 (Washington: Government Printing Office, 1900), 578, Fewkes maintains that any study of Pueblo ruins necessitates consideration of contemporary folklore about the topic because only by considering various folk narratives about the ruins could one achieve knowledge of "the manners and customs of the people who once inhabited them."

23. The article on kachinas appeared in *Fifteenth Annual Report of the Bureau of Ethnology,* 1893-94 (Washington: Government Printing Office, 1897), 245-313; the essay on snake ceremonies appeared in *Sixteenth Annual Report of the Bureau of American Ethnology,* 1894-95 (Washington: Government Printing Office, 1897), 267-312. Both papers include summaries of myths.

24. The paper also includes data on clan ceremonial activities.

25. Washington Matthews, *Navaho Legends* (Boston: G.E. Stechert & Co., 1897), 1.

26. Ibid., 23.

27. Although Matthews concedes that the tales are similar to those told by "other peoples, civilized and savage, ancient and modern," he excuses his failure to deal with the parallels on two grounds. First, space devoted to such comments "would be lost to more important subjects" and second, "many readers of this book may be prepared, better than the author, to note these resemblances." Ibid., 56.

28. This publication was *The Night Chant: A Navajo Ceremony* (New York: The Knickerbocker Press, 1902).

29. William Wells Newell, review of Navaho Legends, *Journal of American Folklore* 10 (1897): 162.

30. Boas was appointed honorary philologist in June 1902, a position he held until it was abolished in 1920. According to Judd, p. 45, it is generally believed that an article by Boas in the December 20, 1919, issue of *The Nation* impugning the veracity of President Woodrow Wilson was the immediate excuse for the abolition of Boas's position, but Judd notes that most of the Bureau staff were glad to be rid of him.

31. Frank Boas, "Tsimshian Mythology," in *Thirty-first Annual Report of the Bureau of American Ethnology,* 1909-10 (Washington: Government Printing Office, 1916), 393.

32. His main work in this vein is "Tsimshian Mythology."

33. Boas's publications dealing with Southwestern folk narratives include "Northern Elements in the Mythology of the Navaho," *American Anthropologist,* Old Series, 10 (1897): 371-76; *Keresan Texts,* 2 volumes (1925, 1928); and "Tales of Spanish Provenience from Zuni," *Journal of American Folklore* 35 (1922): 62-98.

34. The two articles are "Provenience of Certain Negro Folk-Tales, Playing Dead Twice in the Road," *Folk-Lore* 28 (1917): 408-14, and "Provenience of Certain Negro Folk-Tales, II, The Password," *Folk-Lore* 29 (1917): 206-18. Parsons followed these initial articles with essays in the same journal on the same topic in 1919, 1921, and 1923.

35. Ruth Benedict, *Tales of the Cochiti Indians,* Bureau of American Ethnology Bulletin 98 (Washington: Government Printing Office, 1931), x.

36. In a letter to Mrs. Julia Hamilton, March 19, 1934, quoted in Judith Modell, *Ruth Benedict: Patterns of a Life* (London: The Hogarth Press, 1984), 217, Benedict discussed the presentation of narratives and mourned her inability to capture the "heightened handling of the stuff of life itself." She wished for some better method of dealing with the performance of a story as well as just the text.

37. Their reviews are quoted in part in Modell, *Ruth Benedict*, 242.

38. Goddard's narrative publications include "Jicarilla Apache Texts," *Anthropological Papers of the American Museum of Natural History* 8 (1911), 1-276; "Myths and Tales from the San Carlos Apaches," *Anthropological Papers of the American Museum of Natural History* 24, Part 1 (1918), 1-86; "Myths and Tales from the White Mountain Apache," *Anthropological Papers of the American Museum of Natural History* 24, Part 2 (1919), 87-139; "San Carlos Apache Texts," *Anthropological Papers of the American Museum of Natural History* 24, Part 3 (1919), 141-367; "White Mountain Apache Texts," *Anthropological Papers of the American Museum of Natural History* 24, Part 4 (1920), 369-527; and "Navajo Texts," *Anthropological Papers of the American Museum of Natural History* 34, Part 1 (1933), 3-179.

39. The seven myths in "Navajo Texts" were collected in 1923 and 1924. Goddard gives data on the collecting situations.

40. Haile and linguist Irvy W. Goossen are credited as authors.

41. These important collections are *Dirty Boy: A Jicarilla Tale of Raid and War*, American Anthropological Association Memoir no. 52 (Menasha, Wisc.: George Banta Publishing Co. 1938); *Myths and Legends of the Jicarilla Apache Indians*, American Folklore Society Memoir no. 31 (Philadelphia: The Society, 1938); *Myths and Legends of the Lipan Apache Indians*, American Folklore Society Memoir no. 36 (Philadelphia: The Society, 1940); and *Myths and Tales of the Chiricahua Apache Indians*, American Folklore Society Memoir no. 37 (Philadelphia: The Society, 1942).

42. The booklet was published by the George Banta Publishing Company, Menasha, Wisconsin.

43. Margaret K. Brady, *"Some Kind of Power": Navajo Children's Skinwalker Narratives* (Salt Lake City: University of Utah Press, 1984), 11.

Learning to Listen

"TODAY IS SEPTEMBER 29, 1984, and this is Kathy Cunningham interviewing Helen at Zuni, New Mexico," my wife announced as I listened through the earphones connected to the tape recorder—and thus began the first interview of our American Indian research project. I nodded, signaling that everything was working, and Kathy asked Helen the first question on our list about Zuni health, "How would you describe the general state of health of people at Zuni?" We listened to her answer:

❖ There are a few health problems—some with the elderly and some with the younger ones, too. Like, some have diabetes—some in their teens and then a lot in their twenties and on up.

I also know several people who are paralyzed. My uncle, his wife is paralyzed, and they're remodeling the inside of the house, so they are staying with my mom and dad while they get their house fixed up. They're just in a one-room house, and they got aid through the housing, and they're adding on other rooms, I guess, so she can get her wheelchair around. She'd been sick for a long time, and I don't really know what happened, but now she can't even move her arms. She can move her head, and, you know, he feeds her. But she can't use her fingers or hands.

The Senior Citizens bring her a hot meal at noon. There's an old lady that comes from that Senior Citizen Center. She'll fix her bed up, and wash her dishes, and give her a bath, or just little things that she needs done. She helps her that way.

She gets monthly checkups at the hospital. She goes once every month, [and] there'll be nothing but old folks—well, I guess, some of them are young, too. They're seen at a certain time, so they get checked.

I don't know who they are, but I've seen a lot of people in wheelchairs up there.[1]

❖ There are hearing problems, too. I didn't realize there was that many, but Angel had ear infections a lot, and I took her to the ear specialist 'cause they thought if she didn't get any better, they were going to have to put a tube in her ear. I went, and there was a lot of young kids that had already had those operations and had tubes put in, I guess, so that it could drain out better. There were some her age and some smaller. Luckily, she didn't have to, you know, 'cause the wall just collapsed, and all she had to do was chew gum and kind of blow her nose. And that's where she learned how to blow bubbles [*laughs*] 'cause just the blowing of air pushed that wall back up, and she got all right.[2]

We were at the village of Zuni, New Mexico, in Helen's home. The three of us and her younger daughter Angel sat around the kitchen table, and Helen was looking at pictures Kathy had taken of her during an earlier visit when she had demonstrated pottery painting with a yucca brush and traditional natural paints for me to use in an American folklore lecture. In the next room, Helen's other two children watched a movie on the family's videocassette recorder.

Kathy and I were here because of a long-standing desire to experience and understand American Indian stories, their narrators, and their cultures. Our deep interest in Southwestern American Indian cultures generally, and in the Zuni particularly, had begun in 1959—a quarter of a century before this interview with Helen—when one of my professors had introduced the class to what he called "the Pueblo problem." He had assigned us Ruth Benedict's monumental work *Patterns of Culture*, which presents American Pueblo Indian culture as an example of what she termed "Apollonian" culture, "all of whose delight," she wrote, "is in formality and whose way of life is the way of measure and of sobriety." Her famous account of the Zuni made their society seem like a utopia realized.

Then, in marked contrast, the professor had us read Frank Hamilton Cushing's account of his life at Zuni. Although Cushing never actually said so, it was clear from his many anecdotes that he considered Zunis backward, primitive, dirty, and dangerous. After encountering these two very different views of the Zuni, the class read other ethnographic reports and articles—none of which completely agreed with Benedict, Cushing, or each other as to the essential nature of Zuni culture. Kathy and I carefully studied these writings with great interest but without being able to draw any hard and fast conclusions. What we *did* take away was a lasting interest in Zuni.

Partly because I was so interested in questions raised in the class, I decided to pursue some sort of lifelong cultural study. I carefully scrutinized the humanities and the social sciences, but more important than any such theoretical considerations was an old man named Olin Fox. This was the time of the folk music revival, and forgettable groups of revival musicians—the "Palsy Hemorrhoids" and "Uncle Fuzzy's Flexible Jug Band"—were active in and around the university I attended. Having decided to learn the five-string banjo, I started looking for one to buy.

A classmate of mine told me about Olin Fox, someone he knew who had once played the banjo and who might still have one around his house.

So we set off for Ethel, Missouri, where Olin welcomed us to his living room and soon brought out the first banjo he had owned—and had played for forty years—with the comment, "There's a lot of music in a banjo." He knotted together a broken string, caressed the fingerboard with the chord positions worn into its ebony surface, and double thumbed while frailing "Cripple Creek" *(bump-buddle-dumb, bump-buddle-dumb, bump-buddle-dumb, bump-buddle-dumb, dump-dump-dump)* as dead fiddlers danced in the shadows of the room until the broken string slowly but inevitably came apart again, and—as visions of the past also faded— said again, "Yep, there's a lot of music in a banjo."

I was hooked on folklore and soon went off to the University of Indiana and graduate work. Yet, even though I didn't know it at the time, Olin still was sowing seeds. One day I came to see him and arrived a little early. As I started to knock on the front door, my hand—and head—were arrested by sounds I heard coming from his unbelievably agile fingers. It couldn't be, but was, "I Wanna Hold Your Hand" by those hairy English guys—with Olin double-thumbing while frailing! He explained that he was baby-sitting one of his grandsons and had played the song at the boy's request. The performance also frailed my neat little categories of what was and wasn't tradition and made me further realize that, fascinating as Olin's music was, he was even more interesting himself.

HEARING THE SOUND

Several years later, in 1969, I accepted a position teaching English and folklore at Northern Arizona University, and Kathy and I moved to Flagstaff, Arizona—less than three hundred miles from Zuni. We did not, however, actually visit Zuni for another nine years—partly because we were busy with other projects, partly because we were so in awe of the place, partly because our curiosity and desire to experience the Zuni of Benedict was tempered by our apprehension of stumbling blindly into the Zuni of Cushing.

Finally, in 1978, we had an opportunity to see Zuni for the first time. We went along on a field trip arranged by Dr. Charles Hoffman, one of our colleagues who was investigating traditional architecture in eastern Arizona and western New Mexico. On one survey trip with his advanced graduate students, he invited us, too, because there was room in the university van, and because he knew that we had previously conducted research on Anglo-American traditional architecture.

After we spent some time in the Springerville, Arizona, area looking at buildings, we drove on over to Zuni so that Charlie could ask the Zuni governor some questions about structures there. The governor was out of town, but there was a Night Dance scheduled, so we arranged to stay and watch.

Because she was a friend of Charlie's, we had dinner that evening with Helen's mother-in-law, and she volunteered to escort us to the dances. In the dark, bitterly cold night, we parked along a main road and began walking to one of the houses where the dancers would perform. Suddenly, as we moved along a narrow passageway between two buildings, our guide pulled us back against the wall. Turning, we saw a young man dressed in a traditional kilt and moccasins—his body painted half-turquoise and half-white in a diagonal design and his ankles ringed with tortoise-shell rattles and copper bells making an eerie *clink-chunk, clink-chunk* as he pranced by.

The dance was held in an enormous room with a dirt floor. Clan sponsors sat along the walls and the many large windows, while outside in the cold stood the audience: Zunis and other American Indians from many tribes and villages, Anglo-American aficionados of the dance, and rude tourists. Inside danced the Zunis wearing costumes of colored feathers from different birds; gourd and tortoise-shell rattles and copper bells; painted buckskin loin cloths, kilts, and moccasins; and pine boughs. Each dancer was bedecked with turquoise jewelry of various American Indian traditions; owned by members of the dancer's extended family, this jewelry exists to be loaned for the dance. Many Zunis have favorite rings or other pieces of jewelry that they wear frequently, or perhaps favorite necklaces or bolo ties saved for special occasions. But these great necklaces and bracelets and bow guards hang most of the year on the walls of their nominal owners, and are worn only on occasions when—along with other equally spectacular pieces from other walls of other homes—they form major elements in the dancers' costumes.

And the sound! We leaned against the wall. We watched the masked primordial figures dance their primordial dance. We listened to the several separate but united sounds and rhythms—the beat of the drums, the falsetto chanting of the singers, the *clink-chunk-clink-chunk* of the hand-held gourd rattles and the shell rattles and copper bells tied to the dancers' bodies—which came pouring out of the huge lighted room into the darkness. They rolled past the immediate audience, down the winding pathways between the ancient houses, across the Zuni River, on to the faraway foot of Corn Mountain, on to the edge of forever, on beyond time echoed then and echoes still a contrapuntal symphony of sound, a syncopated canticle.

We lean against the wall. We see. And—our hearts, our lungs beating and breathing as one with the sound of the dance—we hear. I still dream that sound.

This night, though, we realized suddenly that the darkness was being dispelled by the low, golden light of dawn. We hurried back to the van and discovered that the rest of our group had returned hours ago and had been waiting uncomfortably for us.

EVERYDAY ART

During the next few years we made trips to Zuni whenever we could to witness Night Dances and *Shalako,* the major event of the Zuni ceremonial year; to research traditional Zuni activities; and to spend as much time as possible with Helen and her family. At the first dance we attended, I noticed that one of the dancers, in addition to his kilt, bells, and rattles, wore a sweat shirt which read, "Evel Knievel Sucks." It was precisely this blend of familiar, even esoteric, aspects of Anglo-American culture with alien elements that fascinated us—and left us feeling that we had been transported to another planet. Helen's family had been leaders at Zuni, telling stories to anthropologists for at least one hundred years, and she told us stories of what her mother told her her grandmother told her Stevenson told the Zunis in the 1890s. Helen was at home in the worlds of the dancer and the sweat shirt, and—after spending some time with her and her family—Kathy and I decided that we wanted to know more of American Indians' stories and their narrators.

The second reason Kathy and I were in Helen's kitchen had to do with *folkloristics.* Even though our fascination with folklore had begun with the so-called folksong revival of the 1960s, that interest soon came to center much more upon Olin Fox than upon the music of Olin Fox. In other words, we began to focus less on the lore of the folk than on the folk themselves and on questions of how people and culture are continually shaping and being shaped by one another. We gradually became convinced by our field experiences that the stories people tell are important indicators of their beliefs and values and behaviors—guides to Benedict's "unconscious canons of choice" which form the patterns of culture. Here, in Helen's kitchen, we could begin to understand Ruth Bunzel's view of her own long research at Zuni—that the purpose of cultural study was to learn what it means to be Zuni in order to learn what it means to be human.

Actually, our developing interests also reflected developments in the discipline of folklore itself. So when we read Richard Dorson's call in his 1973 book *America in Legend* for folklorists to "consider traditional ideas and values which may be expressed within tale and story and other genres *or in ordinary conversation"* (the emphasis is my own), we took it as a charter for blending our interests and concerns into research that looked at lore—including conversation and conversational stories—in order to understand and experience folk and their worlds.

The stories people tell include both *formal* and *informal* performance stories. Through the years, American Indians' stories that have most interested scholars have been formal performance stories such as the great tribal myths and cycles of trickster tales. Visiting with Helen and listening to what she had to say suggested to us that informal performance stories are as important as formal performance items as signposts indicating culture because they are one of the most frequently employed means of communication in small groups. From Helen, we were hearing informal stories in conversation—kitchen-table stories, everyday art of extraordinary people, stories dealing with illness and cures and life itself.

When a new research unit of our university sent out a call for interdisciplinary grant proposals centering upon American Indian rehabilitation, we saw a great opportunity to test our hopes. In a five-year research project titled "Concepts of Disability and Rehabilitation Among Native Americans: A Folklore Approach," we would conduct extensive interviews and tape-record and analyze stories of American Indians of varied tribal backgrounds. Our goal was to experience and better understand stories and storytelling in general; to study American Indians' stories and storytelling in particular; and, with luck, to hear what it means to be Zuni.

And so here we were asking questions and listening to stories:

❖   *Kathy:* I remember when your daughter had pneumonia. Would you tell me about it?

Helen: Oh, Angel had gotten pneumonia. She had it for a month and two weeks, and she had gotten real skinny, you know. Her bones were showing and her ribs. And that's when the girl that works at the store had come over here for a break. She came to have some coffee and a cigarette, and [Angel] was lying on the couch, and she heard her coughing and said that she sounded like she was witched. So I said, "Are you sure?" because I didn't think she was.

I don't know how she could tell or what, but that night we got a medicine man to come check Angel and he took a *lot* of stuff out of her. She had been complaining she couldn't keep her eyes open, and here he had taken stuff out of her eyes! And she couldn't hear, and I guess her ears had been clogged, and he took stuff out of her and her head, and her throat, and her chest, and her arms and legs, and her joints.

Kathy: Oh, that poor little girl!

Helen: And her ankles. Gosh, she was a mess! She couldn't keep anything down, and I guess that somebody had put—She'd throw it up, you know, everything, even liquids, So, two days, right after the next day, she just started eating again, and she kept her food in, and she got all right, and then within that week she was all ready to go back to school. I guess she had gotten over the pneumonia part, maybe, but had the other part, too. She was trying to battle both of them at once, I guess, and just couldn't do it.[3]

❖   *Kathy:* Is there anything the Zunis can do to protect themselves from being witched?
    Helen: You can use arrowheads, you know, to protect, as long as they don't see them. That's why she's wearing—*[Helen checks inside the neckline of Angel's T-shirt.]* She's not wearing it. *[laughs]* She takes a bath, and she'll leave it off, and I always get after her to put it back on 'cause it's mine. She's lost two—Scott's and Franklin's [her father and brother]. But, you know, to have them carry crystals 'cause those work just like arrowheads. Have them under your clothes; then they can't get to you. *[Angel brings the arrowhead from the bathroom.]*[4]

❖   Scott got that arrowhead for me. Some kid came into the store and was wanting to sell it to the owner, and Scott said, "Well, what are you selling it to the owner for? They don't believe in anything like that, you know, and so they probably don't want it." And Scott said, "But I'll take it if you want to sell it." *[laughs]* And he asked him how much he wanted for it, and he said ten dollars, so Scott got it for me. *[laughs]* He had found this one in the forest. It's pretty. He said the tip had chipped a little, but it's still got a point, but that's pretty long, huh? So I have her wear it all the time, and she hasn't been bothered, I don't think, since then. That was the last time, and—*[asks Angel]* Have you been checked [*checked* is the word Zunis use for being examined *and* treated by a medicine man] since?
    Angel: Huh uh.[5]

❖   Oh, it was Peggy [Angel's sister]. She had just been well for maybe three months, and then she got scarlet fever. And then just as soon as she got better, she went the first day of school before Christmas vacation and got chicken pox. *[laughs]* She gets things really easily; that's why I really watch her. She missed a lot of school last year. I was surprised that she passed, you know, but the kids were so nice. They would send get-well cards and little gifts, so I think she likes being home. Likes the attention. *[Angel and Helen laugh.]*
    Peggy had joined track, [and] there was a meet going on, with the Ramah elementary kids running a mile run. She was the first one to come down, and there was a man standing up that she said she had never seen—a young guy, probably in his middle twenties. He just told her if she went down past him, down that hill, that she was going to get hurt.
    She said she was running, and he was looking at her, talking to her, and she didn't look at him that good, but just glanced at him and noticed that he looked like her uncle—as old as her uncle, and he is twenty-six. She said he had long hair and wasn't too big but, you know, was kinda tall but not too big, you know, kinda skinny. By the time she got to the finish line,

she was just having real bad chest pains, and she thought it was just from running, But by the time she cooled down and got home, she was still hurting. I thought maybe—well, she didn't tell me that man had told her anything. I asked her later if anybody else was behind her—if he said anything to anybody else—and she said she didn't know 'cause she never looked back. But that night I just happened to go into the bedroom, and I turned the light on, you know, to get Franklin and them ready for bed, and she was all doubled up. I thought she had gone to sleep, but all this time she was just—She never even called me or said anything. She was crying, not loud, but her tears were just flowing down her cheeks, and I asked her what was the matter, and she said that her chest was just like she had a bad clump in her chest, and she said, "It feels like my heart."

So I—I thought about going to the hospital and then for some reason I just, you know, I just kind of panicked 'cause I didn't know what to do; didn't seem like anything [for] the doctors, 'cause usually when something like that's wrong, they won't, they can't see it, and they'll just let you go back home 'cause they don't know what's wrong with you. And, uh, I got my sister-in-law to go get the medicine man and bring him over here, and he checked her and told *us* that she was supposed to stay in the house for three more days 'cause whoever was hurting her wasn't finished with her, and she would be hurt real bad, worse, if she went outside. So we had to keep her in the house, and I just went and told the track teacher that she couldn't run anymore, 'cause he had allotted them, I think it was, three times to miss, and she had already missed once. I just went and told him that she was going to have to quit. He felt real bad, you know, that she had to leave, but he thought it would be better, too, 'cause he said some people are just jealous. He didn't really understand it either, so we just kept her. He [the medicine man] fixed her up, and we just kept her in the house.

Kathy: Did the pain go away then?

Helen: Yes, right after he started working on her. She just felt all right.

Kathy: Do Zunis have ways to find out who is doing it?

Helen: I don't know. I really don't know. Maybe sometimes you can catch them if they're around your house at night or maybe if they tell you some way—[6]

❖   But I just remembered! The way Angel got witched was when she never used to be afraid of the dark. My mom and dad's house is real dark—no outside light or anything. She was going next door to grandma's and had gone outside and was waiting for Peggy to come follow her. She had gone to the porch and saw that man. She didn't know who it was, but his face was white, and he—

Angel: He was all white.

Helen: Yeah, she said he was all white, and he just came up to her, didn't say nothing, and she got scared. She said she couldn't call anybody for help, you know. She just looked around into the house, and she could hear everybody back there but couldn't say anything. And he just came up to her and touched her right here, huh? Where? Oh, yeah, he just went like that and left. And then, she went back in the house and didn't tell anybody, huh? That's the only thing. I [have] to start telling when anything happens like that; she should tell me right away. That way I can get somebody to look at her right away so she won't be in a lot of pain.[7]

❖   Somebody could be witched, sometimes just from jealousy. They see something you have that they want, or they want to be like you or something. In all my life, that's never ever happened to me except last year. This past summer, it was about this time, me and my mother, we had the same things—everything. I never drink that much, [*grins*] but it was just like if I had gone and drank a lot, and just, you know, stood up. When I woke up in the morning, I thought it was just me being sick: I got up, and the room would spin, and I just felt real awful. I knew I had to get my pottery done, so I started working, but my arms just felt like lead. I couldn't even hold them up.

My mom and dad came over, and they told me not to work 'cause if I felt that bad, I shouldn't be working on my things. And my mom said she didn't feel good either, but she didn't really complain to me about it. I told them it just felt like the room wouldn't stop spinning, and even when I laid down, it still felt that way; and even when I would close my eyes, it was just like my head was spinning around, and I gave myself a massage. I rubbed my head, and then I took a real hot bath, you know, thinking that would work; but I laid back down in bed, and I still felt the same.

I heard some people talking, and I looked out, and my mom was bringing a medicine man [*laughs with relief*] for me, she and my sister. And my mom said, "I brought you—*us*—a medicine man." She said, "I think we should get checked." So I didn't even think anything. I didn't think that anything was wrong with me. I thought it was just me being sick, or something, and he took the same things out of us. And then he left. It went away right away. I just felt real good after he left. [*laughs*] I just was relieved to not have to be feeling that 'cause it felt so awful.

Kathy: When you say he takes things out of you, do you actually see objects in his hand?

Helen: Oh, yeah. He'll just go like that. It's kind of a pinch, kind of, but he doesn't pinch you 'cause you can just barely feel his hands. It's just like he's—just like that, [*touches Kathy's arm with her finger tips*] and you don't even realize that he's got anything till he says something when he takes it out and then puts it in the cornmeal that—See, you have to prepare cornmeal and bread in a corn husk, and it's folded a certain way, like that. And when he holds everything that you give him—the material items or money and the corn husk—he prays and then sets it on the floor by him. And when he takes the things out, he puts them in that cornmeal 'cause he has to go take that to the water—to the river bed. He takes them back. Well, cornmeal is pretty strong, you know, and he takes them—they're usually all—uh, the things that they take out of you are—can be anything. They took—[8]

❖   Well, my brother and I both went up to the hospital. Maybe sometimes, if you're strong, you can keep them from, you know—If maybe you don't believe in them, you can keep them from hurting you; but sometimes if you're not strong or whatever, they can get to you. And they put, uh, it was dead person's—somebody that had just maybe died—It was a human *meat* that was rotting in his ear. I took him up to the hospital, and I was just having pains in my stomach, and I couldn't figure out what they were.

They didn't know what was wrong with me, and I just told the doctor, "Maybe you don't have to even worry about it." I said, "Maybe we're just witched," and he laughed 'cause he didn't believe in it. We were waiting. He didn't know what to prescribe for us, I guess, and we'd been waiting there until everybody left, and I just told my brother, "Let's just go out—" You know, we were talking about it, and I just went into his office, to where there's a door leading into the examining room [with] little desks for them to write their stuff in your record. I just went up to the desk 'cause he was just sitting there with a pencil in his hand, but he wasn't really writing. [*laughs*] He was just trying to think what to put in there, and I told him that maybe, you know, we should get checked, and he laughed.

So we went ahead. He gave my brother aspirin and some kind of pill for infection; but, you know, that night my mom went ahead and took my brother. I didn't go; but they took that—that was in there with hair and some other—It was—had been wrapped in a—[*lowers voice*] It was wrapped in a, a deer hide.⁹

After she had finished telling these stories, Helen gave us more general information in response to our questionnaire and then told us another story about the time her son was witched by a horse:

❖   He had been just playing outside at this lady's—a lady and man that were working for my dad. Ruth had come up, and they were all talking, I guess, and she just happened to look out the door 'cause my mom and dad had their door open, and she saw Franklin going by, and that horse following him. She thought, you know, that horse can do something to him, so she followed them, and here Franklin had gone and just squatted down behind a bush to hide from that horse, and he came up to him and just tapped him on the head. Well, I'd thought he had kicked him real hard 'cause she [the lady] was pretty shook up. But, anyway, it just came and picked up its foot and hit him, tapped him, on the head. I don't think it hit him real hard because he wasn't crying or anything, and then it just went away. That lady is the only one who saw it 'cause everyone else at the other trailer was talking to my dad. It just happened so fast, we decided to see what was going on.

The horse had been around there. I don't know whose horse that was. Franklin just got kind of real ornery—won't even listen, you know. We couldn't get him to do anything. He was so little. My mom and them were going to get somebody checked, so they just said, "We're taking him along!" [*laughs*] "'Cause, you know, you're not listening to your mom or anybody."

And so they went and got him checked, [*laughs*] and it was 'cause of that horse. It was just making him mean and not want to listen. They found—I think it was a leather with some hide with something in it. Every time he would get mad, that knot in it was tightening up, and it was supposed to drive him crazy or something. I don't know what else, what it had in that little bundle, but that medicine man had a hard time opening it up 'cause sometimes things are put in like that. They're in a pouch and like rolled up. It could be hair or whatever.[10]

As I listened to Helen's stories of being witched interspersed with information about diabetes, I felt that our hopes in coming to her kitchen were being fulfilled. We were at Zuni; we were listening to stories told in conversations; we were beginning to gather a view of what it meant to be Zuni; and the experience was everything we had dreamed, and much more. Since this first breakthrough interview with Helen, Kathy and I have continued trying to understand and experience American Indians' cultures by coming to know the people's stories and the storytellers. With the inspiration and example of Clyde Manybeads, our Ramah Navajo co-re-searcher, we have ventured into many Southwestern American Indian cultures.

And so I built this book—a report of our quest—with memories, dreams, and stories. It features several Anglo-American contemporary legends, two previously published scholarly accounts describing and explaining the Navajo Squaw Dance Ceremony, and three stories reported in the body of the book and repeated for analysis in the final chapter. But at its heart lie 251 American Indians' stories framed with their tellers' comments, observations, and interpretations so that others might share the experience.

And thus the adventure begins!

CHAPTER TWO

Zuni Medicine

IT WAS EASY TO UNDERSTAND intellectually that the stories Helen told us as we sat around her kitchen table reflected her reality. It was much more difficult—requiring a great deal of research and listening to kitchen-table stories—to grasp that reality emotionally.

The name "Zuni" refers to a people, their village, and their reservation. The Zuni Indians are a pueblo- or village-dwelling American Indian people living in and around the town of Zuni, New Mexico, about forty-five miles south of Interstate 40 and the town of Gallup, New Mexico, and fifteen miles east of the New Mexico-Arizona state line. The Zunis have a unique, complex system of medicine rooted in their unique, complex culture. Not surprisingly, people's medicine stories offer windows on that special culture itself.

The present-day Zuni Indians are descendants of two prehistoric Southwestern cultures. The Anasazi—known for their multistory towns in adjoining areas of present-day Arizona, Colorado, Utah, and New Mexico—left their villages and fields, wandered southwest, and blended with people of the Mogollon culture—known for their finely decorated pottery—who were moving northeast from homes in what is now Arizona, northern Mexico, and New Mexico.

The two groups formed a new tribe and together wandered across the land looking for a place destined to be theirs: a home which in their ancient stories and present-day speech alike the Zunis call "The Middle Place." Descendants of these two tribes who together became the prehistoric Zunis have lived in the Middle Place for more than nine hundred years, and they call themselves "The People of the Middle Place."

The name the Zuni chose for their land and for themselves describes their culture as well. Students of culture long have noted that the Zunis stress the "middle way" in all that they think, do, and dream. Ruth Benedict, the leading American anthropologist who studied at Zuni in the 1920s, described the ideal Zuni, and thus the Zuni ideal, as cooperative and noncompetitive.

Perhaps because their culture results from the blending of two previous cultures, the Zunis also are remarkably open to new ideas and technologies. When he lived at Zuni in the 1880s, Frank Cushing found that the people were very impressed with Euro-American agricultural tools and wished to have them for their farming. An anthropologist who visited at Zuni in the 1940s noted with some amazement the easy juxtaposition of a terraced bowl, used to contain sacred cornmeal, and a modern radio. The bowl of cornmeal remains today, but the radio has been replaced by a color television and a video-tape recorder.

The Zuni openness to new ideas and technologies from other cultures has not, however, deprived them of their own traditions. While freely adopting ideas and technologies they have found useful, they also have maintained their values, myths, rituals, and dances.

Zuni is one of the most tradition-filled cultures of the world. Zuni time is measured by two ceremonial dances held in association with the longest and the shortest days of the solar year. The major ceremony of Zuni summer is Mid-summer Dance, coming near the summer solstice; and the main winter ceremony, *Shalako,* falls near the time of the winter solstice. The Zuni word *Shalako* refers not only to this mid-winter ceremony, but also to the spirits which the dancers embody, and to the costumed figures of the dance. The date for the Shalako ceremony is determined by solar observations of the *Pekwin* (Sun Priest) and is publicly announced by him and other religious officials by word and ceremony beginning about forty-nine days before the actual event. Shalako to Mid-summer Dance, Mid-summer Dance to Shalako, Shalako to Mid-summer Dance—each is a part of what has gone, each a part of what is to come. Time circles time at Zuni so that after Shalako, people already are dancing toward Shalako.

The dance is long and arduous. Both the year from the winter ceremony of Shalako to Mid-summer Dance and the year from then to Shalako involve major cycles of traditional dance, pilgrimages, and retreats. Chosen dancers start getting ready for Shalako early during the period between the last Shalako and Mid-summer Dance. Preparation involves practice for dancers and musicians; the refurbishing of costumes; bread baking and sheep slaughtering; the learning of long traditional prayers, speeches, and responses; and the building of eight traditional houses. For many Zunis, most waking hours are spent learning and living tradition.

As the announced day finally comes, the air of the village crackles with excitement. The gap between the worlds disappears, spirit becomes flesh, the supernaturals dance among human beings. From the West come the *Ko-ko,* or Council of the Gods, including *Shulawitsi* (the Fire-god), represented by a Zuni boy. His body is painted black and spotted with the colors of the sun according to Zuni tradition (red, yellow, blue, and white), and he carries seeds in a bag over his shoulder and a burning cedar brand.

There also is *Sayatasha* (the Long Horn), the Rain-god of the North, personated by a Zuni man dressed in white buckskin almost covered with turquoise, shell, and coral jewelry. Rattling deer bones as he moves, he wears a mask of black and white stripes with a curved, painted horn on its right side and black hair on the top. There are, as well, others of the Council of the Gods personated by other Zunis. From the West also come the *Shalako* (the Couriers of the Gods) represented by Zunis wearing vaguely birdlike heads and nine-foot-tall conical costumes made of painted and decorated buckskin stretched over willow-wood frames.

After private ceremonies, each of the Shalako goes to the house that has been specially built for his presence. There—accompanied by figures from the Council of the Gods and by the *Ko'yemshi*, or Muddyheads, the sacred clowns of the ceremony represented by Zunis with grotesque, mud-daubed masks, and even more mud on their bare shoulders and chests—the Shalako dance. With their birdlike costumes, clacking bills, and unearthly cooing, they dance for the people and for the people's welfare. Dancing in the enormous empty space in the room at the center of the house, they lean so far from the perpendicular that it seems they must fall, then right themselves and do it all over again and again and again.

The public dances at the houses pause near dawn. To the prayer of dance is added the prayer of language as the Messengers retire for private ceremonies. In the early afternoon they reemerge, cross the Zuni River, and take their places in a large empty field. The tall conical figures form intricate patterns as they run gracefully from point to point planting prayer sticks. The figures dance for all the Zunis; all the Zunis dance with the figures. The dance and the spectators' response to the dance reflect their grace, and they foreshadow fortunes and fates in the coming year.

After the Shalako race for the people, most tourists leave. Dancing actually continues for four more days, and then new dancers are chosen for the new year. The cycle ends; the cycle begins. Life, the secular, and religion, the sacred, are not separate at Zuni, but are one. Zuni life is religion, Zuni religion is dance, and Zuni dance is life. After Shalako, Zuni dances to Shalako.

The Zuni dance of life is among the most frequently observed and analyzed cultures in the world. In addition to Ruth Benedict and Frank Hamilton Cushing (a fieldwork pioneer of the 1880s), Franz Boas, Matilda Coxe Stevenson, Ruth Bunzel, and Elsie Clews Parsons—all masters of American cultural study—conducted fieldwork at Zuni. Perceptive non-academic accounts of Zuni life and culture are voluminous and trace back to shortly after 1539 when the Spanish conquistadors marched into Zuni history.

SAGE PASTE AND VICKS 44

Besides having retained what has been called the most elaborate living costume and religious ceremony cycle in North America, the Zunis also have preserved, created, and adapted complex health-care systems to form a new whole. Home remedies, exercise therapy and preventative medicine, bone pressing, medicine men, and Euro-American technology—all are parts of today's Zuni medicine.

The first system of medicine invoked at Zuni, as in most cultures of the world, is that of home remedies. In the past there was a wide range of herbal and other natural medicines prepared and administered by and within families for common ailments. Suffering from arthritis at Zuni in the 1890s, Matilda Coxe Stevenson noted receiving a paste made from wild sagebrush—and reported that it relieved her pain.

Sagebrush medicines still are used at Zuni to treat arthritis in much the same way Stevenson described, and sage tea still is used to relieve the symptoms of the common cold, just as it was when she lived at Zuni. While people still rely on a number of the old, traditional home remedies, this ethnic naturopathic medical tradition has been augmented by nonprescription medications used all across America.

The initial diagnosis offered for common illnesses by Zuni individuals or their families usually is an Anglo-American term such as "cold," "flu," "stomach flu," or "earache"; and the most common treatments employed first are over-the-counter medicines such as analgesics, cough syrups, antihistamines, and anti-diarrhea preparations. As is also true in American culture at large, some Zunis prefer one brand of medicine (such as Vicks 44 cough syrup or Pepto Bismol) over others of the same general class. They also use various traditional Anglo-American home-remedy medical procedures to deal with certain illnesses. For example, a person who has a "cold" may be told to drink lots of fluids. Minor injuries, too, are most often treated initially with home remedies or traditional advice, and we were told a number of stories by Zunis dealing with home remedies very similar to Anglo-American home care:

❖   Constipation wasn't a problem with the children. In fact, it was more likely the other way around—especially my two-year-old. This one Hopi girl was a little older than he was. He couldn't hold it, poor guy; he just would mess himself, and that girl would say, "Come on. Let's go," and she'd clean him up. I don't know what to call that, [*pauses*] but this Hopi lady gave it to me to mix in with Jello for him. It was already made up. Boiled, I guess, but I can't remember the name. [*pauses*] She was a real good friend of ours. Her children were, too. We'd all eat together, and the kids played together in the yards. We were at Winslow then. There wasn't very many Indian people living there then, and we got acquainted. She was real knowledgeable about those things. She said it was herbs boiled together. She said to mix it with the Jello and have him drink it. Must have been bitter or something because he didn't like to take it. [*laughs*] Maryann is married now and lives in California.[11]

❖ If our kids had a rash, we used cornstarch on them. If they had diarrhea, Mom would always say, "Fix Jello water for them." You just make warm water and mix Jello in it [to] harden the bowel, instead of giving them medicine. That works even though it looks like they're not better: I usually just give it to them about two days. That means cutting out milk, just giving them boiled water and nothing sweet, 'cause that milk just makes them worse. I used to give them crackers and peanut butter and just stuff like that and just stop it. It doesn't look like the diarrhea's going to go away, but what they ate gave it enough time that a couple of days after, you could just go ahead and give them milk, and they'd get all right. My mom told me that.

But my grandmother, my father's mother, was the one that told me—She's the one that used cornstarch 'cause there was no powder. And she said if they had a rash, to lay them in the sun, no diaper, wash them and put the cornstarch on them and just let the sun dry it out, and that would work really good.[12]

Helen was a great help in arranging the Zuni interviews, and she accompanied us on many of the early ones. One day I had such a bad cold and felt so miserable when we were getting ready to drive to Zuni from Flagstaff that I seriously considered calling the whole thing off. But time and grant deadlines wait for no colds, so I put my trusty bottle of Vicks Formula 44 cough syrup in my hip pocket, and off we went.

When we got to Helen's house, she greeted us hackingly and said that she had such a bad cold and felt so miserable that she had seriously considered calling and telling us not to come. She punctuated her statement by reaching into her hip pocket, pulling out her trusty bottle of Vicks Formula 44 cough syrup, and taking a big swig. Kathy laughed, Helen looked puzzled, and—by way of explanation—I pulled my Vicks bottle out of my pocket and took a big swig. We all laughed until, almost in unison, Helen and I started choking, and we spent the day doing interviews and drinking that nasty stuff—and laughing.

Besides using home remedies very similar to Anglo-American cures for illnesses both cultures recognize, or the same over-the-counter medicines, the Zunis also have culturally specific home remedies for *fright*, an illness not recognized by Anglo-American culture. We were told a number of stories that helped us better understand fright and its treatment:

❖   I've cured people of fright. I've done that. I've done that to Helen's kids 'cause she didn't know how. But let's say, maybe my daughter got frightened by older kids who were real rough with her. The way that our grandmother taught us was, like, if the child continually sleeps—not wake up, just keep sleeping—when he gets to the real bad stage, they'll start vomiting and won't keep anything in their stomachs. If you know who the older kids are, you go get a little snip of their hair and the coals that get real hot, and you put it on top and cover them with a blanket and let them breathe the burning hair. After it's done, you get that burnt hair off the charcoal thing, and our grandmother taught us to put it on the eyelids and then one right here, [*points to forehead*] and you just leave that there for about twenty-four hours. But then they'll get okay. That's how it's done.[13]

❖   They had a drama school in Denmark, I believe. They were Inuits from Iceland, Eskimo, and they came here to perform at the middle school where the sixth, seventh, and eighth graders are. They scared those kids to the point that many of them went and hid in their lockers. They panicked. It was terror time. Those kids were terrified, and the director had to *write* to those dancers and get hair to burn from some of those kids being frightened.[14]

The most common response of a Zuni patient to treatment with home remedies for either illnesses recognized by both Zuni and Anglo-American culture or illnesses recognized only by Zuni culture is therapeutic and life affirming.

Adult onset diabetes is much more common among the Zunis than it is among almost any other American group. It is a wearisome disease, often followed by disabling or fatal medical complications such as blindness, amputations, kidney disease, or stroke. Research has indicated that there is a genetic predisposition to the disease, that an individual's chances of developing it are greatly increased by being overweight, and that weight loss and regular exercise can often control the disease or prevent its onset.

One of the newest and most clearly Euro-American medicines at Zuni recognizes these facts, but it also has old, clear ties to Zuni culture. In 1983 a health educator who served the Zunis planned and implemented an exercise and education program to reduce both the incidence and the severity of adult onset diabetes among the Zunis. The program involved a broad range of weight-loss and physical-fitness activities including aerobics, weight training, use of exercise machines, races, and fun runs and walks. The Zuni Diabetes Project, as it came to be known, received a great deal of support from Zuni people and the Zuni government, was the subject of many favorable articles in newspapers all across America, and was featured on a national network television program. The upshot of the program was that all the participating Zunis lost weight and that all twelve in the group who had required medication to control their blood sugar levels were able to discontinue their medicines and still manage their diabetes.

This program of exercise therapy and preventative medicine fits the Zuni idea of wellness as a natural and desirable state reached by working with the world and body, rather than against them, and ties into an old Zuni tradition of running. It has been expanded through the years, and today the Zuni Wellness Center, as the new organization is called, sponsors a broad range of physical-fitness and weight-loss programs for the Zuni population at large, as well as for diabetics. The center was awarded a grant to expand and implement a Model Diabetes Prevention Program, and its activities and events have become very popular indeed. Likewise, the Zuni Senior Citizens Center sponsors a wide variety of exercise programs designed to help elderly Zunis maintain and improve mobility. The Zunis accept and believe in the benefits of exercise therapy and preventative medicine, and two Zuni citizens told us personal stories of success in dealing with their health problems:

❖ My brothers are getting older than me. [*laughs*] My young brother is a sick boy. He came here just about two weeks ago and said he was in good health. "I don't feel any way. I feel all right," he said.

"You watch your diet," I told him. "Don't get into too much of everything. I feel all right, too," I said, "only arthritis on this side [and] my knee—" But then, I go exercise in the morning. I get my breakfast, and then I go out and run around [*points south*] and around here [*points east and north*] and around [*points west*] about two times, and then I come in. I start raising my arms like this [*swings her arms up over her head*] and this way and this way [*completes a circle with her arm swing*], touch the ground, and make my knee fold up this way [*bends knee to her right*] and this way [*bends knee to her left*], lie down and put one leg up like that, and it helps. We go to Senior Citizens, and then we exercise over there. We go out and race. At least I run like that every morning and exercise that way, and I used to have a catch in my arm up here, and now I go up here like this [*claps hands over head*]. I can fold my head down and bend and go around as far as it will go.[15]

❖ Four or five years ago I became a diabetic. I'm a diabetic. I was giving myself insulin every morning, up to sixty units. But last year they kind of checked me, and I didn't put on weight, so they tried me on pills, and I'm taking pills.

I think being a diabetic makes it tough. I have been industrious, like building a house [and] working at this truck station, when I wasn't a diabetic, for sixteen years, twelve hours a day, eight miles or six miles west of Gallup;

so each day I was putting in fifteen hours or so traveling as well as working from six to six in the morning. But when I became diabetic, I couldn't believe it. I don't really know much medical research, but I read somewhere that diabetes is hereditary in some sense. My father was a diabetic, but I think my mother wasn't.

But again, life is too short—When I first approached the doctor and admitted that I was diabetic, I had just about had it—real skinny, loosing weight, so tired and worn out. In fact, when I was getting diabetic, I almost fell off from the scaffold here at the Mission a couple of times till my wife recognized, and she, well, asked me to test my urine. But I kept refusing till finally I just had to go in, and it was four plus, and she told me to go up to the hospital. She said, "Have one of your sons take you up and tell the doctor right away that you're getting diabetes." So I did. I went up there for about a week to get shots of insulin, and finally I just started giving myself the shots, and I started to get better.

But being a diabetic, it distracts you mentally. I don't plan like I did before because the next morning, I may wake up with a different feeling— tired or in mental shock or body aches, so I learn how to do that. If my sugar is level, I feel good. I got this to take care of. I've kind of accepted it. The doctor told me, "If you have licked the problem of alcohol, you can watch your sugar."

I think I'll cope. I do a little jogging, sometimes hiking with the fieldtrips, climbing up the mountain over two miles to see the ancient petroglyph sites that we have around here. So I think walking also helps me, but again, what the heck! I've already had my young years, enjoyed it, although not one hundred percent. Some were hard, you know, adjusting to certain stages of life that I went through. Life is a gift, and I know that however long I have to live, I'll cherish, treasure it all up to that last breathing moments of my life.[16]

Shortly after we became involved in disability research, I became disabled (I have often commented that I was very glad we had not been doing research on death and dying). I had ruptured a disk in my back about twenty years earlier and had managed to live with the condition by ignoring it. When a second one went flat, it was no longer something that could be ignored.

After a great many tests and unsuccessful treatments, my doctor decided that back surgery was necessary, and he did it. I recovered slowly from my operation, and I was even slower at learning to accept and adjust to the fact that I had a couple of pieces missing. For a time, just getting around was painful and difficult. At one point Kathy called Helen and told her we would be coming over to visit. Helen said that if I felt up to it, she would like to take us to see the Zuni Cliffs, a ceremonial site covered with paintings of the Messengers of the Gods, dance figures, and clan totems.

I said that I would like to try, and so—with Helen pulling and Kathy pushing—we made our slow way up the steep slope to a place of magic. Stately they march, these pictographs, around the serpentine face of a cliff that towers above the surrounding countryside. Some of the paintings on the rock are very old and have seen many cycles of dance which are Zuni years; some have joined the collage more recently. The paintings are a whole—a gallery organized around an instinctive aesthetic unity. They are powerful works of native art, and that which they image is at variance with Euro-American views of reality and the expectations of Euro-American art. The skillful, sensitive, lifelike detailing of the mythic figures is arresting—their assuredness of line expressing such a presence that the perfect paintings grow ever more arresting and perfect in the recollection of those who have known their power. Framed in summer by the rust of the red New Mexico earth, the pale green of sage, the yellow-green-gold of native grasses; in winter by the quintessential whiteness of snow; and at all times by the towering rock formation on which they are painted, these figures stand quietly subsuming all their surroundings. They are a part of the Zuni world and the Zuni world a part of them.

Helen and Kathy helped me down the slope at the other end of the ridge of paintings. As we got back to the car and the place from which we had begun the hike, Helen said, "Boy, I'm hot. This being your faithful Indian guide is hard work."

We all laughed. Helen asked how I felt. The trip added visions of power and stark beauty to my life and dreams, and I said with some surprise, "I feel tired out from the hike, but I think I feel much better than I did before we went on the pilgrimage."

Helen smiled her beautiful smile and said, "I thought you would."

CALLING THE BONE PRESSER

In addition to traditional advice or home remedies or exercise therapy and preventative medicine, help also is sought at Zuni from another source. Musculoskeletal injuries and complaints often call into action the bone pressers. Helen told us stories about them:

❖ There was a little white—Franklin's classmate. Her name is Harriet. About a month ago she broke her arm, and her mother and them were on a trip, and she stayed with a Zuni girl. They had gotten a medicine man to put her bones back into place, [pauses] and when the mom came back, she took her to Gallup to have them x-ray her arm because she didn't believe her at first [laughs] that her arm had gotten broken because she fell out of a tree. The doctors there had seen the x-rays and they said, "Yeah," she had broken her hand, and they were asking her [*laughs to the end of her story*] all kinds of questions about how he did it and what did he do.[17]

❖   I just had my back, my spine—Two of them went this way, and two of them went this way, and then my neck—Scott was rubbing my back, and he was saying, "You got a big couple of dips right here." And he said, "You should get somebody to put your—" What is that? A slipped disk? Yeah, and then we just put it off for about a week, and I started noticing my neck was affecting my whole head, you know. I couldn't keep my eyes open, and I was just getting a stinging pain in my area.

So we finally got this old man, and he put me back. I guess something popped out on this side. I don't know what it was—maybe a bone or something. But he said, "What do you want to get fixed?"

And I said, "Well, my back, or, no, my neck," [*laughs*] 'cause I didn't know where, [but] I knew it was hurting. I said, "Might as well just check both places," you know, and they were both off. So he got them put back in place.

Kathy: How did he put them back in place?

Helen: Just pressing it, and it kind of hurt. He asked me how long I had had it like that, and I said maybe three weeks had gone by from the time when it first started hurting till it got real bad. And then just warming it. I liked this guy 'cause he doesn't hurt as much. Some just, you know, don't warm it up. I usually give him a cup of coffee 'cause it warms him up inside, so it makes it easier for him to put—

I went and picked him up. They usually come to your house, and I got all right. It was just out. He said, "If you had waited a little longer, it would have hurt more." And then I had to call him back about four days ago 'cause just after he left, I was pulling the waterbed out and vacuuming through there, and I got my joint twisted, facing this way, and I couldn't pick anything up. It started hurting, and I had to call him back, and he said, "Yeah, it is twisted." And Scott had hurt his hand, too, so he fixed his hand up. After he fixes it, he'll just tell you to exercise it so you'll keep it in place.

Kathy: How many bone pressers are there in Zuni?

Helen: I don't know. I know of that old man and then—I know she's related to us on my mother's side—this lady. I know there's some more. That old man's real busy: he works all day and all night, and he usually leaves early in the morning, walking to his patients; and usually if he's not home yet, they leave word, and he'll either come that night if he's got time or the next morning. He's on the go all the time. There's a lot of people who get hurt, and that's all he does all day long—like a full-time job.

I've given him a head scarf. The first time, I gave him a sack of flour, coffee, and five dollars 'cause he worked on Scott and I; and the next time, I gave him sweet rolls, more coffee, and a scarf and money 'cause he worked on my sister, Scott, and I—and Franklin. Franklin came running in. He was laughing at Angel 'cause she was sitting in the car revving up the gas and holding up the brake because she was on that little hill right there. [*laughs*]

He was running, laughing at her—and he tripped and fell, and landed like this, so all these fingers got messed up. [*laughs*] So he got fixed, too.

But, that's what I paid him. [And] my sister, I don't know what she did. There were some bones popped out, and they'd been like that for a long time, and I told her to have him check her. I said, "'Cause it's not going to hurt," and he put them back in. They were just a couple of lumps in there. I don't know, I guess—

When he worked on my back, I went and got a bench, and I sat. He was sitting on the couch behind me, and he just pushed them back in place with his hand. They use arrowheads, too, to align your back. He just pressed it against my bone after it was in place, and did the same thing right here, too.[18]

The next Shalako morning Helen called. Kathy answered the phone, and Helen began the conversation by asking how we had been. Kathy said that we were fine, and Helen and she talked for awhile about the weather, and then Helen asked if we were coming over to Zuni for Shalako. Kathy answered that we could not attend Shalako this year, and Helen asked again how we had all been. This time Kathy told Helen that we had been awfully busy working but were all right. Helen said that she had been very busy, too, because she had lots of orders for the pottery hanging lamps she had been making and because she had been helping her mother move into a new trailer that her parents had placed between their old one and their son's house. She further explained that she was going to move into the old trailer once her mother moved into the new one. She laughed and said:

❖ I am involved in three movings, and it gets confusing. Last night I got ready to fix supper at our old place and discovered that I needed some of the things I had already taken over to Mom's old trailer, and I had to go move them back again temporarily. [laughs][19]

After Helen again laughed, she paused for a very long time (for an Anglo-American conversation), took a very deep breath, and asked very directly, "How has Keith's back been?"

Now it was Kathy's turn to pause. She decided that a more complete and honest answer was called for than people usually want or expect when they ask how others are, and said, "Well, I don't know if it is the cold weather or what, but he has been having quite a bit of pain and stiffness all fall and is not getting along all that well."

Helen responded instantly, "I knew! I just knew! I thought so! I told my husband I was worried about Keith's back. We talked about it, and the one thing we could think of was having a bone presser check him. Do you think Keith would be interested in doing that?"

Kathy said that having a bone presser check me sounded like a good idea. She would talk it over with me, and we would call her back.

I had been lying in bed while Kathy talked with Helen. I thought that I had been able to follow the gist of the conversation, but it seemed almost too good to be true. I had never dreamed of actually seeing a bone presser "check" a patient, much less of being the patient. I enthusiastically agreed, we looked at our calendar to see when we could make the trip to Zuni, and—within an hour—we tried to call Helen back. Because of Shalako, all of the telephone lines to Zuni were busy, and we were not able to get back in touch with her that day.

Kathy finally reached Helen two days later, and they made arrangements for us to arrive at Zuni around noon the following Saturday. Kathy asked what gift we should bring for the bone presser, but Helen said, "Oh no, you don't need to get anything. Let me get it. I want to do that."

We were very pleased and excited about having a bone presser treat my back, both because of this chance to see Zuni from the inside and because it was caring and considerate of Helen to arrange it.

We left Flagstaff early Saturday morning, and Kathy drove directly to Helen's house. About 11:30 we knocked at the door, and Helen's husband answered and invited us in. He started a roaring fire in the Jotul wood stove and looked through back issues of *Country Living* magazine for his favorite brownie recipe. The chairs in the living room were arranged in a loose sort of C shape with a television in the opposite corner tuned to a basketball game with the sound turned off.

Helen appeared from the back of the trailer, hugged us both in greeting, and led us into the kitchen to show the hanging pottery lamps she had crafted for us. Using commercially manufactured bowls from a hobby shop in Gallup, she had drilled holes in the bottoms with a small electric tool so that she could later insert light fixtures. She also used the tool to cut out designs on the sides of the bowls, applied native paints with a yucca brush to color the backgrounds and highlight designs she had incised, polished the bowls with a polishing pebble, and finally took them to Gallup for firing in a commercial pottery kiln. When they were finished, she and her husband had installed the lamp fixtures.

After we had looked at the two lamps in the kitchen, Helen carefully packed them for us to take home. She wrapped them in multiple layers of plastic wrap and explained that it was the best material for packing Zuni pottery because it cushioned without blotting or smearing the paint. She brought us each a mug of coffee, and her husband gave us some of the brownies he had made. Then he left to take some of them to another friend and to look for the bone presser who was going to check me.

Peggy, Helen's older daughter, visited with us as she sorted through a box of lemons, squeezing them tentatively and picking one out. She rolled it back and forth between her hands, cut it in half, and sucked out the juice. As Peggy went on eating her breakfast, Helen looked through the lemons, selected the nicest ones and put them in a bag. She told us that the bone presser had checked Peggy's arm a week before because she had been having pains from her fingers to her elbow. She said the man had reported that something in Peggy's wrist was out of place and had explained that because young people heal rapidly, it would hurt to move it back. Peggy agreed that her treatment had been very painful.

Helen's husband now returned from delivering the brownies and said that he had gone by the bone presser's house but had not found him there. He and Helen noted that the bone presser was busy most of the day making his rounds and that he did not make appointments but simply went to people's homes as they needed him. They explained that they would use some of the lemons in the box as a part of the bone presser's payment, that he also used money given to him to buy food, and that within four days he burned or placed in the Zuni River a portion of the food given to him, or the food he bought, to feed the Zuni dead.

We sat around the kitchen table with the Rocky Mountain juniper firewood crackling in the fireplace and filling the area with waves of heat and the fragrance of cedar. We talked, laughed, ate brownies, played word games with Angel, drank mugs of steaming coffee—and finally the bone presser arrived.

Helen introduced us, and he said:

❖   I am a real old-time bone presser. I was hit by lightning, and so I became a bone presser.[20]

Helen explained to the bone presser that she wanted to have him check my back and Peggy's arm, and she asked me if I wanted to go first.

I said, "No, I'll go after Peggy."

The bone presser asked Peggy what she wanted him to look at, and she told him about how she had hurt her hand and how he had treated it. He looked at her hand, breathed his breath upon an arrowhead he took from his pocket—and in so doing, in Zuni thought, breathed his life upon it—and stroked her hand and arm gently with the broad side of the arrowhead held in his hand. He told her that she should be feeling better in two or four days.

I was next. After Helen explained to the bone presser that she wanted him to check my back, he instructed me to remove my shirt and to stand before him with my back turned to him as he sat on a stool. He asked me why I wanted him to check my back, and I told him that I had a degenerative disk disease and had had two ruptured disks surgically removed but still had a good deal of pain in my lower back and right leg.

He breathed his life on his arrowhead, showed it to me, and then said:

❖   See this arrowhead? It is my arrowhead. I found this arrowhead one day when I was out walking by Corn Mountain. To find an arrowhead means that it is your arrowhead and you should use it.[21]

He breathed his life upon his arrowhead again, and then he rubbed it slowly over the scar on my bare back from the operation and down my right leg over my Levis. He said, "You will begin to feel better in two or four days, most probably. You should come call me again if you need another treatment, but this should most likely take care of your back."

Helen gave him the bag of lemons, a scarf, and a ten dollar bill. He held the gifts and the money in his hands, moved them slowly in a counterclockwise circle, and recited prayers in Zuni.

It helped. The fact that Helen had arranged for me to be checked by the bone presser took my mind off the pain. In some ways, it was a turning point in my acceptance of things I could not do, as well as an affirmation of things that I *could.* Certainly it added to my sense of what it means to be Zuni.

Bone pressers' treatments involve questioning patients about symptoms and their duration and possible traumatic causes. The pressers usually offer a diagnosis to the effect that a bone or ligament is "out of place" and then "put it back" by pressing on the affected area with their hands or an arrowhead and by reciting prayers in Zuni. Pressers also frequently suggest that the patient will begin to feel better soon, and they sometimes predict that the improvement will begin in a certain number of days.

Bone pressers are believed to be specially chosen for their roles by being struck by lightning or being near where lightning has struck, and they recount their experiences during the initial treatment of patients, much as medical doctors post diplomas on the walls of their offices. Some Zunis stress the training bone pressers receive as a part of the apprenticed relationship they undergo, while others rarely mention it.

There are a number of active bone pressers at Zuni. The tradition is alive and well, and the pressers are reported to be busy from dawn to dusk making house calls. As payment for services, they receive gifts of food, clothing, or money and bless the gifts and the patient with prayers. Sometimes more than one treatment is required, but most Zuni patients respond well to bone pressing.

WITCHES AND MEDICINE MEN

When people at Zuni feel an illness or trauma requires help other than home remedies, preventative medicine, or bone pressing, they seek it. A traditional explanation of such illnesses is that a foreign object has been magically induced into the patient's body by witchcraft.

The first level of defense against witchcraft at Zuni is preventative medicine and home remedies. Just as Zuni homes today have remedies like Vicks cough syrup, borrowed from Anglo-American culture, so some Zuni remedies and preventative medicine dealing with witchcraft also come in part from Anglo-American culture. "New Age" beliefs and practices are among the Anglo-American remedies and preventative practices borrowed by some of the younger Zunis. Both Helen and her husband have at various times worked with and for New Age practitioners in Santa Fe, New Mexico, and both have accepted elements from New Age thought that fit their Zuni sense of form. Once when we were visiting with Helen, I asked her if people other than Zunis could be troubled by witchcraft and, if so, what they could do about it. She said that they could and offered this advice for non-Zunis:

Helen: "Do you know what you could do?"

Keith: "No, I don't."

Helen: "I guess you wouldn't, you being Anglo and all. Well, the first thing is that you could take that crystal I gave you. You should carry it all the time and clean it by covering it with salt and leaving it overnight."

Kathy: "Salt water?"

Helen: "No, just plain salt. I cleaned mine with table salt last week. Then the next thing you do is just stop for a minute before you leave the house and say: 'Father, may the light be with me.'"

Keith: "That's beautiful!"

Helen: "And it works. It just *surrounds* you with light. And another thing: just before you leave the house, stop, stand with your legs slightly apart, and bend your knees just a little. Then just imagine a white flower hovering just above the crown of your head. Then you take deep breaths, and you just draw the flower into your body down to your belly button. Then you put your hands together so they make a pyramid and put it over your belly button. Then you imagine a light coming out of your belly button and making a wall of light around you. Then you imagine the light spinning around you counterclockwise five or six times or for awhile. Then that will make people who wish you harm want to stay away from you. I don't know why, but they can't stand the light."

Keith: "Creatures of darkness shun the light."

Helen: "Yes; and you probably should clean the house. The way you do that—there's two ways—you can take sage and cedar. You know the kind we use for ceremonies?"

Kathy: "Yes."

Helen: "Well, you can take that and burn it and take that to all the corners of the house and you can leave it in the house. It smells real nice. But if you use pitch, you'll have to take it way far away."

Keith: "Why?"

Helen: "Well, it's absorbed the evil, and you need to get rid of it."

Keith: "Oh."

Helen: "You also can use the crystal I gave you. You take it to each of the corners. Start at the end and go to the front door. You wash it. When you get to the door, you back out and hold the crystal in your right hand. Then you make a circle counterclockwise several times around about the door. Then you put the crystal in some water and then you move it around in the water counterclockwise. Then you put the crystal on a paper napkin to dry. Oh, do it on a sunny day; don't do it on a cloudy day. So put it on a paper napkin and let it dry on the porch in the sun. It's flushing the power. Then that water you got to take far away because the power will just come back in the house if you don't take it far away."

Kathy: "Do you have to get rid of the salt when you use it?"

Helen: "No, the salt's all right. That just clears anger. It doesn't clean the house. Oh, there's one more thing. If you see somebody and you think they may wish you harm, imagine them bathed in a pink light. That way they can't be nasty to you then. They won't even want to anymore."

We got out the crystal Helen had given me and purified it—and the house. I began carrying it with me, and we tried performing the light rituals. Then a disaster occurred. Like Angel, I lost my crystal and felt somehow unprotected and vulnerable without it. The next time we visited Helen, I told her that I had lost the crystal she had given me. She laughed and said exactly what I had expected, "Just like Angel," took another crystal from her pocket, and gave it to me, suggesting that maybe I should go to a New Age store and get a pouch for it like the medicine bags Navajos wear. I followed her suggestion and bought a leather pouch. Kathy got me two additional stones for my bag—a forked piece of red coral (two in one) and a half-turquoise, half-malachite rock (a stone on the border)—and, in honor of Clyde Manybeads and Navajo humor, I added one of the pills I have to take every day. So I now have my own personal cross-cultural medicine bag, and I know two rituals not only to combat evil but also to turn evil from its path. That's pretty good, me being Anglo and all.

If home remedies and preventative medicine are not enough to deal with perceived witchcraft threats, Zunis have yet another level of help open to them: the medicine men. From the stories people told us and from our library research, we gradually gained a sense of witchcraft and medicine men. Witches, medicine men, and medicine men's treatments for witchcraft are major topics and themes of Zuni stories told in conversation, and we heard many of them:

❖ I've never seen anything like a witch change into an animal, but other people have. You know, this one guy that was being held in the drunk tank turned himself into a cat. [*laughs*] And everybody had their offices in one side of the tribal building and the courtroom, and the other side was the jail house; so when that happened, everybody went in to see. He was in the cell, and they hadn't let him out. They just came upon it 'cause they were going to feed him, and he wasn't in there. But that cat was in there.[22]

❖ They don't do anything to witches. They used to a long time ago. They were caught and kept—They made them stay awake all night, and if they didn't have a good excuse—this was done by the priests—they'd go—he'd tell them, like, that his sister was sick or something; then they'd send someone to find out if she was really sick, and if she wasn't, then if he didn't tell them the truth by morning, they'd kill him. They'd just club him on the head, and that's how they kept witchcraft down a long time ago. Now, they can't, unless they're in animal form, and you shoot them.[23]

❖ Who was that old man that died, that one that was always hurting everybody? Oh, yeah, there's this one—I won't tell his name—but this one man, I think had gotten shot, but he was in animal form just over here where that gray building is. [*moves curtain and points out the window*] And this one lady was saying that he had tried to get into her house, and they looked out, and they knew who it was, and they knew he was hurt, but they didn't let him in, and he passed away from that.[24]

❖ There's no particular time you're supposed not to discuss witchcraft, but it gets down to where you're talking about a certain person, and they just say not to. Every time I've had a discussion at night, it just—I was talking to the kids about this one person that, uh, is one, and I told them to just be real [*laughs*] nice to this one person. Giving them a lecture kind of telling them, "No matter if you don't like them, you just be real polite and everything," and Franklin just started. He scared me 'cause it's just like his heart was pounding so hard. I felt him on the back, and I could feel it, his heart beating back here, and he goes, "Mom." He was scared, and he said, "Mom, let's don't talk about them anymore." They were supposed to meet that person the next day, and I was just telling them, you know—He scared us—all of us—and the girls started crying 'cause they knew he was hurting. But I don't know. Nothing happened to the girls. It was just Franklin, and we were all sitting on the bed. Maybe that person sensed something. I don't know. But that happened, so we just didn't say anything else about it. Maybe if they sense you're thinking about them—[25]

❖   *Michelle:* The witches can do all sorts of things, whatever they want to do.

Michael: Especially if it starts working in your head, like—I don't know how you can say that. It gets to your head, especially when they're all talking about getting witched and stuff like that, and especially if you're at a weak point or at a vulnerable time. That's when a lot of witches supposedly start using their witchcraft on you—when there's something going on inside your family, like something emotional or something tragic.

The medicine fraternities right after Shalako, they have this religious thing every year, and lots of people go to that place, to their house during that night. They stay all night. They're dancing and doing all of their medicine, all their stuff like that, and people can get cured from whatever sickness they have, and, like, they know where your pain is coming from, too.

Michelle: And your thoughts, too. You have to go with a clear mind. You can't think of them as being weird or anything like that 'cause they can shame you out.

Michael: They can sense it when you don't have belief in them; and if you laugh or stuff like that—if you don't show any respect to them—they'll get rough with you, too, 'cause they've done that to their own people, too, when they start giggling maybe, or when they show disrespect and stuff like that. But usually when you're sick, you'll go over there and sit down, and after awhile they start curing the people, going around, all these medicine men; and maybe if you got problems like headaches, they'll just come up exactly, and they'll know where to take out their, um, whatever they take out. They'll just put their mouth to it and, like, suck it out. It won't be just one guy doing that; it will be different medicine people that will, and they'll come up to the same spot, too. You don't have to say nothing. You just go over there when you're sick, and they know to get it and what the problem is.

Michelle: This is, like, in the wintertime.

Michael: And there's some in the summertime. They have a lot of get-togethers like that, the medicine group, and when it's open you can go, the public can go. Sometimes it's just invited guests. I mean, it's just for certain people.

Michelle: Their own people—

Michael: Yeah. What most people do if the sickness is just more or less starting, if a religious thing like that is going on, they go there first and then after that they go up to the hospital. And if it keeps persisting, then they come back down and seek more help from the medicine groups. They go both ways.

The doctors, they allow medicine men to go up there and practice their medicine, too, in the rooms. My dad's a medicine man, and he goes up there a lot, and he doesn't just help out people. He works with animals, too, like if they have a sheep camp; witches, they go over there, too.

Michelle: Like, if they're jealous of other people having animals and it's time for them to deliver their lambs, they can stop that by doing something not to let them have a normal birth. They get stuck, or they die, or something. He makes it easier by doing stuff for them. And, like, for a human being, if they, I mean, she's going into labor and it's kind of hard for her, he does that. He makes it easier.

Michael: They have special songs—sort of medicine songs that have power to them. They can't just sing them any time.

Michelle: They usually do that in the wintertime. They practice their songs and stuff.

Michael: One time, my dad was singing or practicing, and he didn't know there was a dog around that was pregnant, and he was singing it, singing his birth-giving songs, and that dog—

Michelle: —was in the same room—

Michael: —miscarried, or gave premature birth. Those songs are very sacred, and they're not supposed to sing—They have to watch when they practice them.[26]

❖   They even claim little children are witches. They learn young—five-, eight-, nine-, ten-year-olds. It's kind of weird, too. Like at night, you'll see them running around—little kids—and you'll wonder, "What are they doing out that late," one o'clock in the morning, you know. A little kid will be walking around—But, like, recently, my niece was coming from her grandma's house, walking home just a couple of yards away. She was ready to go into her house, and she noticed somebody standing by her sister's window peeking in. They consider those people witches, and he was standing there—long hair, black outfit—just looking in her window. She ran in, told her dad, and he was gone. But just any age they consider a witch, and if people catch 'em doing it, too, they let [others] know. It's like they have their own little cult somewhere, and you never know where they are going to meet or when they're going—Your best friend could be a witch, and you wouldn't even know it. It's just there, and I don't think there could be a way to cure it 'cause it's every day they're initiating somebody new.[27]

❖   That medicine man is related to my sister-in-law, and if Mom's not around to help me go get him, then I know how to prepare the stuff. But it's just what you have to say when you go get him. That's what I need help on, and that's what I used to go get her for. Just to help me tell him what you're supposed to say.[28]

❖   Witches can put things in you to make you sick. Usually, if you can't find out from a doctor, then sometimes you just sense that, you know, it's not anything a doctor can do. Then they just go pick a medicine man up. Like, when the kids, they're having pains or something and they're really hurting, you know, and uh, I don't know. It's—I don't know. You get to where you know the difference between when you're real sick and when—If I sense anything, I ask my mom 'cause you have to prepare stuff, and when you go call him, you have to tell him "my father" or whatever he is in relation. Like, when my mom goes, I think she would call him "my brother." It's different in the age he is to you. They say something to him, and he tells them he'll be over, and he'll ask you where you live, and then you just tell him, and he comes.[29]

❖ I've gone and seen a medicine man on times [*pauses*] where I wasn't [*pauses*] sure of my behavior. Some people might call it being [*pauses*] bewitched to where you're not actually controlling your own emotions. But maybe somebody like a witch might be controlling your emotions, so I wasn't sure if I was actually being myself, so I had to go see a medicine man to [*pauses*] have him look at me.

I used to just stay at home and not [*pauses*] go out every night and stay away from alcohol and all that. And [*pauses*] all of a sudden I started getting into stuff like that, so [*pauses*] my grandma advised me to see a medicine man, so I went to see one. [*pauses*] I feel that I am [*pauses*] slowly getting back to being myself with his help.[30]

Zuni medicine men are specialists in treating magically caused illnesses by religious ceremonies. This form of treatment, like bone pressing, involves counseling the patient (sometimes including suggestions for behavioral changes) and positive statements on the expected improvement. Stories about this aspect of Zuni medicine describe the nature and behaviors of witches, medicine men's treatments for witchcraft-caused illness, or a combination of these. Members of the medicine fraternities are called medicine men (a term also applied to bone pressers), and they specialize in treating particular areas of the human body. Medicine men are valued for their skill and dedication, but they are not accorded any special stature or privilege; they, too, are a part of the Zuni dance of life. The requirements for membership in the medicine fraternities are a desire to serve people and having been treated by a medicine man. Members of the fraternities join after being cured themselves by this Zuni medicine.

A Zuni feeling the need for treatment by a medicine man may request one at any time of the year. Medicine men make house calls, and their fraternities hold a special annual curing ceremony open to all members of the village. The gifts customarily given to a medicine man who makes a house call are similar to those given to a bone presser. As is true of bone pressers, there are many active medicine men at Zuni.

The most common response of a patient to a medicine man's treatment, as is also true of bone pressing, is to see it as therapeutic and life affirming. Some of the Zunis interpret the medicine man's treatment quite literally, while some see it symbolically as a kind of psychotherapy or stress management, but almost all of the people feel that it is of great value.

BELIEVING IN BOTH

The Zunis have a long history of accepting other technologies that seem worthwhile to them. Matilda Coxe Stevenson brought a supply of Euro-American medicines with her from Washington to use when she lived at Zuni, far removed from the Euro-American medical tradition. She reported that the Zunis with whom she lived in the 1880s and 1890s were very open-minded concerning her medicines and appreciative of her concern and help. Today the Zunis frequently use Euro-American medical systems and medicine for all diseases normally recognized and treated by them—in other words, all problems for which Americans in general seek medical help from doctors and hospitals.

There is a modern Indian Health Service Hospital, Zuni Community Comprehensive Health Center, at nearby Black Rock, New Mexico, where the Zunis go for treatment, and it is always busy. The doctors there also refer Zuni patients to other Euro-American medical facilities near and far for specialized therapies or medical procedures not available at the center. Helen and other Zunis tell stories about this kind of medicine:

❖   They didn't tell me Franklin was allergic to the fat in the milk, and I couldn't figure out why he won't keep anything down. He was just going both ways, and he'd vomit, you know, real far. He was allergic to that formula, and I never gave Peggy that formula. I started to and then I cut her off and started giving her just Carnation. And so I started doing that, and then a couple of months later, my sister-in-law came—and her aunt's a nurse, and she was staying with her. She said, "Oh, I forgot to tell you Franklin's allergic to [*laughs*] that formula, and don't give it to him," after I had found out. In the meantime, I had taken him up to the hospital, and they said that he needed to get on that soybean formula.[31]

❖   Well, I had been going to school, and I got that, um, trachoma in my eyes, and then what made me blind when I was about ten years old, I think, I was getting bad when I was in school, and the things that they put on the blackboard don't show, and I had to go close to the blackboard to copy some numbers and then answer them. But it's getting bad, so that five looks like a three, and three looks like five sometimes, and then when they put six, that's the time I make mistakes. It looks like a five again, you know. My other answers were correct, only I make mistakes in those numbers, and the teacher always hit me on the head or either go like this and spank me back here, and he used to just stand me in the corner because I don't try. "I try," I said, but they treat me so mean, and so I told one time our principal from Polacca. He came up to see his children, the students from Polacca Day

School, and so I told him about it. "I can't see good. Everything look dull, and I can't see far, too, and [when] the sun hit my eye, it hurt."

And so, "I'll take you home." Then he went over to the superintendent, Mr. Brown. His name's Mr. Brown, and so he asked him, and— "Yeah, it can be, it could be treated—somehow." So he took me home. For that reason, I was out there, and then one lady—a wealthy lady was touring, and she came to our place and said, "Is there any vacant place where we can camp for one or two weeks?"

We had a big peach orchard, and my father let them. "Go ahead and just choose wherever you want to stay. It's a big place." It's a nice sandy clean place, you know, where the fruit was growing, so they stayed there. They fixed their camps, you know, everything how the millionaire people are. They just made sidewalks right on the sand, and everything was all built up. And then finally they were staying there a week, and they come to our house. "Why don't you come to our house, and we all talk together?" my father said to them, so they came, and they were talking about how they made pottery and things like that, you know, to make money, and so when it got dark, I come out from the house.

I come out and I walk around when the sun goes down. I could see better that way, being the night time. It's getting worse, and I used to cry, you know, 'cause I'm getting blind. And so this lady talked to my mother if she could take me to California. "You talk to her and I'll take you to one of the eye doctors." And she talked to me, and I said I wanted to go, so I did. In about two weeks' time, they were gathering all their stuff—I don't know how many truckloads they are taking there to the railroad—and [the lady said], "She can stay here for awhile, and then I can send the money. Then she can go on the train." So she did, and the check came, and the superintendent from Keams Canyon came after me, and they said, "We are going to go shopping for some new clothes." So I got in a train and went, and they were already waiting for me over there at the station at Arcadia, California.

She had a race ground there—that Anita Baldwin—and she took me to a ranch. And in no time, in one week time, she made an appointment for me, and so a doctor came and looked at my eyes, and so I went. I had a surgery on my eyes, and so I had to have my eyes closed, and they put some stuff on my eyes, I guess. I don't know what they have done to me. I didn't know. They told me when it's beginning to itch, just don't try to scratch it. Just leave it on like that; it's worse, you know, scratching it. Of course, you feel like just touching it, but don't. I didn't do anything to myself. I'm just pinching myself. [*laughs*]

And so when it's time to take it off, I guess, they took it off. [*speaks loudly*] I see everything as plain as I could see, and I didn't really feel like winking. I thought if I wink, you know, it might go away again. I really feel like I was really dreaming. Maybe it's a dream, you know, and I tried to wake myself up, and then finally I called the lady, Mrs. Anita Baldwin, and she came in and said, "The breakfast is ready for you. It's a late breakfast, but then you eat because you didn't eat anything earlier." And so I went, and I want to go outside. I saw the dogs outside, her dogs, her pets, and so I believe that I can see now. That thing had just gone away—And right away they make the picture of my eye, how it forms and that trachoma, you see. They make a picture, big eyes on the picture in where the doctor's office is. "See, look at your eye," he said. [*laughs*] I don't want to see it. [*laughingly covers her eyes*][32]

❖   Diabetes is very disabling. It can cause chronic renal failure. There are seventeen or more dialysis patients in Zuni. There's also, like with diabetes, gangrene. A couple of people have had their feet amputated. I know my uncle was a diabetic, seventy-seven year[s] old, and he had to have his toes amputated. But he died because of the infection in the blood right after he had them amputated, so there's a lot of disadvantages of diabetes.[33]

❖   He had a birth defect. I didn't go into labor when I was ready to have him. I had problems, so I went to the hospital, and they found it was a prolapsed cord. We had this old hospital then, and from there they sent me to Gallup where they do all that surgery. And I got there, and it turned out that it was that prolapsed cord, and he was already much distressed. They didn't know whether he was going to make it or not, so they did Caesarean section on me. I guess he was really bad when they got him out, and finally they got him to breathing, and I guess that's when he got that—to his brain, in his brain.

He was really a problem. He never learned how to suck on the bottle. He didn't have any strength in his jaws, so when I brought him home, [*sighs*]—he was a normal-weight baby, five pounds, fifteen ounces—we had lots of problems feeding him. I started feeding him with a spoon: thicken the cereal we get in the store; thicken that with a spoon and mix it with applesauce. That's how he survived.

And right now he still has a hard time drinking fluids, but he's a real alert little boy; he seems to understand every word that's said. He talks, but we really can't understand him. We've been with him quite awhile, and he didn't go to start school until he was about maybe nine or ten 'cause they didn't have any schools for those handicapped kids then. I think he would have learned a lot if he had started early, but in late age he is still going to school. They have a special education in school classes that he goes to.

He has this wheelchair that, well, we got help from the Elks Club and different clubs and a couple of counselors, so they finally bought him this battery-operated wheelchair. He uses that, and then just lately they got him a communication board which he is starting to learn to use. They are really something, but what's the hardest thing is to make out the layout. You have to type it in, and you have to print that out for him, and then put this overlay over this expression box, and then he points with a magnet-type light, and the words—The board talks back to him. [*laughs*] It is really something.[34]

While the stories told by the families of those who have incurable or difficult-to-manage conditions are realistic, the Zuni response to Euro-American health care generally is to view it as therapeutic and life affirming. Family, bone pressers, medicine men, and Anglo-American medical services also work *together* at Zuni. Family members suggest bone pressers or medicine men, bone pressers refer patients to medicine men, medicine men refer patients to bone pressers, bone pressers and medicine men refer patients to the Zuni Community Comprehensive Health Center, a medical doctor from the health center is an active consultant working with the Zuni Wellness Center, and members of the health center staff recommend bone pressers or medicine men as adjuncts to their treatment regimens. Zuni approaches to their medicines reflect Zuni cultural values, and people we interviewed told stories suggesting complex interactions of and between the Zuni and Euro-American health care systems Zunis use and between Zuni and Euro-American beliefs concerning health and health care:

❖   Well, when I was having my gall bladder attacks—maybe six before I finally had my surgery—I did go to see my medicine man about it. But, you know, [*pauses*] certain things they can help you in, and it's a relief too. [*pauses*] Well, the medicine man, he told me to go seek professional medical help, the doctor, because I guess they know what is coming about. He did tell me on two occasions, and I did go, and what I was told by him was true. The hospital diagnosis was about the same, and I had surgery.[35]

❖   This one girl has an allergy of some sort, and she thinks it's the witches that are doing it. At the same time, she goes to the doctor, and he gives her medicines that clear it up, so I don't know what to say about that—whether it's witches or not.[36]

❖   I believe in witchcraft, but working at the hospital it's hard to say which side is the really right side. Working more at the hospital, I can see with medication and tests and all, you know. That's there, it's there. But Zuniwise, witchwise, I don't know. You can't really say. They do really strongly believe that it will happen, and that the medicine man will take it out. And he does take things out of them—little things out of them—and tells them what is going on with their life. And then he's like a counselor, too. He'll talk to them and tell if they are having problems, "You're doing this, you're drinking more because of this and that, and it's 'cause you were witched." And he does counsel the person.
     They have doings that go on, and if you're a part of the family, they invite you, and this medicine man will go around. Sometimes there's a lot of medicine men. They just run around, and they see it in you. I guess they see that thing in you. They just—like, I'll just look at you and see it in you now, and I'll run up to you and suck it out, or use a feather or something to get it out. That's how they do it. Wherever, wherever they see it. It could be your

forehead or your arm. They suck it out, spit it out, run around again, and find somebody—I don't know how they do it, but they see it.

I've gotten some out of me. You know, I've gone to those things, and I think every person in the village has gotten something taken out. Well, these things are just like going to clinic. Oh, I don't know how it is—not like a clinic—like a physical. You go for a physical. You're sitting in there, and you just go there to see if you have anything in you. And if you do, they take it out. If not, then you aren't witched, but that's basically what it is—just like a physical exam. But if you're really sick, then they usually lay you down by yourself.

Like my little boy—I'll just give you an example. He was sick when he was about five years old. He had pneumonia clinically, but the doctor that was treating him was a medical student, and he didn't really know at that time what was going on. He kept sending him home, and then my father got worried 'cause he had a high fever like 103 for two days, and he just constantly laid on the couch and cried. I just kept taking him up there, and that guy going, "No, just take him home. He's just got a cold."

They worried about that, so they brought this lady in, and she checked him, and they said he was witched and something was wrong with his collar, or something, and that was why he was having a high temperature. After that I went back to the hospital again, and they gave him amoxicilin—I think it was amoxicilin—to cure the pneumonia. His regular doctor had come [back], and, boy, she just went like this to the medical student, "He should have been in the hospital." You see two sides of it, you know. It's just like a doctor. They call a doctor to the house to try to cure the patient.[37]

❖   They witch babies, too. When I was pregnant, I had a lot of pain in my abdomen, but I thought it was due to the stretching. So they checked and said I was already witched, that somebody was trying to get my baby to kill it, that they didn't want me to have the baby. But it's just widespread; just any little thing, they'll call him in and he'll tell you what's going on. They just called him in like a doctor and said, "She's having problems with her stomach, and we think somebody witched her." 'Cause working at the hospital, I'm in constant contact with a lot of people, and they just figured that. After that, they told me to start walking around in the back offices—not to come up front like I had been doing. Well, the pain did go away. But the midwife, she could tell what I was going to have. She said, "You're going to have a boy." [*laughs*] And I had a boy. Well, I believe both. I don't know. [*laughs*][38]

❖   I think that the old Indian way of understanding things is that there's all purposes for everything around you. I think through early pregnancy that the father, both parents, the mother-to-be, have to be cautious to protect the welfare of the unborn child. Like, for instance, if I am driving down the road and accidentally hit an animal and cause the animal to be crippled physically or killed; if I accidentally run over a dog or cat, rabbit, [and] I cannot take care of my wife immediately, this could cause either a miscarriage or cause the child to be born with a tangled body, no muscles existing, or whatever—disabled because of this accident that I had previous months or weeks.

Usually we contact our medicine man, even though mentally we know, but just to double check in a way. Sure enough, a medicine man could easily identify the need, what you should do to purify, undo all that it causes. If you properly take care of the procedure, do it rightly, the instructions that the medicine man had given to you, it helps the development. It could be like if the infant has been checked, x-rayed thoroughly under a physician's care in any hospital, but yet they could say, "We got to operate this. We got to do this." But sometimes that is not so in [the] Indian way. Of course you have to have faith to have it work, so with the faith as a base part, you just leave it entirely up to that point, and eventually the child will get its own natural development. As it develops from each month to a year, and as years go by, he'll start to walk, just naturally.

Also during the hunting season, if your wife is expecting, you shouldn't go hunting 'cause you're liable to damage the unborn if you kill a deer, even skin it. Even going through the proper rituals as the Indian hunters go by in an ancient setting way, it may cause your unborn child some of these difficulties. So you have to wait till the child is born; mentally and physically if he is all right, then you have a way to fulfill your hunting for that year. All the cautions and instructions come from the parents, paternal as well maternal, to the couple, you know. It's the respected that we listen [to] 'cause everybody throughout the whole world wants a normal baby, you know.

Another thing that can cause problems for the unborn is that if there's death within the family—the immediate family to the unborn, the expectant mother—if you see a dead body being dressed or see a dead body in front of you that you can't miss seeing, or if a dead body is being brought out from the house to the graveyard and you happen to be in the area, just a little glance would psychologically affect your unborn child. When the child is born, the skin is so yellowish. I'm not a medical person to identify these kind of pale infants, and this causes death. Normally we have some midwives in the village that are specialized in certain ways to take care of the newborn infant, and they could have visited one of the ancient archaeological sites where our ancestors had lived long, long time ago—several hundred or even close to a thousand years ago. And also they find a human bone from this area, bring it back, and uh, I don't really know exactly the steps that they take to care for the newborn infant; but they smoke the little infant with this bone and cleanse him, and purify them with it, and that erases the paleness, and again that newborn child will have its natural color of skin.

So again at this time and age, I think our hospital staff members across the nation are kind of dealing with medicine on the Indian side. Well, we have this here in Zuni, the good relationship that has been established through our area office down to our medicine lodge fraternity members here in Zuni. Indian people understand that it is a necessary thing to have it done with medical terms.

I have experienced that myself with one of the young ones that we lost in our family, and they tried to do that medical help. But he died within a few days, a newborn, 'cause he was so—uh. We approached the medicine man before he was released with his mother from the hospital. They really go into that before he was sent for more examination in Albuquerque, but he died within a couple of days later, so they autopsied, which we approved, and a week later or so the body returned back to us for burial. And knowing that, this struck me: I guess my wife was expecting one or two months when I was going to work in Gallup and ran over a dog accidentally without seeing. We should have taken care of that, knowing all this from our ancestors' knowledge, but sometimes it slips your mind, you know. If we had taken care of it properly before it was born, I'm pretty sure we could—But again, it's pretty hard to tell.[39]

These conversational stories tell of care provided by home remedies and advice, bone pressers, medicine men, Western medicine, and combinations of all of these. The same complex interactions of medicines were especially evident and poignant in the story of a Zuni who was himself disabled:

❖   For my part I am paralyzed, disabled, from my waist down because I was involved in an accident which I really didn't expect, and besides I wasn't driving at the time. So I guess I got very unfortunate that I got the worst of it.

      Some people talk to me as, you know, I'm not really on the wheelchair, but others look and look away. Especially when some of my friends or relatives sees me, they all have these hesitations to look at me, or they just walk away, and they don't want to say "hi" or anything like that, which does not bother me at all because I know how it feels to see someone being on the wheelchair or being disabled with maybe a cane or with a crutch, braces, or anything like that. But so far I am very aware of what to expect when I go in public—what to expect and what not to expect.

      When I first got hurt, it took about two to close to four years before I was able to do what I was supposed to do, and it took people awhile for them to begin to accept me. At that time a lot of my relatives could come over to me and say, "Hi, how are you doing?" and all that, and then they would talk about the weather or whatever they had to say as a part of their making a living. And all that was the changes I was seeing in the people around here.

      My being disabled, I usually go up to the rehab center in Denver every year for a checkup. It's more like a physical: they keep up with me as to if I'm healthy; or, if there's something wrong with me, they will let me know. Other than that they just check me over to make sure there's nothing wrong. As far as my health is concerned, it's mostly my kidneys, my heart, and my blood pressure, and then the rest is up to me. Either I take care of myself or I just give up, but that is not my intentions. Sometimes I have a presser come by when I am having trouble with spasms, and he helps me. At times I go for a medicine man; if I see that I have to associate with the Public Health Service, I normally call a medicine man. It's my belief it helps to take some of my depression out of me and helps my health problems.[40]

THE DANCE OF HEALTH

And the meanings of the stories? The long-practiced Zuni cultural trait of accepting technologies from other cultures when the technologies seem to be of value is the major Zuni cultural trait demonstrated by Zuni medicine. The Zuni dance comfortably encompasses video-cassette recorders and prayer bowls. This ease of integrating technology from many sources into their existent culture, one of the major reasons the Zunis remain the same but are always changing, is clearly evident in their use of exercise therapy and wellness medicine and in their use of Euro-American medicines—but for different reasons.

Running was long valued at Zuni; so when a health educator suggested and extolled it, Zuni men, women and children seeking the grace of the dance ran when the rocks burned, when the winds blew ice, when the small rains gently cleansed the earth, when the towering thunder clouds came roaring down. They ran through fields and canyons transformed by crystalline snow, through arroyos tinged lilac by blooms of the wild bee plant, by towering rocks awash with pure golden light. Dancing they ran at Zuni, as the people at Zuni had run before them.

The integrating Zuni cultural value and belief shown in the Zuni cultural trait of accepting technologies like Euro-American medicine which, unlike wellness medicine, are new and different and not a return to old ways is the Zuni sense of the nature of the world—the essence of their culture. At Zuni the successful person is one who serves the common good without attracting attention to himself or becoming in any way the subject of controversy. He is neither rich nor poor, pitied nor envied, and does not stand out from the group.

The single most important moment in the life of a Zuni is the moment when it is revealed to him that the Ko-ko, Shalako, and Ko'yemshi figures he has seen dancing through the village and has respected, worshiped, and even feared, were his uncles and other older males—and that he himself will join the faceless dance. Reactions to this moment vary, of course, from individual to individual; but the traditionally expected response is that at this moment the Zuni child sees and understands the holistic nature of life and reality. He finds that the supernaturals are in and serve the living, that the living are in and serve the supernaturals, that to be a member of the People of the Middle Place is to be a part of the sum and the sum of a part, that life is one. Traditionally, the child is supposed to be reborn at this moment; again in the literal repetition of the moment when he is among those who reveal it to the next generation; and, likewise, in the symbolic reenactment of the moment when he—costumed so as to be indistinguishable from others—joins the long line of dancing Ko-ko, Shalako, and Ko'yemshi that reaches from Zuni prehistory to Zuni posthistory. Before this moment he was a child; after this moment he is Zuni.

The Euro-American views of reality as a series of dichotomies of the sacred and the secular, the body and the spirit, are by this moment defeated and destroyed and made meaningless at Zuni. Family, wellness medicine, bone pressers, medicine men, and Euro-American medicine are by this endlessly unfolding moment made parts of a whole—adjuncts to the dance. In traditional Zuni thought the expected outcome of medicine is that everything—home remedies, exercise, manipulation, prayers, ceremony, pills, surgery, or a combination of these—will hasten a return to health. Those singled out by the misfortune of illness will be reintegrated into the Middle Place, and the dance will continue. On one level, at least part of the time, this Zuni way of seeing the expected outcome of medicine in positive terms may well be the best medicine of all. At one level, at least part of the time, seeing it so makes it so—and the dance continues.

CHAPTER THREE

Tracking Contemporary Legends

CLYDE MANYBEADS, our Ramah Navajo co-researcher, was born and lived his entire life on the borders between cultures. He was raised in a traditional Ramah Navajo family well acquainted with the Zuni and Mormon cultures of his own land, and with other cultures of other lands. He lived in Los Angeles while attending a watch-repair school. He once left home to work on the railroad, traveled across the western United States, and finished the trip by appearing in a movie. (He was employed in Texas as an extra and stunt man during the filming of *Arrowhead*.)

Clyde told us once that he had attended a service at a Native American Church to see what it was like. He described the sacred circle, the drum beat, the ritual ingesting of the sacred peyote buttons, the visions, the dreams, the experience of seeing all things new, the dog near the meeting that was viewed as evil incarnate and was driven off by the chants and rocks of the peyote eaters. It was not, he explained, a completely satisfactory experience. He felt fearful at one point, and the peyote priest and the other participants told him that he needed to let go and become more fully a part of the world he was observing. He told us that he tried to follow their advice but added, "Every time I just got started, I'd notice something else going on I hadn't seen before, and I'd just sorta step back to record it in my mind."

As we drove around the Ramah lands, Clyde also told us about anthropologists he had known. When he was a child, Dorothea Leighton had worked with his mother, and he remembered his amazement at discovering that her thermos jug kept water cold and how he had drunk all the cold water and made himself sick. He also told us about Clyde Kluckhohn's funeral, when the researcher's body was cremated and his ashes spread from an airplane over the canyon sheltering his cabin while Navajo friends stood silent below. He often referred to research that had been published about his own family, his home, and his people. Once when we were talking about Kluckhohn, Kathy asked him, "What would you say if someone asked you about witchcraft?" and he spoke Kluckhohn's words from *Navajo Witchcraft* with the acid delivery of a nightclub comedian: "I would say, 'Who told you I knew anything about *that?*'"

Clyde's wife was one-half Pima-Maricopa and one-half Zuni. He lived at Zuni for several years, both when he was a child attending a mission school and later as an adult living with his wife in her traditional Zuni family home. Circumstances surrounded him with cultural diversity; he welcomed it and sought to experience it to the fullest possible extent. He spoke Navajo as it is spoken in the Ramah area, knew the country and many of the families who lived in the isolated "outfits," observed his mother translate for Clyde Kluckhohn and Dorothea Leighton (her assistance as co-researcher is acknowledged and described at some length in *Children of the People*) and had a great interest and ability in interacting with people cross-culturally. His many and varied experiences, his curiosity, his sense of wonder—which caused him to have the experiences in the first place—made him an indefatigable cross-cultural fieldworker, and that is why and how I came to know him.

MICROWAVES AND VANISHING HITCHHIKERS

Kathy and I met Clyde when we were concluding the interviews at Zuni as the first phase of our grant project to study American Indians' cultures through their stories. Phase one—could there be a phase two? The recording of the Zuni kitchen-table stories had as a prerequisite years of sitting around Zuni kitchen tables sharing experiences and allusions and green chili—becoming a part of a family. Anglo-American grants, however, rarely provide the luxury of the time necessary for establishing such relationships; they often require quick results and very frequently written reports. We decided that a second phase would require working even more closely with co-researchers and depending even more upon them to create opportunities for recording people's stories and lives. And we decided to seek contemporary legends.

Such legends have been collected, anthologized, and historicized by scholars around the world—most notably by Jan Harold Brunvand and the many participants at the various International Contemporary Legend Conferences. The stories are familiar to most Anglo-Americans, as shown by the following examples:

❖   In the late seventies when I was in junior high school, I heard about a lady from Birmingham getting a microwave oven for her anniversary. This was when microwaves became available to the general public and were quite a status symbol. She was so excited about the gift that she would microwave everything in sight. The lady had one small problem. She didn't know how to cook with the oven, so it quickly lost its novelty appeal.

Some time later she was giving her two toy poodles a bath when she remembered an important appointment, and she was already late for it. The lady grabbed her dogs out of the water and started running around like a chicken with its head cut off. She ran into the kitchen to get some towels to dry off the dogs when she saw the oven. She put the dogs in the oven; set it to five minutes; grabbed her coat, purse, and keys. She went back to the kitchen, walked over to the oven, opened the door and fainted. What had been two small poodles five minutes ago was now a bloody mess from a poodle explosion.[41]

❖ A young couple ordered some [fried chicken] and sneaked it into a movie theatre. They munched on the chicken throughout the entire movie. When the lights came on after the end of the movie, the woman found that she had half of a fried rat in her hand. She had eaten the other half![42]

❖ This friend of a friend of mine said she was at the local hangout munching out when across the room all of a sudden this girl started screaming and crying. Well, all of the people in the establishment practically rushed to her and found that she was acting the way she did because there was the remains of a mouse in her [pop] bottle that she had already drank half. This girl who was by now in shock was escorted to the hospital, and rumor has it her family is suing, and it was found that the factory that had bottled that [pop] was totally infested with mice and had to be closed down.[43]

❖ This guy was driving down a deserted country road. He saw a girl standing on the shoulder with a pack on and her thumb out. He stopped, thinking he probably shouldn't. She seemed nice and harmless enough, and he asked where she was going. She said she was going anywhere he was as long as it was a little further down the road. She got in the back, and they continued. She didn't want to talk and said she was going to sleep if he didn't have any objections. Before she slept, she did mention her final, eventual destination, which was a town much further than the man was going. When he reached the place he had planned on letting her off, he stopped and announced that this was the end of the line. Getting no reply, he looked in the backseat and was astonished to see that the girl was gone. Of course the man was badly shaken. He tried not to think about the incident, but it was impossible. When he had a day off, he went to the town further down the road to the address she had given. He rang the bell and asked for the girl. He was told that she had died a premature death a number of months earlier.[44]

We chose stories like "The Vanishing Hitchhiker," "The Mouse in the [Pop] Bottle," "The Rat in the Chicken," and "The Pet in the Microwave" because contemporary legends are told more naturally over a greater range of circumstances and relationships—and with fewer restrictions—than apply to some other types of American Indian stories. (Entire classes of American Indian stories can only be told at certain seasons.) Also, as fully as other kinds of stories, contemporary legends encode cultures and reveal the concerns of peoples.

Plans bravely made, we told Helen we were going to conduct research with the Ramah Navajo similar to our work at Zuni and needed a co-researcher in that other community and culture. Based upon her personal knowledge of the skills necessary for succeeding at cross-cultural research, Helen suggested Clyde. She knew him and his family because he was married to a Zuni woman and had children and grandchildren living at Zuni, and because one of her brothers was married to one of his daughters. We discussed our project with Clyde, his wife Martha, and their daughter Deb, and all later assisted us with our research. Clyde served as co-researcher and translator when we interviewed his father and assisted us in contacting and interviewing a group of non-English-speaking Navajos.

During the year Clyde translated for us, he told family stories about his grandparents and great-grandfather, stories about his boyhood adventures and misadventures, and stories about the landmarks we passed as he guided us through the Ramah country. He told us that he was the great-grandson of Many Beads, one of the seven headmen who with their outfits had settled in the Ramah, New Mexico, area south of Gallup and east of Zuni in the years following the end of Navajo confinement at Fort Sumner in 1868. By stories, comments, and example, he led us to know and appreciate the Navajo culture at Ramah. He was a natural fieldworker with great patience and quick humor and was skilled at listening carefully and responding appropriately. There are relationships in fieldwork, as in life in general, that are characterized by quickly achieved mutual understanding, acceptance, concern, and enjoyment. Clyde and I shared such a relationship.

On the last day of our formal fieldwork together we went—as we had several times before—to interview a medicine man. The medicine man was not at home. Clyde had very much wanted to interview him because he was one of the few Navajo medicine men still active in the Ramah area, but he was out holding ceremonies or herding sheep every time we went by. The drive to his hogan was always a wonderful chance to talk with Clyde, and I shall never forget the many times we took this trip together. But the medicine man was not at home—not the first time we went to see him, and not the last day of the grant when we made the trip again.

Clyde knew that the grant required two more interviews and said, "I'm sorry he wasn't home. What do we do now? Shall we—shall we just go hogan to hogan?" The word *hootaagha* in Navajo is literally translated "to go hogan to hogan visiting," but the clear implication is that the hogans (and the visiting) are within outfits or clans. To do otherwise—to visit strangers—is a very un-Navajo thing.

I said, "Sure." And we went. We visited the very next hogan.

Clyde had no idea who lived in the very next hogan. He didn't know their clan (the mother's). He didn't know the clan they were born for (the father's). We drove off the pavement onto a narrow one-lane, deeply rutted mud road that wound away from the blacktop to a traditional Navajo home with the ground worn bare around it so it seemed a small mound of logs topping a mound of red, red earth. A man moved shyly back around the corner of the hogan when he saw us coming, but a woman came out to greet us after our expected—and required—time spent sitting silently in the car. She spoke no English. Clyde explained the project in Navajo. She invited us in. One wall of the hogan was covered with peyote buttons strung on wires to dry. We conducted the two interviews we needed, and Clyde seemed especially interested when the man said that he was from a Navajo community many miles from here.

After we left, Clyde asked, "Did you see the peyote?"

We said we had.

He said, "We interviewed some members of the Native American Church," and he said, "Guess he must have met his wife at a Squaw Dance."

We "visited hogan to hogan"—each of us rescuing the other from unexpected fieldwork pitfalls—and discussed field observations and ideas with great openness and concern for each other's ideas and opinions. We did not undergo a blood brother ceremony like that pictured in the cowboy and Indian movie which I enjoyed as a child and in which Clyde acted as a young adult. But in a sense we were brother researchers. His help made this chapter describing Ramah Navajo culture, Ramah Navajo acculturation, and their interactions as shown by Ramah Navajo contemporary legends possible; and the jokes he told us as we were in search of contemporary legends made him a natural, major source for our later research on Navajo humor reported in chapter 5. Clyde introduced one of the stories he told us that day by saying: "There was this man, a young boy, and he had just become a *Ye'iibichei* dancer—you know, they wear those big, tall masks?"

We knew.

A purpose of Navajo ritual is to confuse or frighten evil spirits. *Ye'iibichei* dancers personate spirits so powerful that their presence, their dance, and their chant dispel evil and assert balance. One of the most powerful recollections of having seen the *Ye'iibichei* is the recollection of having heard the *Ye'iibichei*. Since *Ye'iibichei* must never use the words of man nor the voice of man while costumed, they speak and perform in a non-human, high-pitched wailing—a wordless chant which communicates beyond language.

After we nodded that we knew the *Ye'ii*, Clyde continued his story:

❖   Well, one of the things about being a *Ye'ii* dancer is that you're not supposed to say anything whenever you've got that mask on. And this new guy who wasn't used to being a dancer, all of a sudden he said, "I almost forget and said something there."[45]

I asked Clyde during our journey—half as researcher half as an aficionado of an arcane art form—if he had heard the story about the old Sioux man who asked what part of the dog his companion had gotten when he got a hot dog, and Clyde said, "No, I heard he said,'That's not the part of the dog I expected.'"

THE PEOPLE

Ramah Navajo stories can only be understood in terms of Ramah Navajo culture and history—to know what it means to be Navajo. Living in the west central area of the state of New Mexico in the southwestern United States, the Ramah Navajo are one of the most frequently studied groups of the Navajo, who are in turn one of the most frequently studied of all the American Indian groups of North America. There are, of course, many reasons for the scholarly interest directed toward the Navajo, not the least of which is the fact that they are the most numerous and the most rapidly increasing of all American Indian groups in the United States.

One other major reason for scholarly interest in the Navajo is that throughout their long history they have been a sort of "living laboratory" of culture. Their lives emphasize and illustrate the basic paradox of acculturation—that a culture can be always borrowing from other cultures and yet (because the borrowing is at its behest, under its control, and subject to its extensive reinterpretation) may retain its essence unchanged and not become progressively more like the culture from which it is borrowing. Classic studies have described Navajo borrowing and re-creation of silversmithing and jewelry making, weaving, architecture, domestic animals and animal husbandry patterns, and religion and ritual at various times in their history.

The vast majority of the Navajo live on the Navajo Reservation, or, as its residents prefer to call it "the Navajo Nation," located north and east of Flagstaff, Arizona, and including portions of northeast Arizona, southwest Utah, and northwest New Mexico. Approximately one percent of the total Navajo live in a much smaller area located around the old Mormon community of Ramah, New Mexico, forty to seventy miles from the large reservation.

Together these two areas include about 25,000 square miles and seem larger than life. It is a land of incredibly rugged beauty bordering Marble Canyon, the Grand Canyon, and Lake Powell; encompassing Monument

Valley, Canyon de Chelly, and sage-covered valleys; and featuring majestic vistas of empty space. Although there is a great deal of variation in climate within the Nation, most of it is harsh. It is a place of extremes—too hot in summer, too cold in winter, too dry when it's not flooded. There are sandstorms, hailstorms, high rates of evaporation, more ultraviolet light than is healthy for most living things, and winds that have to be experienced to be believed. The official growing season is short, ninety days in many areas, and—unofficially—killing frosts can happen any day of the year. Destructive insects compound the drought problem. The smaller Ramah area does not have as many natural wonders as the Big Reservation, but its status in terms of agriculture is similar. The land is harsh as well as beautiful, and it is sacred to the people who are called Navajo.

According to archaeological and linguistic evidence, the people called Navajo (in their own language they call themselves *Dine,* which means "the People") began to drift into what is now the American Southwest from what is now Canada and Alaska fairly recently as prehistory goes. The movement was certainly not a sustained exodus but was accomplished slowly over many generations. The People started arriving in the region perhaps as early as the twelfth century, but the first definite dates for their presence—plus or minus twenty to fifty years—are 1541 (as established by dendrochronology, dating by tree rings) and 1492 (as established by glottochronology, dating by language development). They came from the Athapascan language group of the far north and, once in the Southwest, slowly developed into two major language sub-groups—Navajo and Apache—and a number of sub-subgroups.

The Pueblo groups of the Southwest were well-established city dwellers by the time the People arrived in large numbers. The People, however, had the double-recurved bow backed with sinews, which was a much more accurate and deadly weapon than the single-recurved bow of the various Pueblo cultures. Because of their superior weaponry, the People quickly established themselves as the major military power in the Southwest and came to control a vast area several times larger than the British Isles. The old proverb says that "to the victor belong the spoils," and the People learned agriculture for a hard land from their contacts with the Pueblos. In addition, they greatly enriched their religious and ceremonial life by the process of acculturation.

The People's borrowing, however, was of a particularly Navajo pattern that continues to this day. The core of Athapascan culture was—and is—a concern for harmony and health, a fear of the dead, and a settlement pattern involving small groups scattered over the land rather than centralized villages. The People adapted agriculture from the Pueblos, but not the village pattern associated with Pueblo life. They added many elements from the rich ceremony of the Pueblos but fitted them into their own world view and directed them toward achieving health, harmony and protection from the dead. They remained "the People."

Spanish government and bureaucracy came to the Southwest in July 1598, beginning history as the West reckons it and introducing to the area horses, sheep, and transhumance (a livestock-management system involving seasonal movement of the sheep between mountain pastures and lower ones). The Pueblos were conquered; and though the People were far too scattered and distant to receive such individual attention from the Spanish government, they, too, were greatly affected—particularly after the Pueblo Revolt of 1680, when large numbers of Pueblo people sought refuge with them, intermarried, and accelerated the process of acculturation by increasing both Pueblo and indirect Spanish influence. From the Spanish, usually via the Pueblos, the People received and took sheep and horses and transhumance as ideal adjuncts to their lifestyle. Directly from the Pueblos, they borrowed huge sections of mythology and ceremony.

Yet, it was still Navajo borrowing. The name "people of the cultivated fields" was given to the Navajo because, according to folk history, they camped near the fields of the Pueblos and helped them harvest. From the Pueblos they also seem to have gleaned ideas of mythology and ceremony that they used to build complex, intricate myths and ceremonies which are fully and truly their own. In addition to the new mythology and ceremony, weaving—one of the People's major arts—was borrowed from the Pueblos at about this time. In fact, by the 1770s most of the major features that make the People "the People" were in place. They had acquired sheep, horses, and a management process of husbandry from the Spanish, and ceremony, mythology, and weaving from the Pueblos; but they had reinterpreted it all so that it was their own. Sheep, horses, and transhumance fitted their semi-nomadic lifestyle perfectly and were used to justify it. The new ritual and mythology were shot through with Pueblo elements but in overall form and purpose were unmistakably Navajo. Weaving, a man's art among the Pueblos, became a woman's art among the Navajo—because the culture wished it so. It was the People's self-proclaimed, manifest destiny to occupy and control a vast land bounded by the four sacred mountains, to appease the dead and walk in harmony, to live free and proud on the land, for they were "the People." Until the coming of the Americans some sixty years later, they ruled the region.

In 1846 United States troops marched into the Southwest and, with little opposition, captured the area and deposed the Mexican government. The Anglo-Americans initially must have seemed to the People much like the Spanish and Mexicans who had preceded them (in fact, they usually called the newcomers "White Mexicans") but more efficient and more persistent in their attempts to end the People's raids on the growing population of the area. The People became so disturbed, or perhaps just annoyed, by the White Mexicans that they took the unprecedented act of temporarily setting aside clan, outfit, and family differences in order to organize the largest-scale military action in their history. They made a complex, coordinated attack on Fort Defiance, near Window Rock, Arizona. The attack failed, but to the People's great surprise, the White Mexicans' apparent response was to abandon the place in 1861.

The People, who probably knew very little about the American Civil War, could scarcely believe it when they saw troops leaving the fort. They quickly discovered that the land was theirs again, and that they were once more in control to reign and raid. Forces from the Confederacy actually captured and held Santa Fe for a brief time, but the Confederacy had little interest in, or time for, the Navajo. The feeling was mutual, and the People were again Lords of the Earth until the Civil War began to wane. Northern troops who had recaptured Santa Fe under the command of General Carleton grew increasingly disturbed, or possibly just annoyed, by the Navajo raids and by the fact that their occupation of Santa Fe had removed them from active participation in the Civil War. So General Carleton decided to destroy the People as a military force: he planned, and the old mountain man-frontiersman Kit Carson executed, the most successful war ever fought against the Navajo.

It was a strange war. Carson's campaign lasted slightly less than six months and resulted in fewer than fifty Indian deaths, but it was successful. For the first time in memory—or in the memory of story—the People were not only beaten; they were subdued. Reasons for the defeat were, first, Carson's success in waging a scorched-earth campaign that destroyed the People's food supply; and, second, the psychological effect of his marching through Canyon de Chelly—sacred and heretofore impenetrable. There also is some evidence that the Navajo had overpopulated the area and were defeated as much by their own numbers as by Carson's. At any rate, most of the People surrendered and, as a defeated Nation, were forced to make the infamous "Long Walk" of nearly three hundred miles to Fort Sumner in eastern New Mexico. These were the People's dark days of captivity, when they were forced to live as strangers in a strange land. But they were still "the People."

Carleton's plan was to civilize the Navajo and make them farmers (perhaps even hewers of wood), but he failed miserably. To their credit, the People tried for the first few years; they planted crops and saw them destroyed by drought, grasshoppers, and corn borers. Some died of ex-haustion during the Long Walk, some died of starvation and disease at Fort Sumner, and some died because they felt the People should not and could not live without their land. After four years, a weary federal government proposed, and the People gladly accepted, a treaty establishing a Navajo reservation and allowing the People to come home in 1868. From the captivity, they acquired the beginnings of their rich silversmithing and jewelry-making traditions (in the process counterfeiting the federal ration tags, according to one story) and the fry-bread and coffee that became staples of their diet and symbols of their hospitality. It also produced the only Navajo cultural change ever brought about by force—an end to regular raiding. (The People would fight no more until they went over the water to participate in the White Mexicans' war against "he who smells his mustache," as they called Hitler.) Their culture had again changed radical-ly, yet all these new elements were incorporated into the old way, and the People were still "the People."

The Navajo returned home, but to a much smaller home than they had left. The reservation established by the 1868 treaty was less than one-tenth the size of their traditional land and was, in fact, considerably smaller than the present reservation. In short, some of the People found that their traditional homelands were outside the borders of the new reservation. Some responded by returning to a home that, according to their elders, was not their own. Over time, others separated from the major group and went back to what had been their homelands, even though they were outside the new reservation. One such group of seven outfits settled around the "place of onions" along the base of the Zuni Mountains north of Ramah, New Mexico. The one percent of the People living in the Ramah area today are descendants of these seven extended families.

A century and more of Anglo rule since the return has seen some high points such as the involvement of the codetalkers in World War Two; low points such as the much resented government stock-reduction program of the 1930s; and many promising beginnings that fizzled out, like the Navajo Rehabilitation Act of the 1950s. There were good agents, like Big Belly Bennett, who helped the People and are still fondly remembered; there were bad agents, like the man they called Tarantula; and there were traders, like Wetherill and Hubbell, who made their living buying the People's goods and selling them the products of the outside world and in the process greatly influencing the development of Navajo costume and craft. There was widespread participation of the People in the Second World War (with returning veterans requiring Enemy Way ceremonies to reunite them with the People); there were Christian missionaries from many churches and sects; there were Anglo-American towns and cities springing up around, and even within, the reservation; and there were day schools and boarding schools. The ceremonial system underwent further development and codification. But despite one hundred years of change, the People were still "the People."

The history of the Ramah area illustrates these changes very clearly. The People who returned to their homes there found themselves outside the boundaries of both the original and the present reservation. They came to be separated from it by railroads, highways, and the city of Gallup, New Mexico, and are thus not likely to have their lands connected to the Big Reservation. In the first decades of the twentieth century they almost lost their land to Texan and to Mormon farmers and ranchers who moved into the area. The intervention of an English trader, Old Bald Hood, forced the federal government to give families 160 acres and to acknowledge their grazing rights tacitly. But most of the land granted was south of the original home area and moved the People even further from the Big Reservation.

Today, the Navajo have a complex and rich ceremonial life, a trans-humant sheep industry, many horses, world-famous silversmithing and weaving traditions, a unique culture—much of it borrowed and all of it theirs—and an important place in the history of cultural study. Anthropologists have carefully observed the People's way and have coined the term "incorporative acculturation" to describe how the Navajo borrow elements from other cultures, fit them into their culture, elaborate upon them, and then fit their new elaborations into their culture also—and all so completely and naturally that the borrowed are almost indistinguishable from older elements. They have, in fact, become parts of their new cultural provenance in such a way that its structural framework and integrity are maintained, and the borrowed elements function in support of its essential, pre-existing patterns. Separate from the main reservation, and living closer to Zuni, New Mexico, than to the Nation's capital at Window Rock, Arizona, the Ramah Navajo are the most incorporative subgroup of an incorporative culture. Yet they, too, remain the People.

Culture change among the Navajo in general, and the Ramah Navajo in particular, has increased in the second half of the twentieth century. The pan-Indian Native American Church, a peyote cult, and a number of Christian churches and Pentecostal sects have established congregations in the area. The Anglo-American towns surrounding the reservation have become small cities. The Navajo tribal government, born of the necessity for dealing with the outside world and including local "chapters" and an overall tribal council and president, has become a complex, well-estab-lished bureaucratic system. A number of reservation areas have used existing legislation to establish their own self-governing school districts; and the number of state, tribe, and federal human services offered in and around the reservation has expanded dramatically.

There are, however, many places where the increased changes and contacts are difficult to discern. The reservation's unemployment rate (defined in terms of regular wage-earning jobs) is estimated at sixty percent, and the Ramah rate may well be higher than the average. Most of the Ramah Navajo still live in hogans, the People's traditional low, six-sided buildings, or in cabins in isolated "outfits." Many of their homes have neither running water nor electricity; many of the older Navajos do not speak English; and many people do not have motorized transportation and still depend on horses. Many of the outfits, hogans, and people fit the traditional Navajo lifestyle and, except for the fact that they may use a fast food bucket as a household utensil, show little sign of change.

ASKING THE QUESTIONS

Stories of, or references to, Anglo-American and Ramah Navajo contemporary legends were told or made by a number of the twenty-five Ramah American Indians we interviewed. Although "The Pet in the Microwave Oven" was one of the best known and most frequently reported contemporary legends among Anglo Americans at the time of our work, this story did not seem familiar to most of the Navajos we interviewed, and asking about it through a translator almost always caused a great deal of laughter. After they laughed at the crazy men and their marvelous machines, a number of the people tried to give us the information we had asked for and told us of incidents they had heard of which they felt were similar:

❖ I've never heard that story about a pet in the microwave, but somebody crawled into a refrigerator car and froze to death on the train.[46]

❖ I heard something about drying a cat in a regular oven. The cat died. It was done by a younger person about ten years old who lived next door.[47]

Our first interview using Clyde as a translator was an exciting experience. It also was a challenge for him since the informant was his own father. We noticed that even short questions from us required long translations in Navajo and were curious about the difference in the length of time it took to ask the questions in English and in Navajo. We just felt too new to the experience to understand why.

On a later trip we again needed Clyde to translate, so we picked him up at his wife's home in Zuni and drove out across the low rolling hills south of Ramah. At the Mountain View junction, we drove into a heavy rain storm; but, continuing on to our next interview, we left the rain behind. The air was heavy, and the sound of thunder echoed off the hills behind us.

The interview was with Cora, a ninety-five-year-old woman who obviously understood some English but did not speak enough to answer our questions or to deal with the specialized kind of information we were seeking. She knew Clyde and was obviously pleased to see him. Before the interview started, they conversed in Navajo, and Cora frequently responded to Clyde's comments with a low, soft laugh.

After moving through the questions about health care and disabilities, we started on the contemporary legend survey. Kathy asked, "Has she ever heard a story of someone trying to dry a dog or a cat in a microwave oven?" Clyde translated the question to Cora, talking for more than a minute and using many hand gestures. She nodded, answered "yes" in Navajo at several points in the translation, and finally gave a short answer.

Clyde said, "No, she hasn't heard that one." Cora laughed her delightful laugh as he talked, and he laughed with her. Then Cora added a longer comment in Navajo that translated as:

❖　　　I haven't heard of a pet in a oven. [*laughs*] I have heard of a cat who froze in a refrigerator.[48]

Kathy and I laughed, and Kathy said, "Just the opposite. That's good. Now, I just wish I had pictures of you with your hands when you were asking her about the pet in the microwave." Both Clyde and Cora started laughing, and Kathy added, "That was a hard one to describe."

Clyde said, "Yeah," and laughed again. "Well, I had to see if she knew what a microwave was, so I asked if she had ever seen those sandwiches at the trading posts that you can buy and have them put in a little box, about this-big-by-this-big, that cooks them real fast. I had to do that first, and then I could start to ask the question about the story." With his explanation of what he had been saying, we began to realize how complicated translating for us was going to be for Clyde and how much thought and skill he put into his work.

"Disgusting Objects in Food," one of the broadest and most important categories of Anglo-American contemporary legends, produced a much greater response than we got from asking about "The Pet in the Microwave":

❖　　　I've never heard any stories of [fried rat], but I and my uncles one time had the experience of eating bear meat.[49]

❖   I've heard of the [fried rat]. Well, I pulled a trick like that myself. I was working in Grants for the mines, and there was this one guy, and he was Spanish, and you know how they are. They think they know everything, so one afternoon we were going to have lunch, and I found a rat, a mouse, and put it in his lunch bucket. And I used to work in the welding shop, and they had a little refrigerator like that and brought our lunch and put it in there. And lunch time came around, and that guy got it out, and that mouse was in there, you know. And nobody told him it was in there. [50]

❖   It was when—a long time ago when I used to work down in Zuni. Some company was making cassette players that had to be put together, and we were working. And these boys—it was their lunch break—and one of the men, the boys, got the bottle of pop out, open it. He was drinking half of it, but he found a tail. And then he poured it out, and there was the mouse. [51]

❖   I think I heard one about a dead rat in a bottle of [pop]. It happened in Ramah a long time ago, and I don't remember much about it. [52]

❖   One of my friends was in Gallup at [a fried-chicken restaurant], and he found a rat also cooked like the chicken. [53]

❖   There was one about a potato chips big bag, and there was a dead mouse at the bottom. It was five or six years ago, and one of my aunts found it. [54]

❖   Like the [pop]—I don't know. Like leaves, and I don't know. I heard on the news. Well, my brother found—What did he find in his pop? I mean my own brother found something. What was it? I forget. It's that [pop]. [55]

❖   This one woman was telling me she got a hamburger from this [fast-food restaurant], and there was a cockroach in there. [56]

❖   Her mother [*points to Clyde's daughter who was with us*] said she found a mouse in a bottle of [pop]. [57]

Clyde took interviewing and translating as seriously as he took storytelling. The first day the three of us went out together, we explained our "standard release form" (required by the grant) to one person before interviewing him and to another afterwards. Driving to the next interview, we asked Clyde which he thought was better. He thought about the question for a while and then said, "I think it is better to go through that part first thing so that the people will know exactly who you are, what they will receive, and what to expect."

The next hogan Clyde took us to was that of his aunt Thelma and his uncle John. We interviewed John first, with Clyde translating. He began by explaining the project and the release form, and John signed the form, pocketed the twenty-five dollar interview fee, and said, "Thank you very much; it was a pleasure doing business with you," and started to leave. There was just a split second of silence, he and Clyde laughed, he sat down and grinned, we joined the laughter, and Clyde said, "On the other hand, maybe after is better." Then his uncle told his recollection of a mouse in a bottle:

❖   It was several years ago I heard that there was a mouse or something like that in pop in the bottle—not the cans. So they turned it back to the company.[58]

Others told stories similar in theme:

❖   I attended Fort Wingate about three years. When I was at Fort Wingate, they fed me some bear meat; and when I came home, I had to go to the medicine man.[59]

❖   There's a place up at the other end of the reservation going towards Gallup, right up on top there. They serve barbecue ribs, precooked, and I ordered one there. And we all got out and sat in the shade of a tree there, and I cut it open, and there were worms in it. Since then—That was our own experience there.[60]

❖   I heard a story about a barbecued chicken purchased to eat. So they cut it open, and there was mice in there inside the chicken.
     No one wants to buy chicken now.[61]

When we found that asking if people had ever heard of someone finding something disgusting in an order of food often got a story of—or reference to the story of—someone finding something disgusting in a bottle of pop, Clyde started asking for that story, too. During one interview Clyde had just started to pose the question when he dissolved into an almost silent fit of giggles. The woman we were interviewing started giggling almost immediately after he did. Clyde was laughing almost without sound, but he was shaking all over and having trouble getting enough breath to continue his question. His mirth was contagious, and I burst out laughing just at the pleasure of seeing him laugh so. When the four of us got our breath back, Clyde went on, "Mouse, mouse," he said in English, and then continued talking in Navajo. The woman gave a short answer in Navajo, and Clyde said, "No, she hasn't heard anything like that."

After we got back to the car and started to drive away, Clyde shook his head and started laughing again. "Did you hear me in there? Did you hear me ask her if she had ever heard a story of someone finding a cat, a *cat,* in a bottle of pop? Cat in microwave. Mouse in bottle. Wrong animal."

VANISHINGS

The Anglo-American contemporary legend we asked about that was recognized most often, and retold most frequently, by the Navajos we interviewed was "The Vanishing Hitchhiker":

❖   This person had picked up a rider, and all that time he was there, talking, that guy never said nothing to him, never answered any questions or anything, so he wasn't sure if he could hear or anything. And then, well, this one is sort of different. When he looked down or wondered why he wasn't talking or anything, he happened to look down toward his feet, and he didn't have any, you know. And he just stopped, and the guy never said anything—just got out.[62]

❖   There was one being told by my sister-in-law, and she said that this happened somewhere between Tohatchi and Naschitti. I think it happened because that guy was telling my sister-in-law so, and [he] was driving back from Gallup, so he would have passed Tohatchi. It was [a] real rainy, rainy day, and he said he saw a girl that was standing dressed in squaw dress and real traditional. She was very pretty. She was standing along the road. He said he drove by, and then he had to turn around; he felt sorry for her, so he came back, and she was still standing there. So he stopped by, and she got in, and then he said that he started driving, and he talked to her, and she won't say a word. They just kept going, and finally they came up to Naschitti turnoff. That's the first and the last words she said: "I want to get off here. This is my home just across," and she got off.

And I guess she left her scarf in the truck. I guess she forgot it, and she got off, and this guy took off. Then the next day he came back—to return that scarf—and came up to this house, to the old gray hogan. I guess he honked his truck, and then a man came out, and then he said, "Where's that girl I gave the ride to yesterday? I want to see her."

"What girl? We don't have no girls here."

And then I guess that guy said, "I did! I just dropped that girl off yesterday, and she wore this kind of clothes and that scarf right here. This is hers. She forgot it." That man just got, you know, I guess he was very shook up from it.

And then that man, I guess he was the father of that girl, and he [said], "Go over there to that old house. There's a grave there. Go see. That's where that girl is."

So I guess he went over there, and then the jacket she was wearing was there. That guy didn't know what to do. He just zoomed back out.[63]

❖   Well, this happened to me one summer. We were on our way down to Artesia, south of Albuquerque between Carrizozo and Tularosa. It was in the middle of the night—driving—but this hitchhiker wasn't in the car. I was driving, going about like sixty-five miles per hour, and all of a sudden, I saw a light. This was—I don't know where, you know—I was driving along, and I looked in the mirror, and there I saw this flashlight in back of me, and it was coming closer and closer and then pretty soon I kept looking into the mirror, and then when I looked in the mirror, it was really close—right behind me. It was about to bump into me or something, you know. And then when I looked again, it was passing by me. There was a guy. I don't know if it was a lady or a guy or what was sitting on a motorcycle with a helmet. And it just went right in front of me like that, [*moves hand quickly past her face*] and then I—I was really scared. I was shaking, and I was getting cold chills, and then he just disappeared right in front of me. My headlights were on it, and it was moonlight, too.[64]

❖   He was cruising by some graveyard—I don't know—and picked up some—No, he was cruising by, you know, where they buried all these veterans, and he picked up—Oh, no, he was cruising by himself, and he noticed someone's foot was there. He didn't look sideways. He didn't even look, and he just cruised. I guess after he got out of that graveyard place, that person disappeared. I don't know. It's kind of scary—a ghost—I don't know.[65]

This storyteller was related to Clyde, and he told us after her interview that his niece was retelling *his* story about the appearing hitchhiker and "didn't get it right."

Another storyteller set her scary story along "that 666." Ramah Navajo who are familiar with Anglo-American popular Christianity enjoy joking references to the number of the highway and the number of the beast:

❖   This one is a story I guess was told by a councilman. I think it was a councilman coming home from a meeting somewhere—from Window Rock, or I don't know where it was at—driving on that 666. I think it's that road, and [he] picked up a hitchhiker—I think it was a lady standing by the road—and they started driving. I guess he kept talking, and the person didn't respond or anything, was just quiet, so they went along, and he got to wherever he was going. I don't remember how this story goes, but it must have been raining, and he took off his jacket and gave it to the hitchhiker. And the next morning or somehow—I don't know how this story goes—he dropped this person off and said he would come back for his jacket or whatever he had on. And he later came back and found out that the person never existed, but he found his jacket somewhere at a grave or something like that.[66]

❖   This guy, I guess, was riding a horse along—And, see, in Navajo, they say that if a woman was married, and her husband dies and she remarries, there the husband goes and starts haunting the new husband. So she's supposed to have something done before she remarries, and then that won't happen; but if she doesn't, then that's when, you know, the ghost of her first husband starts coming and starts doing things.

So this one story goes that this guy was riding a horse along, and I guess it got dark before he got back to the house. So I guess he passed this one place, uh, where this guy was buried, and all of a sudden that guy jumped on his back. Well, Navajos also say that a horse is really afraid of ghosts or whatever. So the horse, I guess, just took off and was really going, and big arroyos that horse would just jump over, and that thing was just holding on to this guy. And under branches, through trees, that horse just kept going, and that ghost was just really hanging on, I guess, but the horse knew where home was and just went straight there. Finally, before he got back to the house, they fell off 'cause that thing was just holding on to him so tight that it just finally pulled him off, and he fell off, unconscious. Or something like that 'cause as soon as that person sees a light, like fire, then they just go out. That's what they say. That is one of the stories that was told.[67]

❖   Well, this grandma, she said they were going up to Pine Hill—I don't know whether there's a blizzard—and saw this man going up, walking around. She said this man was wearing a real heavy coat. They stopped for him. I guess they figure that he was cold, so they stopped and he just turned—He won't look at them. He won't face them. Kind of turned his head away, and they asked him where he was going, and he won't tell her. And I guess later he just disappeared, and they didn't see him anymore.[68]

❖   Let me see, who was it told me about that story—just lately? Let me think now. There was one—one right here someplace. That they picked up a hitchhiker—Oh, yes, over on the other side of Gallup, they picked up a hitchhiker, and past Window Rock, and then got to Fort Defiance. Just around the other side of Fort Defiance, they passed a cemetery there—a veterans' cemetery. The hitchhiker asked the travelers to stop, and so they did, and he got out and start walking towards the cemetery. So they were still there watching him, and just when he got off the road, he was just gone right there. So the travelers got scared.[69]

❖   This person was supposed to have been dead, and he noticed this person sitting next to him and recognized the person and knew that he was dead. So he looked, and then he looked again, and he was gone. They were right by this person's grave.[70]

❖   Well, this one is about a guy that was traveling back between Window Rock and Shiprock, and it was kind of during the summertime and kinda late hours. When he was going between Little Water Trading Post close to Window Rock, there was a person standing out beside the road trying to hitch a ride. So this guy picked this person up, and it was a girl. And this girl was dressed in a traditional clothing and was kind of strange because nowadays they don't wear traditional clothes anymore. And I don't know how many miles this guy gave her a ride and drop her off there, and this girl was kind of strange. Had a white face and doesn't have a suntan. So he asked where she lived. Lived just over the side of the mountain, so he asked her her name and gave her his name and wanted to meet again. Started driving back home to Shiprock.

Next day, he went back over there, and when he went back, nobody lived over there. He was told the one person who lived there died a couple of years ago, and so he asked another family that lived there for the name of this girl, and they said she died a couple of years ago. So that's what happened.[71]

❖   It was in a rainy night, you know, lightning—all that stuff. Picked him up on the road, you know. And I guess they went some ways, turned and looked. He was gone.[72]

❖   I have heard of people giving a person like this a ride, and before they know it, this person is gone. I wonder what kind of person this was—a spirit perhaps.[73]

❖   A story like that was told by one of the preachers. He was coming to a service and picked up this hitchhiker, and before he knew it, he had vanished. [*laughs*]

I have heard stories like that about this highway out here, and I sometimes at night go over to the highway and look for them to see if they would disappear, but I never found one. [*laughs*][74]

❖   *Linda:* There's a story about—
Clyde: This is not the dancing partner story.
Linda: There was a couple going to a Squaw Dance. On the way they noticed someone on horseback sitting right there. He was all dressed in black, and he even had a black horse. They asked him how far to the Squaw Dance, and he won't answer. They asked him a couple of times, and they decided this was no real person, so they just took off, and then they realized it was right in back following them. He followed them all the way to the Squaw Dance. There they didn't see him again, but they all agreed this was no regular person. They didn't know if he was some kind of devil or what.
Clyde: Was there anything unusual about his feet?
Linda: Nobody paid attention to his feet.[75]

Linda told this story right after her joking reference to going out to the highway to look for vanishing hitchhikers, but she didn't laugh as she told it.

Others told similar stories:

❖   There was a person in the Thoreau area named John Ralph. He picked up a hitchhiker who was all dressed up going somewhere, so he gave him a ride to the cemetery where he stopped for him. The hitchhiker never said a word or looked back to thank him—just went over the fence into the cemetery. Anyway, this is what I heard.

      About this hitchhiker, when the person talked to him, he never looked him in the eye—always looking away. And when he got off, I guess he went back and wondered if he left any tracks, and there was no tracks where he got off. The weeds weren't disturbed or anything.[76]

❖   This boy went and stopped for this couple. [He went] down the road a little ways—I can't remember the name of this place—but then he looked back, but they weren't in there.

      Well, this person who gave these two a ride didn't know that there was a cemetery there. I guess he was telling another person who said, "Well, we know this place, and there is a cemetery there."

      He was telling this to another person, and so they came back to where he thought that they got off, and then he noticed two cone-shaped hogans there. And then the ground was soft where he let them off, and there was no tracks—nothing.[77]

Clyde told us that he had long been interested in skinwalkers *(yee naaldlooshii,*the traditional Navajo word for witches who assume the forms of other human beings or animals in order to do evil) and stories about them so that he could use the information and belief as source material for his own stories. He told us about how he used to tell *yee naaldlooshii* stories at night to the kids he supervised at a Bureau of Indian Affairs boarding school, how he had twisted the tail of his family's old dog and had tape-recorded the howling for special effects, and how the story and sound effects had been greeted by his audience. He told us all this—including short sections of his obviously memorized text—much as an actor might describe his famous portrayal of a character in a play or a professor might describe a lecture fondly remembered.

We called Clyde one day to say we were coming over to Zuni to see him, and he told us that he had painted a picture, *The Initiation of a Skinwalker,* for us if we were interested. We, of course, were interested, and there was a story accompanying the painting. Clyde explained that he had asked many people about *yee naaldlooshii.* His family and friends had told him that witches give themselves up to evil in order to become *yee naaldlooshii,* and must allow death to claim someone close to them to gain the powers of witches.

The painting shows the inverted ritual that is typically described as the way a person becomes a *yee naaldlooshii.* There is a kneeling figure draped in a bear skin and facing a human skull. Surrounding the initiate are figures stroking him with feathers; and his face has such a look of horror and agony, as he realizes what he has done and the nature of the evil to which he has enslaved himself, that it is the finest vision of the Faustian legend I have ever seen. I asked Clyde about the feathers the men were holding in the picture, and he said, "Now, that's where I almost made a mistake. I started to paint eagle feathers, and then somebody told me that they should be *owl* feathers. Owls are always bad for us Navajos."

Clyde's eyes sparkled as he said, "That's where I almost made a mistake," and he checked to see if we remembered the dancer who almost forgot and said something while wearing his mask. He told us about his painting, and he told us contemporary legends. After we had finished all the interviews called for by the grant, we interviewed Clyde to see how he would tell the stories he had so recently collected. The results of our informal experiment were astonishing. We pulled the car off to the side of the road, set up the recording equipment, and asked Clyde the questions he had asked others. He told us that one of the things he had enjoyed most about the project was getting to learn new stories by hearing other people tell them, and he proceeded to tell the longest, most polished, of the entire project, blending Navajo setting, belief, and custom with an Anglo-American contemporary legend of "The Vanishing Hitchhiker":

❖   Well, this person went back to his home in Shiprock, and then he wanted to come back that same evening, so he started out kind of late. It was raining, and outside of Shiprock—approximately about ten to twelve miles out—his headlights hit this hitchhiker in the road. Came closer, he noticed it was a girl. She didn't have a jacket or anything on—was just wearing a white blouse and skirt. So he decided he was going to pick up this girl and give her a ride wherever she was going, so he stopped and opened the door for the girl, and she was just soaking wet. And he asked her where she was going, and she said she was going a little ways down the road. So he had his jacket there right beside him and told her warm up. Gave her that jacket, and she wrapped it around her shoulders.

Then he went down about a couple more miles, and the girl told him—well, she didn't tell him, speak to him—She just motioned to him to turn off there, so then they just went about a mile and a half down the road and saw a house and hogan there. The girl just pointed over to the hogan, so he drove up in front, and that's where this girl, she got off. And he kind of liked the girl there, so he thought, "Well, I'm going to leave my jacket, and afterward I'll come back to get a chance to see her then." So he didn't say nothing about his jacket, so he just drove off and went to work, and at the end of the week he came back. And he made sure he knew where the turn-in was, and so he went there.

It wasn't raining or anything like that. He drove up to the house, well, between the house and the hogan. A little old lady came out from the house, and she came over and said, "Yes, son, what can I do for you?" She said this in Navajo.

And he told her, "I came to pick up my jacket that I lent that girl that I dropped off in that hogan over there."

And she said, "I'm sorry, son, there's no one living here besides me and the little kids in there." She says, "There's nobody here that lives in that hogan there. That hogan hasn't been used for over two years now."

He says, "No, grandma, I left that girl off here. She went inside there. I was parked right out here."

"You can look for yourself, son. There's a somebody in there, but she's buried in there."

So the boy got out and went over to the door there. And he noticed it was all tied up and locked up, but he could see through the crack in the door. His jacket was hanging way in the back corner there in the hogan—and right beneath was a little bump where there's a grave, and he didn't know what to say, and he just turned around and got back in his truck and took off.[78]

Clyde's story was particularly interesting in its choice of Shiprock as a setting, for it is a place frequently used for stories of evil in Navajo tradition.

Several of the Navajo contemporary legends we collected concerned a participant who disappears at a Squaw Dance, a frequent Navajo summer ceremony and social event. We had Clyde ask people if they had ever heard a story of a devil at a dance because it had been frequently collected from Mexican-Americans living near his homeland, and we wanted to see if any of the Navajo had adopted the story. Some had, as we soon heard:

❖ Several years ago this happened down around the Apache Reservation. There was this man in the bar, you know, buying everybody drinks and everything, and he gave this one guy a ride home, or either he got caught in that bar and got thrown out 'cause they said that when they looked at him, he didn't have any shoes and his feet looked like the devil's.

I don't know what the devil's feet look like, but they had thrown him out, and some guys picked him up—he was walking home—picked him up. They didn't know that he had been thrown out or anything about him, but then they soon realized that his feet were like that. So he got thrown out.

But they said this had happened around White River, and then my mother goes down to around there. I think it's Sells—her other place right by Phoenix—the other reservation right by there. There's another place—anyway down around there, and they have that same story going around, too.[79]

Others had moved the story from a bar or a social dance to an American Indian dance and told a story that was clearly related to the

Mexican-American story of the devil at the dance but had a different cultural meaning:

❖ *Cora:* Well, this person was dancing with a partner which was a female, so they danced awhile, and they went for a walk, went a little ways from the actual dancing place. And all of a sudden, she was gone, and he didn't know where she went, and the next morning he backtracked himself. The track led to a graveyard. He tracked himself, and he could see his tracks, but the tracks of the lady was some kind of a track. He couldn't make out what kind, and they led to an old grave site where somebody had been buried, and that's where she disappeared.

Clyde: What kind of a track was it?

Cora: It was coyote tracks. And this female partner didn't do any talking during the time they were dancing. He had to do all the talking, so he suggested they go for a walk to—And they got to the grave. She disappeared.[80]

One account in particular was so culturally loaded and so elliptical that we shall return to it in chapter 7. According to the storyteller:

❖ There's the lady who was noticed among the singers at a Squaw Dance singing, so this man went over and asked her if, you know, could take her some place, and so she went, and when they got there where they were going, she disappeared.

She didn't talk.

Her tracks were the tracks of a coyote along side the man's tracks.[81]

Similar stories were told by other storytellers:

❖ There was this real nice lady at the Squaw Dance, and this man came up to her, and I guess he was asking her for a dance, and they danced, and they got to know each other, and then they took off together, and then they slept somewhere, and in the morning the lady was gone, and there was just footprints of coyote.[82]

❖ Well, this man came to dance, and he wanted to dance with the woman. He start dancing with this lady, asking all kinds of questions, you know, wanted to meet a lady just like he was talking about. So after they got through dancing, this lady went over to the side into the dark, standing over there, and she was wearing black clothing; and pretty soon when this man came back to that lady—where that lady was standing—she doesn't have a face. And only the clothing was standing there. And he got real scared and just ran away. That's what happened.[83]

❖ They danced, went for a little walk to spend the night there, and when they got ready to get down, she disappeared.

This person reached for her, and there was nothing but a little dried up stick.

He didn't bother to check for tracks.[84]

Clyde had never heard the story of the figure at the dance, and he shared our excitement at discovering it. When we were recording him by the side of the road, he told us his version and explained why it was his favorite:

❖   Well, the one I heard was where this dancer man thought that this girl was—He noticed this one girl there. So he kept an eye on her and then pretty soon she came over and got him to dance with her, and so he went along and danced around maybe two, three, or four times. Then he asked her if she was willing to come over for a little walk, and there he found out that it wasn't no—not the girl that he'd expected to see. And the way that she was dressed—all dressed up with silver belts—And then he didn't know what happened to her. This is the way it was told by one of them, and this is the best one.

With the dance going on, that many people walking around there, it would be hard to find the—to track anything.[85]

Clyde's reference in this story to his previously told story about the old Sioux who did not get the part of the dog he expected was an unexpected gift.

The Ramah stories clearly demonstrate that the contemporary legend is a part of culture. During our very first interview of the project, Clyde's eighty-two-year-old father told us a dramatic first-person story of a figure that suddenly appeared beside him in his truck as he was driving it and just as suddenly disappeared when he pulled off to the side of the road and turned on the interior light. When I asked him what the figure had been, he gave a concise answer:

❖   This happened here in Ramah where I picked up a rider at night, and this person was a female sitting right next to me. I didn't know how this person got on, and it caused me to pull to the side of the road and stop, and I opened the door to where the dome light would shine and found nobody there. And this is one of the experiences I had here in the Ramah area.

Anything like that that happens to us Navajos, we always call it *ch'iidii*—which is a ghost or something evil.[86]

Clyde had many times heard his father tell his story. He had a similar version himself, and so did others:

❖   Oh, my girl was the one that told me about it. I don't know too much about it. But she was telling me one day that she heard this from one of her friends, I guess it was. Somebody was riding up to Shiprock. I guess that's the famous story. There's a lot of people know about that. Anyway, she's the one that told me that this person was going up, and all of a sudden he noticed somebody sitting by him; and the next thing you know, he kind of recognized this girl that was a young lady—a young woman—was riding with him. But I guess they never talk or something. Anyway, she told me about what it was, but I don't know. Just kind of knew about it 'cause I heard it elsewhere but didn't really pay attention to that at that time. And she was kind of talking about it one day.[87]

❖   This was the time I was going back from Albuquerque. On my way outside of Grants, I didn't pick up no hitchhiker. I was just driving along, and I had all my clothes in back on a hanger in the back seat. I went a little ways outside of Grants, and then I saw somebody's feet right beside me— from the knee down—and this person had on old work shoes that were all scuffed and needed a good shining. And I looked at it. And every time I looked down there, it wasn't there. And this kept up until I was about halfway to Gallup. About halfway, yes, and then pretty soon I started reaching over there, over to the seat next to me. I didn't feel it, and then I got to where I would quickly reach over there. I didn't feel anything. When I looked down there on the floor, I could see the shoes. And we got outside—about six or five miles outside Gallup—I look again, but I didn't see the feet there. And then I just drove on into Gallup.

        Well, on the way about halfway, I started talking to him. I told him, I said, "I don't know who you are, what you want, or what you're doing in here, but you're welcome to ride with me." So I said that to him, and that was it. And I never said anything more to him. By the time I got to Gallup, I just lost my rider. That was all. And then after I got off, I went into the bus station, and the bus hadn't come in yet to where I was supposed to meet my wife. When I walked into the bus station, everybody looked at me, and I thought I was—that there must be something wrong with me. I checked my shirt and all that, and then later I started thinking maybe I looked scared or something or pale or something, and so I was. I had chills down my back.[88]

The Anglo-American "Vanishing Hitchhiker" legend and the Mexican-American "Devil at the Dance" tale are both well-known in New Mexico and have been frequently reported from the area. It is tempting to identify the "Vanishing" and "Appearing Hitchhiker" stories, "Disappearing Dancer" stories, and stories of other disappearances as borrowings from these traditions. If they have been borrowed, however, they have been borrowed in terms of the Navajo incorporative acculturation. The People adopted and reworked contemporary Anglo-American legends because they were in many ways similar to a much older, much more important Navajo story form: *ch'įįdii* stories.

Though *ch'iidii* most often is translated into English as "ghost," that is only approximate. A more accurate translation would probably be "the evil part of the spirit of a dead person"—a formulation reflecting the Navajo belief that the evil in each person (except for children who die before they speak and old people who live blameless lives and die naturally) is released at the time of death and is the primary cause of illness, disharmony, and most of what is wrong with the world. According to traditional belief, *ch'iidii* linger near the body's place of burial, and this is the reason that in the past the People abandoned or destroyed hogans where deaths had taken place. *Ch'iidii* are believed to use animal forms, particularly those of coyotes or owls, to visit the living during times of darkness. They also can assume any human form and frequently are not recognizable by people who knew them when they were living. Thus unusual behavior of something that is a part of the normal world (for example, an owl appearing in the daytime) may suggest a ghost *(ch'iidii)*. *Ch'iidii* appear and disappear inexplicably; they do not talk to people; and one of the most widespread beliefs about them in the past was that they jumped on horses and rode along with their riders, exactly as reported in one story in our collection.

Contact with a *ch'iidii*, whether recognized or not, has been seen as an ever-present danger requiring complex ceremonial cleansing. *Ch'iidii* sickness also has one other aspect that seems strongly like Western science: as with asbestos poisoning, its effects may not appear until years after the actual event. In case of any illness or misfortune among the People, one of their most common assumptions is that there has been contamination by a *ch'iidii* at some time perhaps unknown to the sufferer. The pervasiveness of *ch'iidii* belief, the power to do evil attributed to them, and the ceremonies designed to counteract their effects were once the center of Navajo life and were, indeed, the major manifestation of the fear of the dead which anthropologists described as intellectual baggage brought from the north.

THE MORNING STAR

Navajo Christianity has developed in a distinctly Navajo fashion. Most of the churches that have been successful on the reservation itself are Pentecostal sects which stress spiritual healing, value local autonomy, and lack centralized authority. These groups generally do not require or expect their pastors to have specialized ministerial training or formal education, so many of the congregations on the reservation are led by Navajos who have organized, and in some cases, financed their own churches. The result is that Ramah Navajo Christianity is extremely varied and has been acculturated by the People as much as it has acculturated them.

During my first year at Northern Arizona University, one of my students was a Navajo lady who had become a teacher's aide at a reservation school after her children left home. In one of the class essays she wrote: "Navajos get up early and face to the East because they can see the morning star and the Bible says, 'Jesus is my bright and morning star.'"

I have remembered her comment because it seemed to me a perfect example of Navajo Christianity. One of the most important Navajo household rituals has long been rising before dawn to honor the morning star. The student's family retained this ancient Navajo custom but reinterpreted it so that the old became a part of the new.

Back in the field, Clyde's half-first cousin once removed seemed uncomfortable when Clyde asked him about vanishing hitchhikers and dancers. Later, as we were driving to our next interview, Clyde explained that Mr. Lopez was a devout Navajo Christian and said he thought that some Christian Navajos had renounced the old Navajo ways and would feel that telling stories about vanishing hitchhikers was non-Christian.

Most of the Ramah Christian Navajos, however, did not seem to have a hostile attitude toward "vanishing" stories. In fact, many of ours were collected from Ramah Navajo Christians, and two informants said they had heard the "Vanishing Hitchhiker" stories from their preachers.

Still, in one basic way the vanishing and appearing hitchhikers of the stories are radically different from those before Christianity was widely accepted. Traditionally, the *ch'iidii* were consistent; they always and indiscriminately caused trouble. In the new stories, many malevolent spirits have become merely mysterious. Yet Navajo culture and belief are always in the background. Only people for whom bear meat is taboo would have contemporary stories of unknowingly eating bear meat. The disappearing dancers leave coyote tracks; and hitchhikers appear mysteriously, disappear mysteriously, and cannot be in the presence of light. The Athapascan fear-of-death lore has reshaped "The Vanishing Hitchhiker" and "The Devil at the Dance" stories that may well have been borrowed from other cultures, and the power of the old underlies the attraction of the new. From the point of view of most of the Ramah Navajo, the *ch'iidii* have not gone away but have been incorporatively acculturated. Appropriately enough for Navajo evil spirits that traditionally assume any form, the *ch'iidii* now appear and disappear as hitchhikers and dancers, demonstrating that contemporary legends and their performance are a part of culture, just as culture and its enactment are a part of contemporary legends.

And the Ramah Dine are still the Ramah Dine.

CHAPTER FOUR

Conversations with Kuiceyetsa

CHAPTERS 2 AND 3 center upon large groups of stories collected from many American Indian storytellers. This chapter centers upon twenty-seven stories told by Kuiceyetsa during conversations we recorded in 1988 and 1989 plus four stories told by her daughter Helen and seven by her son Norman when they came to visit their mother and joined the conversations.

Kuiceyetsa. Our grant required that the actual names of the people we interviewed not be released. We discussed this regulation with Kuiceyetsa and some of her family one day while we were visiting her. They thought the requirement was a little humorous but agreed that there might be situations where some people we were interviewing might not want someone else to know what they had said. I explained that we would make up names for those who had no preference and asked Kuiceyetsa what name she would like to have us use for her. She first laughed at the idea of making up a name; but, after giving it some thought, she said, "You could use my Zuni name." Her idea sounded good to us, so we asked what the name was. She said *Kuiceyetsa* over and over, and we tried to write it down as it sounded to us. Helen helped by suggesting how parts of the name might be spelled in English, and we worked on it until we were all comfortable that we had a spelling that came close to the actual pronunciation.

Kathy asked, "What does it mean? How did they select that name for you?"

Kuiceyetsa laughed, "It's a Laguna word. I don't know that it means anything. It was the name of an old lady here who had lived a long time."

To live a long time at Zuni is to become one of the "elderlies." By this English word adapted and added to their speech, the Zuni emphasize the role of the elderly in their society. The beginnings and the endings of lives are especially cherished at Zuni: babies and small children because they are the future, and the elderlies because they are the past. Such a one has known overt persecution and discrimination; technological revolutions; periods of intense world, national, state, and village upheaval. Such a one is acquainted with death. Such a one proclaims by persistence, patience, and presence the path—the road—the way. To know such a one is to know something of what it means to be Zuni.

Something of what it means to be Zuni is to know that Zuni tellers of conversational stories often include their endings in their introductions— and I shall always remember the first time ever I hugged Kuiceyetsa.

Kuiceyetsa is an elderly; Kuiceyetsa is such a one. She combines a regal presence with a childlike playfulness and enjoyment of life in an easy juxtaposition, but it was her graceful, assured aura of authority that most impressed us during our first visits with her. Kathy and I always exchanged hugs with Helen whenever we saw her, but we were simply too much in awe of Kuiceyetsa when we first knew her to presume to greet her in the same manner.

On our first visit to Helen after her move to what had been her mother's trailer, we knocked on what used to be Kuiceyetsa's door. Helen called for us to come in. As I stood outside in the bright sunlight, I could only see darkness inside the open doorway, and I started in. Kathy was just in front of me and stopped because Helen was right inside the door. I realized why Kathy had stopped when I ran into her back. Helen was hugging her. Helen saw me behind Kathy, reached around her, and included me in the hug, so I reached around Kathy and hugged Helen. "Wow!" Kathy laughed. "I'm getting the best of this deal."

"We're an Oreo cookie," I said.

"No," Helen laughed. "We're a Zuni sandwich, and you and I are the bread."

As we let go of each other and started into the dim light, we saw Kuiceyetsa standing at the end of the hall watching us and smiling. "What am I?" she asked, throwing open her arms, "chopped liver?"

After we initially interviewed—and hugged—Kuiceyetsa as a part of our funded Zuni research, she quickly and naturally became one of our major Zuni co-researchers; we visited with her whenever we were in the area; and we interviewed and recorded her comments, observations, and stories whenever we were working on a specific project.

Because she is an elderly, many of the younger members of Kuiceyetsa's clan call her "My Grandmother" even though they are not her biological grandchildren. "My Grandmother" is a role she fulfills not only naturally but abundantly. Kuiceyetsa teases her grandchildren; they roast chilies together over the open flame of the gas range; they joke and laugh together; they eat and drink together—coffee and canned pop, mutton stew, Zuni sheep stomach sausage, chicken enchiladas, or luncheon meat sandwiches—and always they share the ever-present elements of the traditional Zuni affirmation of Zuni culture: salt gathered from the Zuni

Salt Lake (which, according to traditional Zuni stories, moved from near the village to its present location long ago when the people insulted her by their behavior) and Zuni bread baked in the traditional shapes in the traditional domed outdoor ovens in the traditional manner. They all adore her and laugh and talk with her; and her house is always open to and filled with sons and daughters, grandchildren, great-grandchildren, and clan grandchildren. Kathy and I consider ourselves fortunate, indeed, to have sat in this circle of open arms, salt, teasing, Zuni bread, light.

Our first interviews on the Zuni project were conducted during warm weather, and Helen, Kathy, and I occasionally stopped at Halona Plaza Grocery Store and got food for a lunch to eat outdoors. Luncheon meat, sandwich spread, sandwich bread—it was the picnic fare of my midwestern childhood. Anyone who experienced the Midwest in the 1950s remembers these sandwiches; they were home. Helen chose the sandwich bread because she could tell which loaves were the freshest. We added whatever fruit looked best and something cold to drink and ate sitting out in the sunshine talking, telling stories, creating stories.

As cold weather came and the outdoor part of the lunches no longer seemed so inviting, Helen suggested we hold our picnics at her parents' home, and so we began taking our supplies to Kuiceyetsa's and her husband Max's kitchen. Kuiceyetsa teased us and laughed when we told her luncheon meat and sandwich bread must be traditional Zuni foods because they were the foods we had traditionally eaten at Zuni.

When Kuiceyetsa laughs, she looks down—often holding her hand above the dark glasses she wears because her eyes are very sensitive. Her laugh is a low, soft chuckle. The sound is light, but it envelops her entire being, and she shakes with her laughter. Kuiceyetsa's laughter is the joy of her family. Whenever her children and grandchildren who are in her home—those seated around the table, those watching cartoons or movies on the the large screen of the satellite-linked audio-visual center, those talking quietly among themselves in other nooks and corners of her combined kitchen and living room—hear her laughter, they smile to themselves and to their world. Kuiceyetsa laughs well and often.

After Kuiceyetsa laughed at our description of "traditional Zuni foods," she began introducing truly traditional Zuni foods to our indoor picnics. First: Zuni bread baked in the Zuni outdoor ovens. The bread had been shaped by forming the dough into an elongated oval and folding one end back over itself before baking. Helen sliced the sourdough bread starting at the more narrow end; we cut the luncheon meat to fit the bread.

On a later visit we discovered that Kuiceyetsa had anticipated our indoor picnic. The odor of roasting meat greeted us when we walked into her house. It was so pleasant that Helen, Kathy, and I laughed together because we were each sniffing the air. Kuiceyetsa had sprinkled an herb she had picked and dried over the top of a roast. She kept the herb stored alongside commercial containers of cinnamon and cloves and told us that the Zuni name for it was *hambassa* (cinch weed).

We sat down around the kitchen table and waited for the meat to finish roasting. When Max came in, Kuiceyetsa spoke to him in Zuni, and he opened the oven door, checked the meat, and adjusted the oven temperature. Kuiceyetsa laughed and explained, "All the time I was going to school in California, I practiced my Zuni words. I said I would never forget how to speak the Zuni language. At night before I fell asleep, I said Zuni words over and over. When I got home several years later, I discovered I knew the words, but I had forgotten the order to use the words in sentences. What I said to Max just now was Zuni words in English word order. It wasn't easy for him to know that I wanted him to see if the meat was done."

"Well, I knew you were using some kind of language on me," he said as he laughed and reached for her hand.

"When I went to school in California..." Thus people all across the Indian lands recall the days when the federal government tried to force American Indian children to renounce their heritages and replace them with Anglo-American culture. Youngsters from a variety of tribal backgrounds were rounded up—sometimes by force—and sent off to schools in a world not of their making, not of their choosing. One story widely told by American Indians of a certain age who "went to school" vividly describes being forbidden to speak their language and of being punished for violating this rule.

And so the child Kuiceyetsa who would become "My Grandmother" put herself to sleep saying over and over in her mind the words of home because she was afraid of losing her native language that she needed to communicate with the older members of her family. There was a strength and courage in that child; that strength and courage—refined, purified—is also in Kuiceyetsa.

The roast with a light sprinkling of the coarse Zuni salt was perfect on the Zuni bread. On our next visit Kuiceyetsa replaced the sandwich spread. She roasted about seven large green chilies in the oven broiler, checked them, and turned them when they began to brown. After they cooled under a towel, she peeled off their skin and put them in the blender with a couple of minced cloves of garlic. Helen added a bunch of fresh cilantro to the blender, and they blended the ingredients briefly and put the salsa in a bowl. Several of Helen's nieces and nephews were at Kuiceyetsa's that day, and they ate the chili mixture spread on buttered Zuni bread.

At one point Kuiceyetsa got a bite of a particularly hot chili, and her face broke out in a sweat. She took off her glasses, mopped her face, and laughed. "I'm so blind without my glasses," she said, "I'm lucky I can even find my face to wipe it."

LEFT WONDERING

One of the times when we tape-recorded Kuiceyetsa after our funded research project, her son Norman was visiting. Norman has an advanced professional degree from one of America's most prestigious graduate schools and has managed to build a life working with, and for, his people in his village. The day he came in the kitchen to visit with his mother and eat lunch, he had just driven all night across New Mexico, returning from a meeting.

It was just before Halloween, and we asked Kuiceyetsa if Zuni children went out trick-or-treating. She said, "Yes, they go out."

Kathy asked, "Do they wear costumes?"

"Oh, yeah." Kuiceyetsa laughed.

"Good," Kathy said. "That's such fun."

Norman was just coming to the table and asked, "Who? The tribal council?" Everyone laughed, and he said, "Every day."

Kuiceyetsa continued her conversation with Kathy. "They wear all sorts of costumes. They come and scare us first."

Norman said, "Oh, the kids," and we all laughed again.

Kuiceyetsa commented on the nice weather, and Norman said, "Yes, last night was so bright, three-quarter moon. It was just—You could see a long ways."

"It's beautiful to drive at night," I agreed.

"Well, I came the back way through the Continental Divide," Norman said.

"There's a stretch of road back off there after you go through Ramah," Kathy said. "When we went to Santa Fe with Helen, she was telling us that that's where the UFO-type strange lights have been seen."

"Oh, yeah," Kuiceyetsa said.

"Toward Fence Lake?" Norman asked.

"Yes, down in there," we said. The tape recorder was running, and it captured Norman's fascinating stories of unidentified flying objects. Stories of UFO sightings are widely told across Anglo-America and stand in a long tradition. Norman's first story was a personal experience of seeing "with his own eyes"—in the company of other responsible witnesses—a flying object that could not be identified:

❖   One of our board members and them have a ranch out there toward Fence Lake, right on the edge of the reservation. See, if I didn't see it with my own eyes, I wouldn't have believed them. It was from here to Janice's house, I guess. Came out from behind a mountain like that. It was hovering, and then it chased Harris about fifteen miles, and he was going 80 and 90. [*laughs*] It's a—It's kind of a saucer-shaped object with lights going around it, and there is a light that comes down. They don't know what it was, but they got a real good look at it.[89]

Norman's use of onomatopoeia in the second story of his UFO cycle echoed one of the major performance characteristics of Zuni language formal storytelling:

❖   The only thing I've seen similar to that—Well, twice we were doing some night patrols over in Vietnam, going from one place to another, and all of a sudden these big lights came on—great big lights, and they were powerful lights, and they were in a line. Looked like about two miles away, and so we were calling in and seeing who was in the area. Nobody was in the area. We were describing the lights, and they told us to see if we could get a closer look, and so we went on up toward it. And those helicopters only have an operational ceiling of about ten thousand feet, so we got up to as far as we could go, and it seemed as though we were staying about the same distance. And we did get a little closer, and we were describing them, that they were a set of lights that looked like—at least—forty-five feet between them. There was about six of them like that across, and while we were describing it, they just got really bright, and then it just *chu-u-u-u-u*, just took off and disappeared, and we were left there wondering what is going on. [*laughs*] And I don't really know what it was.[90]

Norman's third story followed another major characteristic of Zuni-language formal storytelling—the use of a great deal of direct quotation. He described another UFO sighting and referred—only half humorously—to the widely reported Anglo-American stories of abduction by aliens that have been the subject of so much controversy across the country:

❖   And then, a few years ago Tommy Nelson and I were coming from Santa Fe about twelve o'clock at night, the back way. We kept seeing this real bright star, and it was real bright, and you know, we were both looking at it. We hadn't said anything about it.

Finally he said, "Do you see that star? Seems like it's getting closer."

It would go out, and it would then, you know, come back on, and it would be closer. It kept doing that, and finally [*laughs*] I was going all over the road.

I said, "Let me stop, and we'll look at it."

We were watching it, and here it comes, and it came over. Then a mesa to a side of us about a mile and a half away, and it was up there. And then the light went off again, and you could see. It was a kind of a moonlight night, and you could see the—an outline. And I thought it was a helicopter at first, but it wasn't. There was no sound, and you couldn't hear anything. Then another light came on, and we were looking at it, and he said, "It's going away."

And I said, "No, I don't think so. I think it's coming here."

'Cause it was; it was coming across this way, and it looked like it was going that way, but it was really coming across, and it got bigger and bigger, and it was just dark—It was a real—kind of like, like that, that kind of shape. You could see some kind of structure there.

I was telling my— "It's a chopper you're looking at." And I said, "No." It was close enough so you— I can't hear any blades or anything. No sound.

And he said, "Watch. A green light'll come out and transport us up there." [*laughs*]

And just when he got through saying that, a light did come out, and it was a yellow—you know, just a regular light, you know, but it wasn't— you know, how a light is instantaneous. It went across the sky like this— about that fast—and it went up in the trees on top of us like that. Then it started down, and we jumped in the truck and took off. [*laughs*] We were watching it, and it came, and I told him to keep his eye on it. It was right above us for a little while, and then it crossed there towards Grants, but there was no—If it was a regular aircraft, they have nav lights on it and rotating beacons and things like that. There was nothing like that on it, and there was no sound of it.[91]

His fourth story was the retelling of an account he said that he had heard from a Zuni man we all knew and admired. The person to whom he attributed the story was, in fact, one of the best-known, most frequently collected tellers of the great Zuni myths. He was just as well known among the Zuni for his personal story of seeing a UFO explode:

❖   One of the most interesting descriptions that I've heard was from an old man that I used to work with. Very, kind of sober type of person, but he said he was going to Gallup one day about in the mid- or late-sixties. He said they saw this thing. It looked like an airship, you know, a blimp, or something similar to that. He said it came across Zuni this way, and they saw it, and so they stopped, and it was making real funny noises like something was wrong with it, and it came across fairly fast that way down the valley. Then they saw it coming back across this way, and it flew over toward this area like that. That's when they were building that subdivision right around there.

They were sitting on the road observing it, and it came across back towards Zuni, and it was heading in that direction. All of a sudden, they said, it just kind of went up in the air like that, and there was an explosion. It blew up, but you couldn't really hear that much sound. It was just—You could just see it, you know, disintegrating. And he said out of the middle of all that fire there was, he said, four, or five bluish-looking like balls of light that went up, scattered out, and then regrouped like this in some formation. And then they flew back this way, around the village, and then it just took off. But he said they watched it for about three or four or five minutes—all of this thing happening, but he said that big ship or whatever it was just exploded. He said they were much smaller. They were some kind of objects that were blue, real bright blue, that looked like they were lights, and they all pulled together, and then flew around a little bit, and then they just *chu-u-u-u-u,* took off.

He and his son were together, and they were telling me that one. He was saying there are beings from other places that we don't know anything about. That probably could be an explanation, he said. They didn't, they couldn't, there was nothing they could connect it with 'cause they just thought it was one of those airships at first—those blimps—'cause it looked similar to that, but it wasn't really. But he said it was making noises like something was wrong with it when it flew over them. It was, you know, five thousand feet or something. It wasn't that high. Said it sure sounded like there was a problem there. Something was happening, and it was kind of flying funny, he said. It was going that way and came back. But a number of people have seen things like that, and you just don't know what—[92]

After Norman had told his first four stories, he paused to drink some of his coffee, and Kuiceyetsa told a brief, elliptical story referring to her son's previous reference to abduction by aliens:

❖   Someone from the place down here by Heber—What is that little place called? Taylor, or something? Two people were taken right in there.[93]

After her story, Norman put down his coffee mug and continued to tell his stories of experiences with UFOs. His last story on the subject cited more physical evidence for them:

❖   Well, we had a friend here named Bill Casebeer. We used to work together, and he used to do a lot of hiking around here. He found some, ah, some kind of imprints and burn marks over here by Twin Buttes, and he was telling us about it, and so we said, "Well, one day after work let's go look over there." So we drove out, and we walked over there. There was three spots on the ground that were about as big as this—well, maybe a twenty-foot diameter. Kinda cupped out and depressed, and there was—The bushes and stuff were scorched, and there were kinds of imprints, you know, like something had landed there, you know, or pushed down on the ground. It was pretty interesting to look at, but we didn't—You couldn't really explain what it was, you know. You could only imagine that maybe something landed here.[94]

After telling his series of stories about UFOs, Norman began to talk about rumors and reports of sorcery in the public schools. The story he told to illustrate and explain his concern is a fascinating blend of a contemporary personal-experience story and a condensed portion of the traditional Zuni origin story (a text collected by Stevenson is included in the note to this story for comparison). The old and new work together to create a powerful, artful story:

❖   We've been running into one kind of enchantment that we don't like here with young people. It's getting into that witchcraft, sorcery area. The kind of belief system here is already strong enough without them having a how-to manual to enhance their skills. They don't need that. Lots of the non-Zuni people—not a lot, a few, of the teachers—refuse to believe there's anything like that, and that's their prerogative. But we know what we have to deal with on a daily basis, and it's very real for us—for all of us that are tied into any kind of political responsibility. It's an occupational hazard we have to deal with because that's why we see our medicine man so regularly [*laughs*] to keep us, all of us, cleaned because some of that stuff they take out of you—

I mean, how are you going to explain away something that's sitting right in front of you that was inside of you. There's no way that the guy's going to carry it in, you know. He doesn't have anything up his arm that he's going to pretend that he's taking out of you. It's [the tendency for people who have political responsibility to be a frequent target of witchcraft] true for tribal council men, for other people, and private individuals that are doing well, that have kind of a directed purpose in their life; but the people who practice that, I think are fairly labeled kind of the loser types. They want to find a shortcut to personal or other kind of success, and they don't want to put in the work that's required, the patience, and maybe the self determination to do something either for themselves or for their families or their tribe.

It can come out in terms of—like, Santa Fe Public Schools is having a problem with devil worship and Satanism, based on some kind of medieval practice. Upper-middle-class affluent kids are getting into that kind of. They're making a connection with those negative spirits and forces that they don't know anything about. Well, here we have a long-standing, centuries, thousands-of-years-old practice that's part of our lives that is based on a certain kind of practice but is really the same kind of thing that they're practicing at a different level. It's the same source, you know, which is the thing about good and evil.

You know the story about—We're asking our parents and other people, "Why do we have witches? Why do we have to deal with these people? Where do they come from?"

Well, as the development of the Zunis is told, you know, we're coming up from another level of awareness and development, and we're coming to this new one, and everybody's development or transition is going to be together. If we have our prayer bundles and we have our prayers, we're a religious people and everything except—

They decide to leave all the sorcerers and those evil people and the witches and everybody behind, and the one who they hoped to leave behind has grabbed the bundles of corn and the corn and cornmeal and things like that, and he's hanging onto them. So, "Do you want those things up there? Then you'll have to bring me up with you." So there's a connection and a continuation of that. They have their own practice, and we know quite a bit about it. But we're not at the same level as they are in their own practice because to be at that level, we wouldn't even be talking about it. We wouldn't be able to because they have secrecy in their society, and they won't talk about it, but if you catch them, then they better talk about it.[95]

THE GRANDPARENT'S WORLD

After finishing his coffee and his stories, Norman excused himself and left to return to his profession. Kuiceyetsa and Kathy and I began to clear the coffee cups off the table and wipe the table off. As we worked Kuiceyetsa said, "I like your bolo tie."

"Oh, thank you," I told her, and we looked at the piece which was shell carved in the shape of an eagle.

"You know, Max has one in the same shape. He has one from Alaska," and she went into the bedroom to find Max's bolo tie so that we could compare it with mine. "I don't see his eagle. He must have worn it today. It's that shape. It's an eagle."

She came back into the kitchen carrying an American Indian necklace. It had slender leather thongs that tied in a bow knot behind the neck. Below the thongs on each side was suspended a pattern of three translucent, glowing, amber-colored beads, followed by a white bead, a long, flat, purple bead, three more of the amber-colored beads, another white one, and finally a long, tapered, gently curved white spine from some sea creature. The pattern was repeated until the two cords met at the top edge of a polished and shaped abalone shell which reflected pearl, purple, green, gold, and silver iridescent light. A short combination of the beads and spines in a slightly different pattern was suspended from the softly glowing shell.

"This," she said, "is from the Northwest. I'll give you this one."

I was speechless for a second and then managed to say only, "Oh, my goodness!"

Kuiceyetsa laughed, "I don't think anybody will ever wear it, so you can have it." We all laughed. "It's from Oregon, I think. It's made from shell."

"It's gorgeous," I said, taking off my carved eagle bolo tie and putting on my new American Indian necklace.

"I see you wearing something, you know, big. It matches," she said and laughed.

All I could manage was, "Thank you," but I wore the necklace Kuiceyetsa gave me when I presented a paper at the Pre-General Meeting of the Folklore Society in London and told them about her and it.

The conversation turned to Kuiceyetsa's memories of her early life, and we began to ask her questions about what it had been like to be a child at Zuni many years ago. Across cultures and time, the stories grandchildren most like to hear grandparents tell include accounts of when the old were the young and the snow was *this deep*. Across time and cultures, stories grandparents most like to tell grandchildren include accounts of halcyon times when the days were right. Between those new to the world and those soon to leave it, there is a bond—most often by unspoken agreement—to listen and to tell so that the long-dead past lives again through this celebration, the bonds of time are unfettered, the child lives in the grandparent's world, the grandparent lives in the child's world, the past and the future meet in the now. Such stories teach that all things can be endured, and such stories have lives of their own. By their nature and by their telling, they provide precious glimpses of the everyday minutiae and emotions of being. Kuiceyetsa's next three accounts were such stories:

❖   I remember coming back from Ojo Caliente with my grandpa—on his back—and he'd set me down, and I had to walk a little ways, but I don't know how old I was. I remember a little doll I had, and it was so old and kind of cracked and made out of some kind of—It was a ceramic, something like that. China. Yeah, I remember that—[*laughs*]—remember having a doll.

My cousins, they took me out there when my brother was born. I guess I made such a fuss that they said they would take me out there. They did take me, but I remember a pond, you know, where there was some ducks. I would sit out in back and watch the ducks, and she had Mexicans coming all the time. I don't know what they did, but they were rowdy, and I was just scared to death of them. [*laughs*] I don't know how old I would be. Let me think. I would be about four or five, but I remember real well.

I cried a lot, I guess. My grandpa came out to get me. He didn't have no way to bring me home—just on his back, [*laughs*] and it's quite a ways—brought me home.[96]

❖   Took me to my mother's—they lived together. She really wasn't my grandmother. I don't know my grandmother. I guess she died sometime—when my mother was born, I think—and so I didn't know her. But her sister—I didn't know her either; I just heard them talking about her, and [*laughs*] he, he called her Mrs. Bently, and that wasn't her name, but—'cause she was bent over, you know, and his name was Ta'tan. He was high priest at that time, and they used to call her that, and he got to be real old.

I remember him sitting out, out in the back. He'd have this rock he'd—I don't know how he placed that board—that turquoise on a board, and he would rub it to make it shiny. But he was real old. He had kind of white clothes on, and I remember he would always scratch himself. [*laughs*] He had this woolen, you know, what they knit; he had those on, no shoes, just those, and he'd forever scratch. [*laughs*] The early part of my years I remember.[97]

❖ I heard them talking, you know. They'd go out somewhere this way, clear to that place—uh, what is that? Out towards Hopi and then down below in the canyon. Who are those people that live down there? Havasupai! Yeah, they said they were part of us and separated from them, I guess a long time ago, and they used to go over there. He'd have his donkeys loaded down with stuff that he got here, and he would go a long ways. And he said oftentimes they would run across—hide, you know, hold on to the muzzle of their animals so they won't make any noise. I don't know what they called—Texans, I guess. *Tejja:na:qe,* they used to say. They'd go by, and then they would continue on their way. They were afraid they would take their things or kill them. But they would, you know, just travel that way, and when he gets there, I guess he does trading with whatever he had for the people here, and then when he'd come back, then next day or so they would have things out there. People would come: "This is yours." "You got this." You know, and that. Cooking pots, I guess, and cloth. I don't know what kind.

I just remember my mother described an old lady. She was up this far with all kinds of bracelets—almost to her elbows. [*laughs*] When I was little and I would get something, I put it on, you know, [and] she would say, "You're just like your old grandma, you know." I didn't know her, but— [*laughs*]

He did trading. Whatever he brought back, well, the people come to get, and then the extra things, you know, that he'd traded over there. He'd lay them out, put a price on it, I guess, and that way the people would get what they want—something like a raffle or something. [*laughs*]

Just in snatches, you know, I remember the things the old people used to say.[98]

After we had attended Shalako several years, Kuiceyetsa said we also should see the Mid-summer Dance held following the summer solstice. She made it clear that she found great meaning and pleasure in this dance and told us Helen would let us know when it would occur. When Helen called, she told us to be sure and come for supper and be early enough to see the dancers enter town. "They'll come across the Zuni River before sunset," she said.

We arrived at Zuni a little after noon and spent some time visiting with Clyde's wife and her family before we drove to Kuiceyetsa's. As usual, several of her children and grandchildren were there along with a niece fixing Kuiceyetsa's hair. We all talked, catching up on the news of everyone's health, new babies, and events in the village. Kuiceyetsa then served a special meal of *tsu'balonne* (sheep stomach sausage made from a mixture of sheep's blood, cornmeal, and chilies stuffed into a cleaned sheep stomach and baked in an outdoor oven). In addition, there was tossed salad, rolls made from the Zuni sourdough, watermelon, and chocolate sheet cake. All of this was served with cold pop or hot coffee. Kuiceyetsa's home was the center of much activity, with friends and family coming and going, plates of food being passed to people as they came in, and empty plates being passed back to the kitchen as people left.

As the afternoon wore on, I began to worry about getting to watch the dancers arrive. I checked my watch several times and peered out at the west to see how low the sun was sinking. In her usual observant manner, Kuiceyetsa saw my concern and suggested we all go to the center of the village to await the dancers. When we got to the stone ledge along the road the dancers would be using, Kathy and I were surprised to see only a few Zunis were gathered on the rooftops across the street. I put my cushion that I carry on the ledge and sat awhile. We had a good time visiting, but I was getting stiff, and my back was hurting. I got up and walked around, trying to get the muscle cramps out of my legs and back.

"They will be along pretty soon," Kuiceyeta said, and we could see more Zunis were gathering along the road. I realized that years of attending classes both as students and as teachers had made Kathy and me think in terms of *melika* (white people's) time.

"Next year," we promised Kuiceyetsa, "we'll wait until you tell us that it's time to go watch the dancers."

Kuiceyetsa told a story of her grandson Franklin—sometimes as impatient as we were—after the accounts of her own childhood:

❖   We always stayed at that one motel when we went to Flagstaff. One summer we were staying there and walked over to the K-Mart. It started to rain, and when we got to K-Mart, we were soaking wet.

Right in front of everybody, Franklin took off his pants. [*laughs*] At first he rolled them up. He tried, and then he came back and took it off. Peggy was so mad at him. She was just yelling at him, "Put your pants back on you." [*laughs*] "There's lots of people here. They'll see you." He took it off and just started running.

That was a flood all right.[99]

PART OF LIFE

With the joy and pleasure of meeting people of like minds in different cultures, comes also—all too often—the pain of losing these friends to death. We have attended more than our share of funerals at Zuni, and one cold day in January we attended Clyde's mother-in-law's funeral. She had come to Zuni as a young bride more than fifty years before from her Maricopa-Pima family in the Phoenix area and had quickly been accepted by the Zuni community because of her sweet and sunny personality. We first visited with her while waiting for Clyde at his wife's home where she also lived, and we soon began to look forward to seeing Mrs. Flores. She was retired, but her life and her work continued. In addition to helping her daughter care for her great-grandchildren, she did the mending for the entire extended family. Her Singer sewing machine was often set up in the living room of their home, and she was usually busy using it.

We went to Kuiceyetsa's as soon as we arrived at Zuni and changed into the clothes we had brought to wear to Mrs. Flores's funeral. Kuiceyetsa was not feeling well enough to attend herself, but she told us to come back after we had seen the family and been to the funeral.

By the time we returned to Kuiceyetsa's, we were chilled to the core. She had fixed hot blue cornmeal mush and gave us each a steaming bowl, which at first we just used it to warm our hands. Then Kuiceyetsa showed us the various ways we could eat the mush. She had small bowls with dried, crushed red chilies and coarse Zuni salt for sprinkling over the top. In addition, she said some people liked to put sugar and milk on the mush. We ate in silence for awhile, still thinking of Mrs. Flores. Kuiceyetsa looked at our solemn faces and touched Kathy's hand.

"It's part of life," she said.

Kathy told Kuiceyetsa, "My dad's family was from Scotland, and his idea of the thing to eat if you were sick, upset, cold, lonely or in any other way unhappy was oatmeal."

Kuiceyetsa laughed as she sprinkled red chili on her mush. "That's much the same way with our blue cornmeal mush."

The hot food began to revive us, and Kathy asked, "How do you cook this?"

"Just the way you do oatmeal," Kuiceyetsa laughed.

It was soon after that Kuiceyetsa began telling us a series of stories about funny funerals:

❖   The funniest funeral I have ever been to [was at] that military cemetery. There was a whole line of people going, and when we got there, the snow was on the ground, and it was real cold, but they had a sort of little shed that they put out. They did the service and the burial service, and when they came to the end where he blows the bugle, the "taps," this young man [*laughs*] couldn't even—his face was just red—he couldn't even get anything out. He kept blowing. [*laughs*] And then the grandchildren, one of them started to laugh, and they looked at each other, and they all giggled. They started laughing—[*laughs*] Everybody was laughing 'cause he couldn't blow the "Taps." He finally made like keening; he just continued until he got a few notes out. [*laughs*] It was funny.[100]

❖   I don't know what Joe did, but he worked in Flagstaff for quite awhile, and he married a Navajo. Joe was one of these bow priests, and he came one time to visit us, and he had become a Christian and said he didn't need those anymore, but he didn't want to give it to just anybody. He didn't know what to do with it, but he said it was his. It was one of these—what do you call those?—a sash with a pouch; but the sash, they're woven with enemy hairs or whatever, and when he brought it in, I said, "What's in there?"

And he said—he pulled it out—and he said, "This is my sash."

"Hang it outside." I told him. 'Cause we were told not to receive it into your house, and so he left it hanging out on the porch, and he came in, and he was telling us about the Lord and everything, and then he went. Soon after that, he was, ah, hit by a car right over there by the pass going out towards Ramah, and I guess it was just instant death, you know—'cause his body was just quivering. My son came up on that scene—he and some other people—but he died, and then three days later they had to send him to Albuquerque, I think.

They had his funeral, and we all went, and they had a nice service for him, graveside services. While they were saying the service, I looked at the coffin, and I looked at the place where they were going to put it, and it didn't look like it will fit, you know. [*laughs*] And so when they finally were trying to lower him down, it started going, you know, sorta sideways. I guess one of the relatives or somebody stepped on the other side, and he went in. [*laughs*] They were laughing. They just crunched him in.[101]

❖   I think the nicest funeral we went to was Bill Martinez's funeral. He was here for a long time. His wife taught school—Oh, I don't know. I can't tell how long they stayed here, but he really took his wife's going hard. Come to visit us, he'd come in crying, and then he'd go out crying. He didn't last very long. But they had a nice funeral for him, and we all got lost. [*laughs*] It was a procession, you know, of people. We had two police escorts. The line was real long. He was a Mexican, but he could talk Zuni, you know. Well, we all went over to Albuquerque to the services. They took Maxine and Janice, and one party went one way, and the others stayed and went another way. [*laughs*] I don't know how we got separated, but we finally all gathered over there.

They had the service there. They had a whole bunch of flowers, and we took a flower and threw it in. Afterwards they had a reception for him, and everybody had a good time. They were here a long time, and Mrs. Martinez was a teacher at Zuni, so they got to know the Zunis.[102]

Kuiceyetsa returned to the question of witchcraft in the schools that her son had raised earlier. One story dealt with her own grandchildren:

❖   I didn't realize that Ouija boards were becoming a problem. I heard about them a long time ago, but, you know, Peggy and Franklin and their cousin, they had a piece of paper, and they go put it on a board and use it. Helen had to run them over here to her brother to talk to them not to use it, and he destroyed it. It's hard to believe, but I guess the people that do evil just think nothing about that. They devise ways and means to draw their attention to themselves or whatever they believe in. We're all told in our old, old times, too, that these things will come about, that we're not surprised at anything, you know, new—or something happening. It's been done before, and it's going to repeat itself in time, but all those things will come along. But you have to seek the truth to know the way—how to get out of it. I guess it's just like being a drug addict or something. They get into something and can't get out of it. I guess they were talking to the board. They would ask questions, and it would point the way—Whatever it answered, they wanted.[103]

She followed her story of Ouija boards with another describing the proper remedy for them and other temptations of witchcraft:

❖   I know there's students that were doing that in Santa Fe at the dormitory, and in one of the girl's rooms these girls were just going wild. Peggy was there at the time, but she didn't take part in it. She heard them just screaming and screaming, and they got caught, you know. They were sent home. There's ways that you can keep yourself from those things. Our old people used to say, "Keep yourself busy. Don't be chambering," or something. "Don't be idle 'cause it brings wrong things into your mind," they would tell us. "You think too much. You don't do any work or anything. You'll get into trouble." That's what they used to say to us.[104]

After Kuiceyetsa's stories about evil, Kathy asked her where evil comes from, and Kuiceyetsa answered by telling her synopsis of the relevant section of the Zuni origin story Norman had summarized earlier:

❖   *Kathy:* When we were doing the urban American Indian interviews, we kept getting stories about places where evil things happen repeatedly. What makes a place evil? Was it evil before human beings came? Do people create evil?

Kuiceyetsa: Well, in our origin, the Zuni say they had to let the evil one come. He was the last person to come. "Well, we don't want you," they said. "We don't want you."

But he says, "I have the things that you need, so you can't exclude me from," you know, "from taking with." 'Cause he had the seeds of everything, so that's how he was allowed to come. That's how they had it. They say it takes four nights of telling about that origin and how we came about. And they talk about the ten idiotic children of a brother and sister that became Mud Heads. Those things they carry on their head, they take a little portion of sand from everybody's house and make it up. And when they come, why you give them something to eat, and they bless you, so there's a spiritual meaning, too. Those things and other things that the dancers do—well, just the men that are initiated. But I always wonder, what about the ladies? Don't we go to the same place? [*laughs*] If I don't get accepted—[105]

"Spiritual meanings" and spiritual concerns led Kuiceyetsa next to the story of a near-death experience:

❖   For instance, in my life, well, a blood clot gets into a vein. They don't expect you to live 'cause it will go to your brain. Well, I had that happen in me, and it dissolved. I prayed about it, and they put me in one room and by myself. I knew it was really hurting bad, but I didn't seem to care, you know. I thought if I went to sleep, I'll never wake up, so I kept repeating the names of my children, my sisters' children, my sisters—I keep doing that over and over. In the meantime, I was real sick. I kept throwing up, and they gave me a morphine shot, too, 'cause I held on to the bedstead, you know, and I wouldn't let it go 'cause the pain was so bad.

My folks weren't there, or any other, but then I began to pray, and every time it hurt me a little bit, I start praying again, and His grace was sufficient for me, you know. Towards morning, the pain eased, but, you know, I had a funny feeling that my grandpa was in the room, but he wasn't dead yet. It was like in a dream, but I woke up, I guess, when the door closed. He went out. The door closed, and I looked, and I said, uh, "Are you there?" I looked around. Nobody was in the room.

I had had my son, and I had a problem with the leg here. It was all swelled up, and I guess a clot from that got in, and then the next morning everybody looked in at me. They say, "You look different." They thought I was going to die. I didn't.[106]

Kuiceyetsa next returned to stories of Franklin getting wet as a child:

❖   The next day we went down to Walnut Canyon, and we were down there all right. We were looking into those little rooms down there, and going up I knew it was going to rain. I said, "Hurry up! It's going to rain." And sure enough, we got caught—just a downpour. We were just soaking wet. We couldn't make it up the steps. [*laughs*] And we were just squishing in. [*laughs*][107]

❖   When Franklin and Peggy didn't go to school, I took them with me. Oh, he was onery. He wouldn't stay in the room. He had long hair with a band around his head, and the guys that stayed there at the motel—I think they were workers of something, you know—they'd get off work, and they'd go to the swimming pool, and that's where Franklin would be. [*laughs*] And he'd play ball with them, and they'd throw it to him. He was all wet. He didn't even get in the water. [*laughs*][108]

After telling more stories of Franklin as a child, Kuiceyetsa returned to memories of her own childhood. The art of telling stories of childhood is to remember *as* a child, to become a child again, to communicate the experience of childhood. It is the art of Kuiceyetsa:

❖   I couldn't tell if I was unhappy as a teenager. I stayed in a dormitory all the time. We had to always do what we had to do. One day they got me a job in Los Angeles. I was terrified. They got jobs in Beverly Hills, and it happened that I had to work for an Episcopalian minister. [*laughs*] Everywhere they put me, I'd go to. [*laughs*] I took care of an old lady, and they lived near L[os] A[ngeles] J[unior] C[ollege]. I had to walk down five blocks, I think, to the street car, then I get on the street car and go around twenty blocks to Virgil High School that was on South Vermont, if you know where that is. [*laughs*] Well, it was a street next to Santa Monica Boulevard. Nothing was there hardly. You know, there was shops and all that, but you could walk down to—I always wanted to go down to Western. That's as far as I'd gotten and turned back.
     On Saturdays the grandma and I stayed and [I] took care of her. I didn't give her shots. I didn't know I would be doing that to myself [*laughs*] one day. I couldn't understand why she couldn't eat anything sweet. When her daughter's gone, she'd say, "Sneak over. Go get me a raisin pie or something." [*laughs*] I didn't know that wasn't good for her. I went over there for a year, just a companion to her—plus housework—and Dr. whatever-his-name-was. I can't remember. Harris. Dr. Harris, he had students coming in all the time. He taught theology, I guess. That got me away anyhow from the school. [*laughs*][109]

❖   I used to get—kinda got lonely, you know, 'cause in a big city you don't know anybody. Everybody on their own. I used to watch the kids next door—a deaf and dumb boy and the younger boy. There were two boys, and they were always making sign language and everything—playing. I didn't have anything to do. I wandered along and watch.[110]

❖   My sister went to church all the time over there. We lived on that side [*points south*] with my aunt for a short time, 'cause my mother got married again after my father died, and she went out to stay at Hill Ranch. I stayed with my aunt, my father's sister, and I had the hardest time. They had a hard time with me. I didn't get used to them for a long time. Everyday I just would take off.[111]

❖   I'd go out there. I'd get there in the evening, and I'd stand in the shadows in the dark, you know, and they'd discover me and bring me in. [*laughs*] About three times I did that. Finally I got used to them, but I'd walk every day over there. I was lonesome for my mother, but she had to stay out there because my stepfather had sheep and horses and fields to tend. But after that, every weekend we'd go out there. We'd all gather over there by the field on the west side and wait for each other, and there'll be a good group of us going. I had a real hard time getting used to living with my aunt.[112]

❖   Most of the time I remember we had to be dragged out of bed by my sister and taken to the mass at six o'clock, and then at eight o'clock we go to school and go back and go to mass again. So when I went away to school, I never did set foot in a Catholic church again. [*laughs*] I wanted to go with the others to the other church. I was drilled and drilled over there. We had to form up and go to catechism, and then we made our first communion, and I don't know why we had to march to the Old Mission. They don't do that anymore. Father would [go] with that cross and with that altar, and whoever served—the little boys—they'd go, and they'd all go to the church. They don't do that anymore. I was always ashamed to go there. I'd hid behind the next person. [*laughs*][113]

❖   Those sisters were nice, some of them. I know we got our teaching, our ABCs from them. These were kind of old-fashioned ones that were here. Only there was a sister—I can't remember her name—but she wore those looked like work shoes, you know, that come up to here. I used to look at them real good. But she really used to cook, and they had their own garden, and I was hanging around over there to see if she'd give us cookies, you see. And I think they were Italians. They talked a funny language.[114]

❖   I guess it was strange for them to be here, but they had a purpose, and they used to give us clothing over there 'cause we were poor. We didn't have no shoes. They issued up clothing. I know my little brother, one time he had a fur coat in the winter. I guess donations come in, but he had a fur coat. He looked like a bear. He was just round. [*laughs*] And every morning we go to school. I remember it was real cold, but we'd take off his coat and slide down the hill, you know, over there where they have that wall now. We lived up there when my mother was here in the winter. We'd ride down on his coat. [*laughs*] In the mornings when we'd get over to school, we'd get punished. [*laughs*] We'd get so busy playing on the way. [*laughs*] We'd go to mass first and then go to classes.[115]

THE ZUNI SPRING

Twenty-seven stories later, after many cups of coffee, my favorite green chili and cilantro salsa lavished on buttered Zuni bread with a sprinkling of Zuni salt (and the salsa Kuiceyetsa makes for Kathy from cooked chilies because they are easier on the stomach), the conversation tapered off into pleasant, comfortable silence, and we left for home with a loaf of Zuni bread Kuiceyetsa had given us.

We returned to see Kuiceyetsa again several months later, and the conversation seemed to continued right where it had left off. First, she told us another "funny funeral" story:

❖   They all have different things that they do for their dead. Like the Maricopas and Pimas, they burn their dead. They put them on a rack, and they *cry* all the time that that's burning. One time their aunt Janice was there, and she cried so hard and cried so long, [*laughs*] and they brought to her—they keep putting stuff on her like a gift or something—and the more she cried, the more things they brought. [*laughs*] And her mother said, "Don't cry anymore." [*laughs*] I remember she told me that.[116]

Stories of those who have collected stories are common among the storytellers they have studied. Kuiceyetsa next told stories of three of the leading researchers who had worked at Zuni over the last one hundred years:

❖   Leslie Spier came and stayed here. He was an anthropologist and, of course, Mrs. Stevenson. She was an ethnologist, too, and also an anthropologist and, of course, Cushing, as you remember. One thing that she [my mother-in-law] said that he was like. He didn't like the kids running around after him. They did that to white people. They would trail after them, and he'd leave them by the door, you know, wherever he was staying. He didn't want them in the room 'cause he told her they were unclean. They followed him everywhere he went and sat outside sometimes and waited for him to come out. [*laughs*] Once in awhile he'd come out with candy or something, you know, and give to them. Must have been interesting to see a person like him. But he [Cushing] said there were always kids around him. Curious, kids are.[117]

❖   Elsie Clews Parsons stayed here, too, and when Max was little he said she left her shoes in there, and they were those high tops. He pretended he was a cowboy. Put those on, got up on the bedside, and his mother's girdle was on the bed rail, and he was sitting on it like a saddle pretending he had a horse. [*laughs*]
       And he'd always pick up those cigarettes that she smoked. They were scented, I guess, or something, you know. And he'd always look around to see if she would drop some, and he'd just latch on to them.
       Parsons would always have pancakes, and she [my mother-in-law] said he always said, "Pancake ready." Max would go to the door of the house and knock and say, "Pancake ready." They had it fixed, you know.
       He remembers Elsie Clews Parsons. She stayed quite awhile, I guess, while she was here.[118]

❖   Grandmother said that Mrs. Stevenson was a hard person to get along with. She would order the men, you know. She'd go tell someone, "Go get me some water from the spring." They would have to run all the way over there and get her some water. I don't know what was with the water. That spring was on the side of Towayalane [Corn Mountain].[119]

While Kuiceyetsa was telling her stories of anthropologists at Zuni, Helen came in, and Helen, Kathy and I smiled at each other after her mother's story as we remembered what was with the water and *our* going to get it from the spring on the side of Towayalane. We were driving back to the village after Helen had served as "our faithful Indian guide" and taken us to see the rock paintings along the Zuni Cliffs, and Helen said, "You know what I think would taste really great right now? Some water from the Zuni spring on this side of Corn Mountain would be just right. It's always so cold and tastes so good."

Kathy and I had been thirsty before Helen's loving description of the cool waters which came down from the Zuni spring; now we longed for them.

"Where is the spring? Could we get there in the car?" I asked.

I was tired from the hike around the Cliffs and was not sure I could walk much farther. Helen assured me we could drive a good part of the way, and we decided to go to the spring rather than waiting until we got to the village for a drink. We turned off the highway onto a gravel road, but the gravel soon thinned out and we found ourselves driving on a sand lane. Several hard rains the month before had packed and smoothed the sand, so we went along safely but slowly. We crossed a series of small rounded hills and entered an area thick with desert willows and bee plants covered with purple blooms. We drove until we reached a place where the thicket grew across the road. I stopped the car, and we talked about going on.

"The spring is just there at the base of those rocks." Helen pointed ahead, but the plants blocked my view. "You can wait here, and Kathy and I will bring you some water. There's usually some kind of cup there."

I appreciated her offer, but I did not want to lose out on any of the adventure. We left the car and started walking through the willows and bee plants. The air at Zuni is usually very clear and dry, but here along the base of the mountain in the middle of all the vegetation, it was heavy and wet. Insects and small birds filled the low trees, and their calls and voices sounded, echoed, and reverberated around us. I lost sight of the car, and when we topped a low hill, I turned back to see if I could find it and get some sense of how far we had walked. Helen saw I had stopped and suggested a rest. We stood on the crest of the low hill and looked out over the copse of willows below us. We saw the car to the east of us, and further to the east beyond the thick growth of vegetation we saw a Zuni runner. He was a man in his late twenties wearing a tee shirt, shorts, running shoes, and a sweatband. He was concentrating on his running, and he did not seem to see us watching him from our hill. He glided effortlessly along the path, moving at a steady, even pace, and swinging his arms gracefully as he ran, apparently at peace with his purpose, place, and progress.

As the runner disappeared from sight, Helen said, "He may be getting ready to dance at Shalako. Dancers have always run here to build their stamina for the dance. He might also be someone taking care of his health. Lots of Zuni run out here to stay in shape."

We turned back toward the mountain. We walked toward the spring. There in the heart of this dry land, on the side of this dry mountain, under this brilliant sky, the cool waters came trickling down and came forth. Some earlier visitor had fashioned a trough from the body of an aluminum pop can, and a stream of iridescent water ran away from the face of the rock down the trough and splashed to the ground, reflecting, intensifying, re-creating the light that shown on, through, and from it. Helen stood below the end of the trough, filled some kind of cup that was there and drank, then splashed the trickle gently on her forehead and chin with her cupped hands.

The spring was about level with my head, and I thrust my face below the trough, and drank and drank and drank and drank, and the cool waters enveloped me.

Kathy and Helen laughed. With the sound of their laughter and the touch of the water there came an intense, achingly clear, total awareness and experience of this moment, the knowledge that even as I felt it so deeply with such clarity it was passing away and could never return, and the certainty that it yet had been always and forever would be. We took turns drinking and letting the cool water run on our faces and hands. When Kuiceyetsa told her story of Stevenson at Zuni, the moment was once more.

Helen poured herself a cup of coffee, refilled our cups, and joined the conversation. As always when another person came to join the circle around her kitchen table, Kuiceyetsa pushed her chair back enlarging the circle, gestured with her arm to bring the new person into the circle, and welcomed the addition.

Helen expressed concern about the fact that the village was having a problem with violence, and Kuiceyetsa told a story of the origin of violence in the recent past:

❖   They found a man buried in the kind of soft sand, and he was out there tending his orchard. That's where he had peaches out there, and he would stay out there. They didn't know he had been killed until they started looking for him. Then he was buried up to his neck—right here—[*puts her hand to her throat*] I don't know how long he had been alive, you know.

This was somewhere around the 1940s. That's when we started having violence around here. The beginning of that.[120]

Within each culture is an ideal—a concept of the way things should be. Within each culture is a reality—the ways in which members of the culture depart from its ideals. Stories tell of the ideal and what should be, stories tell of departures from the ideal and what should not be—and what the culture most fears. Helen told stories of deviation from the Zuni ideal, and in them—as in the dismay and disgust they evoke in her—is the chance to see another part of what it means to be Zuni:

❖   You know that kid that ran into all those police cars? When we went to town that day to get her [Mom], they were having her put those tubes back in 'cause they were clogged, and she couldn't go through dialysis, so they had to put her tubes in. I think I called home, and they were talking about it. Someone told me about it—Janice or somebody. But this kid that crashed into these police cars was trying to get away. I guess he was in jail for a little while, and then he got out, and then he—

    This Navajo family lost their daughter, and so they got a medicine man to look. You know, they use those crystals to find out where the person was. And they said that the girl was buried in a shallow grave, and she's buried by something metal, and they—he—could see who the person was that did it. The medicine man brought the family down here to this one kid that ran into the police car a few weeks before, and he denied it, and so they couldn't prove anything, so the family just left. They got another medicine man, and he said the same thing, brought them to the same house; but this time they brought some police, and they said, "If you know anything about it, let them know," and so he finally told them he had buried her out here at Vanderwagon, and he had. She had died from a blow to the head. I don't know what he hit her with, maybe a pipe or something. I don't know what's going to happen to him. I haven't heard anything. I guess when the veterans had their meeting, they were talking about it.[121]

❖   I guess that guy is weird. He's just—He ran over a kid. School had just gotten out, and he hit a kid and then took off without finding out if that kid was hurt or anything, and he made off quick to the other side of the village. The police were trying to stop him 'cause he was going so fast, and he went sideways, I guess, and he smashed two of them. And then he got out and started to run across the fields 'cause his house was just over on the other side, and they caught him. [*laughs*][122]

❖   There's a couple of guys like that. There's another guy that's like that. He just buried—They were taking some clothes over to Roxanne's on Friday for their little boy 'cause they moved. They were right behind the trailer, and this guy comes up and asks them where they were going, and he just started to fight them and won't let them—They wanted to go inside the house, and he was just saying that he had guns at his house, which was just a little ways away. He was going to kill them, and they were asking why he was doing that 'cause they said they hadn't done anything to him.

He said, "Well, do you guys want to join the Mafia?" [*laughs*] He's just—He's got guns. I don't know where he gets them. That's why—[123]

❖   We went to a graduation party last year, and his grandmother was sitting there, and she wanted to go home, but everybody else wasn't ready. The grandmother just didn't want to leave with him. He said he'd take her home, but she said, "No!"

And he goes, "I don't know why she's afraid of me." Now I know why she just didn't want to leave with him. And then one of her daughters said, "Yeah, she's afraid of him."

And we were getting ready to leave, and she said, "Well, take me." The neighbors have a bed over there for her when her daughter doesn't come home, so she goes and sleeps until her family comes. So we took her there. She didn't even want him to help her outside, so we took her out.[124]

SHARING AND AFFIRMING

Helen paused after her stories of deviance and sighed. Kuiceyetsa resumed her storytelling with a personal-experience story of asking directions from a mounted policeman in Washington, D.C. She clearly conveyed by her smile and laughter her delight in the memory of seeing someone on a horse in a city and asking him for directions:

❖   When I went to Washington, D.C., with Max, I went to the building where all these other Indian ladies were, and they had to go a block down to the left, and I had to go a block down this way, and I started walking down. The buildings all looked the same. I walked down one, and I said, "I think this is where I cross," and I crossed, and I was supposed to cross this way. I looked there. The buildings are the same. I walked down this other way. I walked and walked, and I wondered. I begin to wonder if I'm lost. Then I look real good, and I saw this man on a horse. [*laughs*]

I went over there and asked the man and then, "You're down to the levels in the Interior [Department] and the other federal building central offices."

"I'm not lost," I say, "I just couldn't find my way." [*laughs*] Then I started walking away from there. I had to cross one street over and down into the next one. I was right there.[125]

Kuiceyetsa may have told us the story of her almost getting lost in Washington, D.C., because of Kathy's reputation for getting lost at Zuni. On our first trip to Zuni with Charlie Hoffman, we had been driving the university van with Kathy giving directions when she sent us up a road that was too muddy. We got stuck and had to have two young men with a tractor come and pull the van out. They asked what we were doing on that road, and Kathy said, "We were supposed to turn left at the beige house with the Toyota truck in front of it."

"Oh, yes," they agreed. "You should have. Not at *that* beige house with the Toyota truck but at the one before it."

Several years later Kathy was driving at Zuni. This time she was looking for a pink house with a silver hatchback in front of it. She turned at the pink house, but the hatchback had been gray, and she ended up driving further and further from town. Finally she stopped and got new directions, and the kind lady went in and called the people Kathy was trying to find, who then stood out in the road and flagged her down as she drove back into town. Kathy's getting lost at Zuni is a source of amusement and concern for Kuiceyetsa.

Amusement and concern. Unlike their neighbors the Navajo, Zunis do not have a tradition of jokes, but many Zuni conversations allude to shared past occurrences and function thus as stories recalled but unspoken. For example, Kathy and I were buying materials for lunch at Halona Plaza in Zuni one day when Helen walked up behind us and said, "Mister, your car is running." We laughed as we turned around, hugged her, and made arrangements to stop and visit with her on our way back from interviewing a Ramah Navajo medicine man.

Helen's quip referred to the experience we shared touring Santa Fe with her as our guide so that we not only saw Santa Fe but also saw Santa Fe through her eyes after making a research presentation. Our car has a radiator fan that runs after the engine is shut off. It seemed as though everywhere we went that day someone noticed the fan and said, "Hey, Mister, your car engine is running." The situation and the phrase became one of Helen's and our favorite shared references. She employs it frequently, and it is funnier every time we hear it.

Helen listened to her mother's stories carefully, and the last seemed to remind her of another. She asked Kuiceyetsa to tell us the story about the haunted motel in Washington, D.C., Kuiceyetsa's kitchen table and personal-experience stories often contain a good deal of humor. They simultaneously affirm and strengthen the close, accepting personal relationships sought by the Zuni. Her final story featured a level of language play unusual in Zuni and contained within it a magnificent tall tale in delightful, exquisite miniature:

❖   *Kuiceyetsa:* That was the old motel where we stayed. I used to go and stay there, and they said the roaches know Max. They all stand and salute. [*laughs*] They see how long he had been going there. [*laughs*]

It was one of the real old buildings 'cause just the bathroom down on the end, everybody used that, and we always stayed there to save money. [*laughs*]

Helen: But anyway when he found out there was a ghost, he turned the light on 'cause they don't like the light.

Kuiceyetsa: I know! They turned the tap water on, and it would be running. Max would turn it off, and then the light in the next room would turn on. [*laughs*] I hesitated about wanting to spend my days and nights there. [*laughs*] I wouldn't even get out of that one room. [*laughs*] When it began to be dark, I just turned all the lights on.

They didn't know why there was a ghost. He wouldn't hurt you or anything, but he moved—[*laughs*] I would leave the room opened, the doorway opened. Max came one time [and asked], "Why is the door open?" [*laughs*]

"Because I'm afraid!" [*laughs*]¹²⁶

THE ZUNI WAY

Kuiceyetsa seemed very tired, and we left early that day. We saw her again at Shalako. She was lying down in her room when we came into her home filled with her children and grandchildren. She came out and said that she had heard our voices. She sat in her usual place at the table and talked to us while we ate mutton stew and Zuni bread. She seemed very, very tired, and we left after a very short visit. Kathy called Clyde's wife about a week later, and she told us that Kuiceyetsa had collapsed the day after we saw her and had been taken to the hospital in a coma.

Kathy said, "Oh, my goodness, she had just been telling me stories of funny funerals."

Clyde's wife said, "She obviously was preparing you."

Kuiceyetsa survived her coma. We have been fortunate enough to speak with her again, and we have her with us yet awhile, but her efforts to prepare us seem obvious in retrospect.

Norman and Helen's stories tell of ideals not achieved; of things unidentified (sorcerers, flying saucers, and psychopaths); and of evil conceptualized both traditionally and in terms of acculturated beliefs. They show that what the Zuni fear most is an experience or person beyond reason. All of these stories acknowledge the existence and the reality of evil, but all of them also affirm their tellers' convictions of the supremacy of the ideal—the tendency for people and cultures to become what they say and feel they should be.

Kuiceyetsa's stories, by contrast, show only passing acquaintance with or interest in UFO abduction stories and stories of community tragedies. Her stories concentrate upon her life, its meaning, and its aftermath.

Kuiceyetsa has been a member of a Catholic church and a Baptist church, has spoken to presidents, has edited a book, has spent a good deal of time in Washington, D. C., on tribal business. She *is* Zuni and tells Zuni stories.

"Life," Kuiceyetsa's stories say, "is difficult and has always been difficult; death is part of life as evil is part of man; and a Zuni death should be observed and honored in the Zuni way." The purpose of cultural study is to *know* what it means to be Zuni—not to cry anymore, but, as we have done before at Zuni after death, to gather around the kitchen table, drink coffee, eat traditional Zuni foods, tell pleasant stories, and laugh.

CHAPTER FIVE

Navajo Humor

ANGLO-AMERICAN CULTURE has a remarkably consistent view of American Indians as verbally deficient Tontos who possess no jokes and never laugh. In reality the Navajo possess many jokes—a deep and wide body of jokes—and much laughter. This chapter examines Navajo culture, Navajo humor, and the workings of both in Navajo stories.

Clyde's career as a cultural instructional aide in a Navajo school district required him to tell stories to the children, both to entertain and to instruct them about their heritage. He told us other stories about stories in addition to his account of twisting the old dog's tail so he could record the howl and use it as an audio aid when telling the children at the dormitory a *yee naaldlooshii* (skinwalker) story. When a performing arts center asked me to recommend an American Indian storyteller who might appear before a festival audience of several hundred people, I checked with Clyde. He was interested, so they called him and also asked me to serve as master of ceremonies and interpreter for the storytelling section of the festival. For once, I was to act as *his* interpreter.

All too soon I was seated on a chair in the center of a stage with a spotlight shining in my eyes, an Eastern Pueblo professional storyteller to my right with a spotlight in her eyes, and Clyde to my left with a spotlight in his eyes. The director of the festival introduced me, and I began by suggesting to the storyteller that she tell a story I had heard her tell before.

She did. It was a highly polished performance of a classic folktale which was very well received by the audience in the steeply tiered gallery that almost surrounded us.

Next I introduced Clyde. He told a story that he said had been one of the children's favorites at the Navajo school where he had worked. It was a story extolling Navajo values and skills—and the Anglo-American audience didn't understand it.

I went back to the other storyteller. She performed another carefully crafted, fixed-form story. The audience loved it.

Back to Clyde. He told another very Navajo story about tracking sheep. Again the audience did not appreciate it.

Back to the lady. Another crowd-pleasing performance of a dramatic, fixed-form folktale.

I asked Clyde to tell about his movie career. He looked surprised—but desperate—and launched into his story about the filming of *Arrowhead.* As they always say in old movies, a star was born. The listeners loved it.

When it was the other storyteller's turn, she—not to be outdone—told about the time she participated in a movie that had been filmed at her village.

Clearly there were lessons to be learned as an interpreter. I had seen firsthand the difficulties in translating stories from language to language when Clyde, Kathy, and I had interviewed non-English-speaking Navajos, but now I was seeing firsthand the difficulty of translating stories from culture to culture. Stories are set in culture and are judged by culturally relative standards of excellence and appropriateness. To understand a Navajo joke and *why* it is funny is to know something of what it is to be Navajo.

Once, the three of us—Clyde, Kathy, and I—were on our way from his wife's home in Zuni to the far southwest boundary of the Ramah Navajo Indian lands to interview a medicine man. We drove by the base of Corn Mountain, the mesa to which the Zuni temporarily moved after the Pueblo Revolt of 1680, and the setting for much of their mythology; past Boy and Girl Rock, named after the central characters in a major Zuni myth; and past the unmarked primitive road leading to the Zuni spring where Helen had shared water with us. We went on past Black Rock, the Indian Health Service Hospital near Zuni that serves both the Zuni and the Ramah Navajo, and the new Zuni housing development that dwarfs the hospital; past Salt Women Rock; past the road leading north to Gallup, the city of evil in Leslie Silko's novel *Ceremony;* past the road leading south to the trading post; and then past a lane curving up into the trees where Clyde's mother Hazel (Clyde Kluckhohn's translator when he conducted cultural research in the area) has her log cabin and where Clyde's "outfit," or extended family, lives.

We saw the Ramah Chapter House at Mountain View, a community of fusionist hogans combining Mormon and Navajo folk-architecture in a blend vaguely familiar—yet, at the same time, vaguely disturbing—to other members of both groups; and we drove past Pine Hill, the Navajo Housing Project, which in basic design looks like federally funded housing projects all across America, but which in setting and decoration is as indisputably Navajo as the individual hogan built nearby by the Navajo Council. After the road became dirt we traveled to the far corner of the Ramah Navajo Indian lands—and all the way Clyde told stories.

We saw a heavy, localized rainstorm off in the distance, and Clyde said that it reminded him of a story:

❖   This man was out—out in the field. He was herding sheep, and then it started raining, and there was no trees. So he went to this cave where a cliff was overhanging, and then he went under this. And then he saw some something moving out there coming towards him. As it came closer, he noticed it was a coyote. He just sat there watching it, and pretty soon it came right up to that cave there. And the coyote came in, shook himself, and sat down, looking out to where he came from, and then this man said, "Boy! It's really raining out there, isn't it, cousin?" And then the coyote just got scared and just fell over dead when he heard this man talk from behind him.[127]

Kathy and I were particularly pleased to hear Clyde tell this story because we had previously collected two other versions similar enough and yet different enough to demonstrate that the joke was indeed traditional:

❖   One time it began to rain, and the old man looking for a place to find shelter (he was away from any house) decided to shelter in between some large boulders. While sitting there looking out at the rain, an old coyote came up the path and sat down beside the old man not noticing him. After a long time in silence, the old man turned to the coyote and said, "Sure is raining, isn't it?" The coyote fell dead.[128]

❖   A man was walking, and it started raining. He found a cave and went in to wait the rain out. There was also a coyote who was walking when it started raining. He also saw a cave and went in. Unfortunately, it was the same cave that the man was in. The man was sitting quietly way in the back of the cave when he saw the coyote come in. The coyote didn't see him. The coyote sat with his back to him watching the rain. The man was very uneasy with all the silence in the cave, so he said, "It's raining really hard, isn't it?" The coyote was so stunned that he fell dead right there. The coyote didn't have a chance to think or do anything else.[129]

As we were driving further along over the unforgettable route from Clyde's wife's home in Zuni to the medicine man's home, Clyde began another story by pointing out the window:

❖   It was right around here my aunt had some sheep, and my cousin and I had a sheep camp and were watching them for her. Well, she came around one day and told us we had to drive those sheep way over there to the other side of that big hill. [*points off into the far distance*] That would have been all right except she also had a few chickens, and she told us to drive them over there with the sheep.

Well, after my aunt left, we packed up all our stuff and got ready to drive the sheep over there.

When we were all ready, my cousin said to me, "*You* drive those chickens."

And I said, "I'm not going to drive those chickens. *You* drive those chickens."

And my cousin said, "I'm not going to drive those chickens. *You* drive those chickens."

So we decided to catch those chickens, put them into a couple of gunny sacks we had, and carry them. So we caught them—chased them all over that canyon. Well, we finally got them all in the sacks, and my cousin said to me, "*You* carry those chickens."

And I said, "I'm not going to carry those chickens. *You* carry those chickens."

And he said, "I'm not going to carry those chickens. *You* carry those chickens."

So we tied those gunny sacks over the back of this old ram that was with the sheep, and *he* carried the chickens. When we got there to where the new camp was going to be, all those chickens were dead; they had suffocated in the bags on that ram's back.

She asked us what happened to the chickens and we said, "Guess they just couldn't keep up with the sheep." She never said anything more about it.[130]

Part of the humor of this joke was the fact that it built upon the popular television commercial of a few years ago for a breakfast cereal called Life. The advertisement featured two small boys saying: "I'm not going to try it. You try it," and Clyde mimicked the Anglo-American boys to represent an incident from his boyhood.

The medicine man was not at his hogan.

FINDING GRANDFATHER HORNY TOAD

The only extensive discussion of Navajo humor in cultural research literature is a 1943 article by W. W. Hill. Hill termed a popular fallacy the idea that the American Indian in general, and the Navajo in particular, is a stolid, unemotional individual incapable of the expression or the appreciation of humor or wit. From his own fieldwork and research, he gave examples of puns, practical jokes, and obscenities, as well as institutionalized humorous behavior associated with kinship relations, ritual performance, and oral literature.

Although Hill dispelled the idea that the Navajo are a people without humor, he reported that it was almost always spontaneous rather than planned and concluded that Navajos did not manufacture jokes or puns deliberately. He reported, in short, that in the 1940s they employed a great deal of humor in the course of ceremony, in formal oral literature performance, and in the events of day-to-day living but had little if any fictive joke or punning tradition.

Hill carefully categorized Navajo humor but did not attempt to analyze his materials in terms of their structures. Even so, his categories and rich examples suggest a contrast between that which should and should not be. (For instance, the complex clan-relative teasing he and others have described seems to be based on sexual innuendo within the context of culturally mandated asexual relationships.) Grounding humor in what should not be was typical of Navajo humor in the 1940s, and it still is in the 1990s. A new form based upon old structural principles and expectations also has risen to prominence over the years—the fictive, preplanned joke.

As we drove back to Zuni from the Ramah Navajo Indian lands, we three told all the Navajo jokes we knew during a bicultural, bilingual, co-performer, co-researcher session. Kathy and I made an appointment with Clyde, and we three met again at his wife's home in Zuni to have him explain the humor of Navajo jokes. We asked him what the jokes meant and why they were funny. Analyzing his extensive comments, which we tape recorded, we found that most jokes fit into ten basic categories.

A number of jokes in the collection clearly derived their humor from Navajo words or expressions which have differing usages that must be determined from context. The most widely distributed, most frequently reported Navajo joke, for example, uses the fact that the word for *grandfather* also refers to a well-known creature:

❖   One day a grandchild came running home and told her grandmother that her grandfather was dead. She said that he was run over by someone. The grandmother then started crying and cussing as she ran to the highway after her grandchild. She kept saying, "I told that old man to stay away from the highway since he cannot see good." When they reached the highway, the grandmother found a horned toad lying dead on the highway.[13]

❖   One day when the grandma was staying with her grandchildren, they saw a horn toad in the grass. She told them that the horn toad was believed to be their grandfather. The children went herding sheep that day. When they were coming back, they saw a horn toad that was runned over by a car on the road. The children hurried back to tell their grandma. The children told their grandma that their grandfather had been runned over by a car.
       She said, "Where?"
       And they replied, "He is lying on the road." She started crying, saying that their grandfather had gone to look for the horses that morning. They took her to the place to see for herself.

When they arrived at the spot, she said, "Where?" because she didn't see her husband lying anywhere. They pointed to a horn toad lying there on the ground. All this time she was crying her eyes out. When she saw the horn toad, she started laughing. She said, "I thought you were talking about your real grandfather."

The children said, "You told us that the horn toad was suppose to be our grandfather, so we told you about it."[132]

❖   A Navajo lady and a Navajo man couldn't get along with each other, so the Navajo woman chased her husband out. The Navajo man left to visit relatives over the hill. The grandchildren were playing, and they seen a dead horned toad on the road, so they ran back to their grandmother's house and told her that their grandfather had been run over. The grandmother started crying, and she told the children to take her to where their grandfather had been run over, so they took her over there. When they got there, the children showed their grandmother the dead horned toad, and she started laughing.

In the Navajo culture the horned toad is a sacred animal. The Navajo people refer to the horned toad as their grandpa, and when the children were telling their grandmother about the dead horned toad, they called the horned toad their grandpa.[133]

❖   An elderly man and his wife are having a talk. The talk soon becomes an argument, and he leaves very angry. A little while later, one of the grandchildren walks into the house very upset and says, "Grandfather has been run over by a car." The grandmother starts crying and tells the kid to take her to grandfather. The grandchild brings her out to the road and shows grandmother a flattened horny toad.[134]

❖   This happened over here where my grandpa lives. The grandpa is inside, and all the kids are outside playing, and I guess they find a horny toad, and I guess my grandpa overheard them. They said, "We're going to kill grandpa," you know. So my grandpa figured they were going to kill him, you know, so he came out, and the kids were there fooling around with a horny toad.[135]

❖   A little boy, I guess, was staying with his grandma. I think [he] was running around outside, playing by the road. And then he came upon a—what do you call it? A horny toad. Then I guess he got kind of scared. And then he ran. I guess they told him that horny toads are our grandpas first. He came on back into his grandma's and then he said, "Grandma, my grandpa got ran over."

Then the grandma goes, well, I don't know, "For Pete's sake," or something like that. I can't say it in Navajo, but they went over there where the grandpa got ran over, and there was a horny toad sitting there ran over.[136]

❖   In Navajo we address a horny toad by calling him grandfather because, I guess, there's stories related to that. A long time ago when there was monsters or whatever around this area or wherever it was—I remember my dad telling me that a long time when I was a kid, and I guess that was just in respect to the horny toad. Because that was one way we were instructed not to kill horny toads or other things because they have sacred meanings to them, I guess. So that was my dad that told me about that one.

He said that this horny toad had a great big crown that he wears. And one day this giant person came around, destroying people or eating people, and so this horny toad was at the site, I guess, at the time that this monster came again, and I guess he made sounds so that this giant kind of didn't really know for sure where the sound was coming from. He kept looking around, and pretty soon it was just under his foot, and there it was. The little horny toad holding his cap there—his crown. And then, I guess, the giant just got frightened. I don't know, maybe there was horn on the crown that's frightened him, and so he fell off the cliff, and that was the end of him.[137]

❖   There was an older couple, I guess it was, staying with their grandson, and the grandmother was cooking, fixing something, so she sent out her grandson to get his grandpa to come and eat. So he ran out, and then he came back, and I guess he seen this horny toad that was runned over on the road. [*laughs*] He came back, and he told his grandmother, "Grandpa got run over on the road," and the grandmother just, you know, got all paranoid and everything and ran out, and here was the horny toad that he was talking about. [*laughs*][138]

❖   It was some years ago that I heard about that story. That there was a grandfather and a grandmother living with their grandson. So they were all together all this time, so the grandfather went someplace, and the little boy was with the grandmother. The grandpa was watching over the sheep, so the grandmother told him, "Better go check on the sheep again." So he went running around out there with the sheep, and then he find out someone ran over a horny toad, so the old people used to say that the horny toad was our grandfather.

So the boy just came running right straight back to the hogan and says, "Grandmother, grandmother, my grandfather got ran over there. Somebody ran over him." And then the grandmother got scared, the grandmother got scared. She was all shook up there.

"What happened? Who did it? Where?" So they all just start following him—couldn't find nothing and just kept going—and the boy stop right there.

"See, grandmother, see here's where my granddad is, right there." And it was a horny toad. [*laughs*][139]

❖   This grandpa took his little grandson to a Squaw Dance nearby, and so they walked over there and left the grandma at home. Later that day the little boy came running back and got to where his grandma was and said, "Grandma, my grandpa got run over. He's over there laying in the road."

This grandma got scared and says, "Where? Take me to him. Let's go to there. Show me."

So they went over there, and sure enough, there was the grandpa, which is the horny toad in our language.[140]

❖   This boy was out with his grandpa, and grandma's staying at home, and later this little boy came running back in and told this grandma his grandpa was run over and was out there in the road. And he took his grandma to the place and saw the horned toad which was the grandpa.[141]

❖   A little boy came around back to the grandma, and he said, "My grandpa has been run over out there in the road."

And then the old woman got up and said, "What do you mean? Let's go over there and see."

So he took her over there, and there was the horny toad in the road.[142]

❖   The toad is called grandfather in the Navajo way, and the little boy says, "Grandma, Grandma, my grandpa has been run over."

The old lady runs, "Where? Where?" And he shows her the toad.[143]

One of the Ramah Navajo women we interviewed was ninety years old. Her kitchen table held a carefully cleaned Kentucky Fried Chicken bucket that she used to store kitchen utensils. On the wall hung a beautiful Mickey Mouse sandpainting. (Sandpainting is a Navajo folk art in which colored sands are dropped upon a plain surface to create complex and striking designs. Once it was practiced only by medicine men as a part of ceremony, with the paintings destroyed afterwards. In later years, Navajo artists have made permanent sandpaintings designed to be sold.) This sandpainting—the lady explained that it had been made by her grandson— was a playful piece with Mickey showing forth in Disney Technicolor from a traditional Navajo art form.

The lady herself now turned to a horned toad story from a time long ago when things were right:

❖   This story goes way back. Small children always call the horny toad their grandfather or their grandpa. It's just that the story is told like that to the kids, and that's how I think that this boy told his grandmother that his grandpa had been run over and was out there in the road. I think this goes way back to when people called the horny toad their grandpa.

Everything's changing right now. Even the weather and the places around here aren't like they used to be. There's something wrong here and the same with our people now. It's just not like it used to be when everything was plentiful. Even the days are not right now.[144]

Other Navajo, too, remembered and told the story:

❖   There was this little child. He was out some place along the road and
ran over to his grandmother's. "Grandma, grandpa got ran over. He's lying
over there in the road."
          So this grandmother started crying, says, "You take me over there right
now. Show me where it is."
          So the little boy took his grandmother over there, and there was this
horny toad right in the road all squashed.[145]

❖   This boy was out herding sheep, and he came across a horny toad that
had been runned over, so he went back home and said, "Grandma, I just
found my grandpa over there in the road. He's been run over."
          And this lady says, "What do you mean?" and got mad at him and
said, "You take me over there right now!"[146]

THE SOUNDS OF JOKES
          A second category of Navajo jokes depends on different meanings for
the same sound in Navajo as it is usually spoken. Clyde stressed that these
jokes are oral, not written, and depend upon sound rather than upon the
appearance of the words in written form.
          Since the Navajo population of the Ramah area is descended from only
seven families, Clyde was related to many of the people living in the area.
Although he tried to make sure that not all the interviewees were his
relatives, he asked us one day if we thought it would be all right to meet
with one of his cousins. Not only did he want us to meet this man, but he
also felt his cousin would provide good information because he had lived
in the Ramah area all his life.
          We drove a long way until we were at a higher elevation than the area
around Pine Hill and Mountain View which we had just driven through.
The hills were not so bare as those below and frequently had stands of
Rocky Mountain juniper. In the distance we could see a hogan atop a long,
sloping rise. We wound around the base of the hill and finally approached
the hogan from the west. The view from the top was spectacular: we could
see all the way to El Morro, approximately twenty miles to the east, and
the hills in front of us ranged lower and lower into a haze. Now that we
were closer to the hogan, we also could see that it was unusual. Navajos
traditionally build their hogans so that the doors face east toward the
morning star. The door here had this traditional orientation, but it was the
only hogan I had even seen built with a porch over the door. The dirt floor
of the entryway was swept clean, and there was an old truck seat beneath
the porch overhang next to the door.
          Clyde's cousin Charles Lopez was sitting on the seat, enjoying not
only the magnificent view but also the company of two chickens there on
the porch with him. Mr. Lopez stood up and came toward us as we climbed

out of the car. When he recognized Clyde, his face brightened into a wide smile, and they greeted each other very warmly in Navajo. He invited us into his hogan and told Clyde to put a narrow board across the doorway to keep the chickens out. It was a fiction which the chickens seemed to understand. They could easily have walked across the board and joined us in the hogan, but they remained on the porch just outside.

The interior of the hogan was as striking and pleasing as the outside. Just to the right of the door was a woodburning cookstove polished to a soft black gleam. Opposite the door was a neatly made double bed, and in the middle of the hogan was a kitchen table with a clean oilcloth covering it. Above the table, suspended from one of the ceiling beams, hung a healthy Boston fern, and from every window there was a wonderful view of the receding hills. The hogan was filled with a sense of art and life resembling that of the American Shakers in its order and functional simplicity; like Shaker houses, it seemed bathed in light.

Clyde introduced us and explained our project. Whenever Clyde, Kathy, or I spoke, the chickens were silent; but when Mr. Lopez gave one of his slow, thoughtful responses, the chickens would answer his voice with low crooning calls. Clyde was very familiar with the interview form by now, and he started by asking Mr. Lopez when he was born. Mr. Lopez answered slowly in Navajo.

"He was born in June. He doesn't know the year," said Clyde.

"Ask him how old he thinks he is," I suggested. Clyde asked, and Mr. Lopez answered in Navajo.

"About seventy-four," Clyde translated. Mr. Lopez then gave more information in Navajo, and the chickens answered the sound of his voice. "There was a guy across here who is deceased now. He figures he was a couple of years older than him."

"Where all has he lived?" I asked. Clyde asked the question in Navajo, Mr. Lopez answered in Navajo, and the chickens responded again.

"He's always here. He's always been here, and it looks like he'll always be here," went Clyde's translation.

"Has he ever heard the story about grandfather horny toad?" I asked.

Again Clyde translated my question, and Mr. Lopez launched into a story in Navajo. When he finished, Clyde and Mr. Lopez laughed. The chickens echoed their laugh. They both laughed at the chickens, which made the chickens respond even louder. The two men glanced at each other briefly as they realized they would have to stop laughing to quiet the chickens, and we all waited for the cackling to stop before Clyde translated the story, which derives its humor from the fact that, depending upon context, the same set of Navajo sounds can mean either "they are dead" or "they are ten":

❖ This is not the horny toad story exactly. The grandmother sent her grandchild to the next hogan. "Go see how many people are in there and let me know how many people are in there." So he went over there and he came back. This is one of those things that sounds—instead of saying ten in there, he said, "They're all dead."

The grandma says, "What do you mean, they're all dead? What about your grandpa?"[147]

There are many other stories that also depend upon different meanings for the same sound in Navajo:

❖ A long time ago this happen on Navajo Reservation. This Navajo family got use truck first time in their life. They got vehicle. In those days few Navajos had vehicles. One day the old man and the brother-in-law decided to go after some firewood. The old man didn't know how to drive, but the brother-in-law was the driver since no one in his family didn't know how to drive. They got to the place where there was lots of dry firewoods. They got lots of dry woods and load up in no time with the two of them. When they were on their way home, they got stuck in the sand out in the desert country. So the driver said to the old man to check what was wrong with the wheels. The truck's wheels were just turning. The old man said, "It's just turning (or spinning)."

The driver got off the truck and head down the road. The old man said, "I didn't mean for you to leave."

In Navajo language, one word can mean more than one thing depending on how you understand it. The words *t'oo naalwul* means "it's just turning or spinning" and can also mean "run along or go home." So that's how the driver interpreted.[148]

❖ Two little girls were riding a horse, and they saw a man herding sheep, so they rode over toward him. There was a little colt running after the horse. The man then asked the two girls who the horse belonged to. The two little girls said, "It belongs to my grandfather."

The man asked, *"Bi'aad ish?"* which can mean "Is it a girl?" It can also mean "spouse."

The two little girls answered, "No, it is just my grandfather's horse." The two little girls mistook the word for his spouse instead of the horse being a girl or a boy—sex of the horse.[149]

❖ This joke was told to me by my great-grandmother Ashkaydebah Deel. It was in the wintertime during the night when we were allowed to tell stories. It was about this little boy taking the horse to the water hole for the horses to get a drink of water. There was also another at the water hole. The man said, "You have a real nice colt there. Who does it belong to?"

The little boy replied and said, "It belong to my grandfather."

The man asked, "Is it a female?"

The little boy really got embarrassed and said, "No, it is only my grandfather's horse."

The little boy misunderstood and thought the man said, "Is it his wife?" In Navajo both interpretations are the same for "Is it a female?" and "Is it his wife?" In a way, the little boy was right, too.[150]

❖   There was three of them: the grandfather and someone like you and me. You would ask, "Does your grandfather have a, what we call ah—" Well, we have to tell it in Navajo to get the true joke there, but you asked me if my grandfather had a [wife], and then somebody says, "No, it's my grandfather's horse."[151]

The fact that, as Clyde explained, the same Navajo word means in a literal sense "stick" or "twig" or even "log" (and in a figurative sense "mile") helps make other Navajo jokes understandable:

❖   A girl came home from school and then started out with her grandmother to the store. The girl called, "Grandma, how many miles is it from here over to the store?"

The grandmother replied, "I really don't know, my granddaughter. Who counts them? They are scattered all over here."[152]

❖   One day a little boy asked his grandmother, "How many miles is it to the trading post?"

The grandmother replied, "I don't know. You see, you have logs lying all over the place."[153]

We asked Clyde about another joke we had collected and not understood. He said, "Yeah, that would be a tough one in English. When the Navajos started dealing with American money, they didn't have any names to call it, so they went by the color of the coins and called the nickel and the dime by the names they used for the colors":

❖   This happen on Navajo Reservation. A long time ago, a Navajo man was looking for his horses. He was on foot looking all morning. Finally he seen a distant neighbor herding sheep nearby, so he decided to ask the sheepherder if he seen his horses. He went to the sheepherder and just talk about the latest news. Then the man asked, "Have you seen my horses? I been looking for them all morning. I need to haul water."

The sheepherder said, "How do they look?"

The man said, "One brownish and the other one is grayish in color."

The sheepherder said, "So it fifteen cents. Somebody probably spend it."

In Navajo language, brownish also means "nickel" and grayish also means "dime." Depend on how you interpret it.[154]

Clyde said that a third category of Navajo jokes derive their humor from Navajo words that sound somewhat similar in conversation but have very different meanings:

❖   The father says to the boy, "Go out and track the horses." He goes out, gets his bow and arrow, and shoots the horses. The father is quite upset.[155]

The humor in this story derives from the fact that the spoken Navajo words meaning "track the horses" and "shoot the horses with a sharp object" are similar in sound, and other Navajo jokes illustrate the same principle:

❖   A young man attending school was having a traditional ceremony done. He wasn't a very fluent speaker. His entire family was present—father, mother, sister, brother. Other friends and relatives were also in attendance. From the beginning of the ceremony the medicine man gave instructions to the young man to recite whatever he said. Then the medicine man started praying. The young man did well with some and not so well with some parts of the prayers. The medicine man said, "*Sha bilajichi*" (sunset). The boy had a hard time pronouncing it, and he said, "*Sha'di bi' jil-chee*" (my oldest sister's ass). The sister was present, and she blushed with embarrassment as the remainder of the attendants laughed.[156]

As is true of all languages, Navajo does not include some sounds found in other tongues and *does* include some of its own—all of which accounts for grandma's disappointment in a fourth category of Navajo joke:

❖   Grandma sent grandson to the trading post to bring back some salt. He was informed to keep repeating "salt" while on his way to the store. Why? Because the grandson didn't know how to talk in English, and the trader was a white man. So grandson takes off running, repeating to himself, "Salt. Salt." On his way, he trips over a rock, gets up and takes off running again. This time repeating to himself "Shorts." He enters the trading post, walks up to the counter, the trader comes over and asks, "May I help you?"

The boy replies, "Shorts." The trader hands him a pair of boy's briefs. The boy dashes out the door and runs home as fast as he can go.

Grandma, with a disappointment, "I asked you to bring back some salt, so we can use it on the mutton stew."[157]

Many contemporary Navajos speak English. Their knowledge of the English language offers them delightful opportunities for a fifth category of jokes based on the similarity of sounds of some English and Navajo words:

❖   One day an Indian boy said to his grandmother, "Grandma, I'm going over to Johnny's house to watch television."
         The grandmother asked, "Why in the hell do you want to go over to Johnny's house to watch a donkey urinate?"[158]

The term "television" when spoken by a traditional Navajo is pronounced more like "telebision" or *"telli bializh,"* which means "a donkey urinating."

❖   Two mens get together and were discussing where they were at a long time away. And then, the [man] that wasn't really educated asked the question, "Where were you all this time?"
         And the man with the bun said, "Um, I was at Seattle, Washington." In Navajo ways, saying "Seattle, Washington," means "your bun flew off" or something like that, and the uneducated man [told] that to him.
         The man with the bun got really mad about it and said, "You're stupid." So he said, "I was working in Seattle, Washington." So the [other] man understood what [he] meant.[159]

Yazzie and *Begay* are the Navajo equivalents of the Anglo-American names *Smith* and *Jones* in their frequency of appearance, and their widespread occurrence adds to the humor of jokes based upon their similarities to English words:

❖   A daughter took her mother to the P[ublic] H[ealth] S[ervice] hospital for an examination. When the examination was through, the doctor told the old Indian lady that she had arthritis and would have to have medical treatment right away. The old lady replied, *"Who?* Did you say Arthur Yazzie? He must have witched me!"[160]

❖   An elderly Navajo goes to Public Health Service hospital, and her knees are hurting. They had told her before that she has arthritis. And so she had come to the PHS for medicine. She said to the doctor, "I already have Arthur Yazzie. Now let me have Ben Begay."[161]

A sixth category of Navajo jokes is based upon similarities in *English* word sounds:

❖   A Navajo boy came running into a trading post. He asked the storekeeper for help in Navajo. The statement was, "Betty and Jenny are fighting. I need some help." The storekeeper could not figure out what he was talking about. The boy kept repeating the statement, "Betty and Jenny were fighting and killing each other." Finally the storekeeper called the police. The police took the boy out where the trouble occurred. The boy showed the police the trouble. It was only the battery and the generator of his grandfather's truck throwing sparks back and forth.[162]

❖ A young Navajo boy was riding along with his father in a pick-up truck when the engine stopped. The man got out and raised the hood. Then he said to the boy, "Run back home and tell them the battery and generator shorted out."

The boy ran back home and said, "Betty and Jenny got into a fight, and Shorty can't break it up."[163]

❖ An old man and his wife were traveling on vacation from New York to California when their mobile home broke down in the middle of the Navajo Reservation. Since sheep is the main source of economy, there was nothing around except for sheep and a hogan. The Anglo man goes to the hogan and tries to explain to the old Navajo man that he needs a monkey wrench to fix his car and then he will be on his way. The Anglo man notices that the Navajo man is puzzled, so again he tells him, "A monkey wrench."

The Navajo man looks at him and says, "This is not a monkey ranch. This is a sheep ranch!"[164]

ON MY BILL

An interesting, and by no means uncommon, seventh category of Navajo jokes consists of English-language puns that have been adopted and retold more or less as they are performed in Anglo-American culture. Well-known, frequently reported English-language puns become stories that Clyde said would be meaningless in Navajo but often are told in English by Navajos as jokes:

❖ There was this white man who wanted to buy this beautiful horse from an old Indian man. The old Indian told the white man, "He no look good," in describing the beautiful horse.

The white man said, "What do you mean, he no look good? This is a beautiful horse." The white man brought the horse from the old Indian, and he came back a few weeks later complaining about his purchase. The white man told the old Indian that the horse was blind as a bat.

The old Indian said, "I told you he no look good."[165]

❖ It was about this duck, I guess, walked into this drugstore. He needed something. And then, "Put it on my bill," he says.[166]

This joke may very well be based upon the Chapstick double pun television commercial where the bird wants the Chapstick put on his bill.

What a wonderful example of acculturation since the storyteller may have remembered and appreciated the joke because it echoes the form of Navajo humor even though he speaks only English.

When we went visiting hogan to hogan, we encountered another story centering upon the same principle of Navajo humor:

❖   This grandson, his grandma got sick, so there was nobody else there to go with her, so he went along to interpret. He wasn't very good at it. He was just starting to understand English, so they got to the hospital, and then the doctor wanted to weigh the grandma and then after that give her a shot. So the little boy did his best explaining to the grandma. He says, "First they're going to hang you and then they'll shoot you."[167]

As we were driving away after visiting hogan to hogan, Clyde asked if we had seen the fifty-pound sack of feed tied to a rope thrown over a branch of a tree in front of the hogan.

We said we had.

He explained that the sack was used as a scale and that a person could tell if an item was lighter or heavier than fifty pounds by tying it to the other end of the rope. We laughed as he explained, "See, in Navajo to 'weigh someone' is to 'hang someone' because it refers to that old balance scale, and to 'give somebody a shot' is the same as to 'shoot somebody.' The boy was saying that the doctors said they were going to weigh her and give her a shot, and she thought that they were going to hang her and shoot her 'cause that's what he said."

A number of less common jokes made themselves known when people told us their favorites. When we asked Clyde himself for his favorite, he gave another example of an English-language pun also popular as a Navajo joke:

❖   Well, there's this time. I don't know whether I told you this before. I was driving to Gallup one morning. It was in December—the first week—or no, it was the last week in November—what year, I don't remember. But anyway I was traveling along to Gallup, and then I saw this hitchhiker along the road. It was cold, and I decided to pick him up, get him out of the cold, so he got in with me, tried to talk to me in Navajo, and I noticed then that he was a Zuni. So I start talking with him, and he said, "Well, you come—you come to my house Shalako time. You come to my house. You eat at my house. I cook myself."[168]

This Navajo appreciation of English-language puns is shown in other Navajo jokes:

❖ There were these people coming back from a Squaw Dance; they got a flat tire. The driver got out to check the tire and noticed they got a flat. There were several men sitting in the back of the pickup truck, and one of the men was named Jack. The driver said, "Throw out the jack." Then Jack said, "No, no, I can get out myself."[169]

One of the longest and most dramatically performed of the Navajo jokes told us as a favorite story depends on misunderstanding of referents:

❖ This boy is out herding sheep, and it started raining. Pretty soon it was really pouring, and he wanted to find shelter; but under a tree, I guess, he was getting wet, really wet. So then he looked, and there was a little shed or something like that on a hill, so he thought, "Well," you know, "maybe I can run in there and dry myself."

So he took off; he took off, and he got to the shed. I guess somebody was living there, but it looked like a shed, so he got there, and then he heard some noise inside, and then somebody was saying, "Pull harder! Pull harder!" and he kind of got interested. He walked in, opened the door real slowly, and then walked in, and he found out the house was kind of divided to two rooms, but there was a curtain hanging there—just a blanket. And then he walked in, looked around, and there was a stove; and then he just stood there, and all that commotion was still going on from the other room. There was a man talking, and then he heard a lady's voice, and the man kept saying, "Pull harder! Pull harder! It's coming. It's almost coming," and then, "Twist it! Twist it! Twist it around! Twist it around!" He kept saying that, and then I guess that little boy kept getting more interested and interested. [*laughs*]

All this time, you know, this guy kept saying, "Pull on it! Pull on it!" "Twist it some more. Twist it," and, "It's coming! It's almost coming!" and pretty soon I guess that little boy was just really wondering what's going on in there. He opened that curtain, and here I guess the grandpa was sitting, and the old lady—I guess it was his wife—was trying to pull his boots off of him. That's what all the commotion was about. [*laughs*][170]

This well-crafted, well-told story reflected the Navajo appreciation of the apparently obscene, as did others:

❖ There were two Sioux people—one was an old Sioux man and the other an old Sioux woman. They were at a fair, decided to eat, and saw a sign reading HOT DOGS, so they ordered two. When the old Sioux man opened his and saw what he had, he quickly covered it and turned to the old Sioux woman and asked what part of the hot dog she got.[171]

An eighth category of Navajo jokes is built on onomatopoeia of animal sounds in the English and Navajo languages. Both the last joke and the next three also find humor in playing with cultural stereotypes.

❖   There was this Navajo—assume he was a male—went to visit a Sioux family. And while he was there visiting these people, he learned to eat dog, and he didn't really like it that much, but he got used to it. And finally when he went home, he was asked by his relatives what he was fed while at the Sioux people.
       "They fed me dog meat."
       "Oh, how awful! How did you ever get used to it?"
       "It was ruff."
       Then a man from the Sioux came to visit this Navajo guy. And while he was there, they fed him mutton. He wasn't really sure he liked mutton, but he got used to it. When he returned, he was asked what those Navajos had fed him. He told them they fed him sheep meat.
       And the relatives said, "Oh, how awful! How did you ever get used to it?"
       And his reply was, "It wasn't too b-a-a-a-a-a-d!"[172]

❖   A social worker comes to one of his client's homes out on the reservation. Nobody is home. The social worker wanders around the house, sees a cat sitting outside by the doorway. The social worker didn't want to leave the place without any information as to whereabout his client is. So he figures that maybe the cat will give him some information, if nothing else.
       Social worker: "Are you the only one home?"
       Cat: "Ummh?" [*purrs*]
       Social worker: "Where is everyone?"
       Cat: "Ummh?"
       Social worker: "Where is everyone?"
       Cat: "T-o-w-n-e-e"
       Social worker: "Town?"
       Cat: "Ummh."
       Social worker: "Why did they go to town?"
       Cat: "W-i-n-e-e."
       In Navajo, the *ummh* sound would be conversing to another individual that one is saying yes.[173]

❖   One day a whole family went on a trip and left their cat, dog, and rooster behind. After they had departed, some visitors stopped by. Upon learning that the family was not at home, the visitors then questioned the animals as to the family's whereabouts.
       When asked where the family had gone, the dog barked: "Rough Rock." When asked when the family would return, the rooster crowed: "*Aa ii aa o (a ee ow)*" or "About sunset."
       When asked what they went for, the cat meowed: "W-i-n-e-e."[174]

MISS-SEEING

       The ninth category or type of Navajo joke Clyde identified was what he termed "a visual pun."

There is on the Big Reservation—and there once was among the Ramah Navajo—a traditional hogan style that was a circular earth-covered dwelling. The materials, the circular shape, and the overall appearance of this simplest of hogans is widely said to have been taught to First Man and First Woman by the ant people in imitation of their own homes. The stories—as the hogans—have disappeared among the Ramah Navajo; the only complete story Clyde translated was told by the man who "met his wife at a Squaw Dance" and moved to the Ramah area from the Big Reservation. This animal tale about the grasshopper and the ant illustrated the principle of Navajo humor "miss-seeing" (as opposed to miss-hearing):

❖　　　But anyway the grasshopper's telling the ant something and then maybe criticizing him for his size or something, and the ant says, "Did you know that you're all backwards or that your knee is?"[175]

❖　　　I heard about the grasshopper and ant, but I don't know how it was told. Maybe the ant does more thinking than the grasshopper because the ant gets ready for winter—he knows what to expect—so maybe that's why the ant tells the grasshopper that his legs are on backwards.[176]

❖　　　I guess this ant was busy piling up all those little pieces of gravel—real small, ant-type, you know—to make this ant pile. So the grasshopper confronts him about this: "You crazy? Getting all that many rocks?"
　　　And then the ant turns and asks him, "What's the matter with you? Are you crazy? You've got your legs on backwards."[177]

One delightful lady said, and Clyde's eyes twinkled as he translated, that she had not heard the story but *had noticed* that the grasshopper's knee is indeed on backwards. We found many more visual puns:

❖　　　Last year Desbah came into town with her son and grandkids. She had bought some wrapped intestines in a local trading post. Toward late afternoon she and her family caught a ride in the back of a pickup truck. About five miles outside of Shiprock, the pickup had become involved in an accident. People and packages flew every which way. When all was quiet, Desbah checked her grandchildren. They were crying but appear uninjured. Her son was laying amidst packages, dazed but moving slightly. Desbah ran over crying, "My child, don't move. Lay still; your guts are hanging out." The package of wrapped intestines had broken across the son's midsection.[178]

❖　　　This man was getting off work, and he worked in a sheep shearing and butchering company, and he had just gotten paid, and he wanted to go and have a good time, so he went down to Gallup and drank up his money.

He realized he had spent all his money, and he was getting hungry, so he made his way back to the shearing company. He went to the place where they throw all the guts, and he pulled some out, like the heart, the liver, the stomach and stuffed them in his coat. Then he went back to the bars to use the toilet and went to one of the stalls and passed out.

An Anglo man came in and went in the stall next to the passed-out Indian. The Anglo was buzzed, too. When the Anglo looked down, he saw the organs coming underneath the stall wall, and he thought somebody had thrown up their organs, and he died of shock sitting on the toilet.[179]

❖   It was December, and the snow was falling. A man went out to look for his horse. He had tied the horse's legs the night before. His horse was all white—no spots. He was blinded by the bright snow. The snow had covered the horse's tracks, and he had a hard time finding fresh tracks. He followed the tracks and was so occupied with it that he didn't see the horse. He walked right smack into the behind of the horse. Of course, the horse kicked him.[180]

❖   A grandmother had a nephew who went overseas. When he came back, the grandmother went to town one day and, meeting a friend, said, "Did you know that my nephew went overseas and came back with a scooped-out watermelon for a hat?"[181]

❖   There were these tourists traveling from the East. They visited the Pueblo in Santa Fe, New Mexico. The tourists bought a yeast bread which was baked in an adobe oven, and it was delicious. It tasted really good. They continued their journey into the Navajo Reservation. Along the road they saw an adobe like the one they had seen in Santa Fe. Thinking they would get some yeast bread, the tourists stopped and were getting closer to it. It kinda felt funny to find the clothes around. Just then a man came out nude, and the tourists just look and say, "This must be the gingerbread man."

They didn't know the sweathouse in Navajo is almost similar to an adobe oven that the Pueblo Indians bake bread in.[182]

❖   A family was living in the woods. One day the father was going to the store. He was going to take the sheep skins over there. The children asked for candy. As he was going through the woods, he went under a branch of a big tree where a bobcat was sitting. The bobcat jumped on the sheep skins, and the horse began bucking. The man fell off the horse. The horse turned around and headed for home with the bobcat still on its back.

As the horse emerged from the trees with the bobcat still on its back, the children saw them and said, "There comes our father with the candy." As the horse came nearer, they said, "Looks like he bought himself some glasses, and he also has on a beautiful furry coat." The horse was coming very fast because of the bobcat on its back. When the horse passed by, they saw that the rider wasn't their father. The bobcat jumped off and ran back into the woods.[183]

❖   Two couples were living alone together. The woman was very jealous of her husband, so she lets him stay at home while she herds sheep. One day she went off to herd sheep. Her husband stayed home. He usually stays home and makes lunch for his wife. He was going to make bread. When he found out that they were out of flour, he decided to grind some corn. He brought the grinding stone and some corn outside to grind it. While he was grinding corn, the wind began to blow. He put a blanket over him and the grinding stone and went on with his grinding.

        While he was grinding under the blanket, his wife came back. As soon as she saw her husband, she assumed that he was with a woman under the blanket. Without hesitating, she picked up a stick and hit him over the head.[184]

❖   It was raining very hard, and the family were in the hogan. The day became night without the rain letting up. The old man went out to go to the outhouse. His grandson wanted to play a trick on him, so he took a flashlight and a whip and went after him. The old man didn't see his grandson come out after him.

        The grandson sneaked up on his grandfather and flashed on the flashlight like it was lightning and right after that he whipped his grandfather on his behind. He quickly went back into the house.

        The old man didn't know what hit him, and he rushed back into the hogan shouting that he was struck by lightning. He told his family not to come close to him because he was dangerous. He went on and on about dying.[185]

❖   A Navajo family summoned an old medicine man to do a sing for them. The old medicine man said that he would do so. The family made the necessary preparations for the ceremony right away. Then it was time for the medicine man to leave. He saddled his favorite mare and rode out to the family's home with the mare's colt following behind.

        In the meantime, the family kept looking for him across the desert. They finally saw him coming about a mile away. The family was happy, so they went inside the hogan and sat in there quietly and patiently waiting for his arrival. The old medicine man got to the hogan, and as he was getting off, the mare's colt decided to drink its mother's milk. Not knowing this, he sat backwards on the colt. The colt was so startled that it took off with the old medicine man the way they came. The mare was following them close behind.

        The family heard the old medicine man yelling for help, so they rushed outside. All they could see was a big cloud of dust moving away from them. They just looked after them, not knowing what to do or say.[186]

❖   A lot is expected of a Navajo husband. Anyway, this was quite awhile ago. This man marries the daughter in a family. The morning after the wedding the husband comes to the door of the in-laws asking for a hoe. So the father-in-law directs him to where the hoe is. The husband explains he is going to weed the cornfield. It is before dawn. He completes the task of hoeing just after sunrise. Next he asks the father-in-law for the bridle so that he can bring the horses back. As he's getting off the mare, he sits on the back of the colt who is nursing. The last time he is seen, his dust from riding the colt goes off over the hill. He never comes back.[187]

Clyde explained that for the Navajo the major source of humor in all these jokes was centered in *appearances.* The term, the concept, and the words "visual pun" are his.

DEALING WITH DISHARMONY

A tenth source of Navajo humor is inappropriate behavior at a ceremony. Many Navajo jokes center upon this disharmony of situation:

❖   There's this one about a little boy. I guess his mother and him live alone, and so one evening they were going to go to a sing, you know, maybe at another neighbor's house. Little kids being so vocal about a lot of things—they don't really know when not to say and when to say—she instructed him not to say a lot of things. I guess that one day she was really bloated, and so she told him not to say anything about that part of it when he got there. And then he says, "Okay, okay, Mom, I won't say anything," and so they left and got to the sing. Then they went in the hogan, and just right about the time everybody got real quiet, this little boy came up and says, "Mom, remember you told me not to say anything about you being bloated?" [*laughs*][188]

❖   This happened in White River, Apache country. A Navajo went for his first time to one of the Apache celebrations. And you know these Apaches are always very friendly with their home brew, so he tried some of that, and then got to where he ended up getting drunk on that. So after he got drunk, he wanted a partner. He was unmarried or single himself, and he wanted a squaw. They said, "Yeh, sure, but you can't take one away once you get one. You are just going to have to stay here. They don't want you taking her home. Once you get one, you belong here. There's a tent here where you can stay."
     By this time he was coming out of it, so he thought everybody was making fun of him, and he got mad at everybody. So he went away over a hill and sat there the rest of the night. They sent someone over to get him to chow down on this feast they were having. But he said, "No, I don't want to stay here. I want to go home now." So this is where he made his mistake of getting too much of that home brew.[189]

❖   There was a healing ceremony going on. The hogan was full, and the medicine man was sitting at the opposite side of the door. The medicine man started the ceremony by starting the traditional songs. As the medicine man and some of his buddies were singing, two women came in and sat next to the door. One was old, and the other was middle aged. Normally, you just don't walk in on a healing ceremony when it is started, so they got a lot of attention.

The medicine man started the songs again as soon as they settled down. As he was singing, he noticed the two women by the door were whispering to each other. When they stopped for a breather, the two women stopped also. That went on for awhile, and the medicine man decided to do something about it. He was curious about what the two women were gossiping about, so he told the men to stop in the middle of the next song. They started the song, and when they got to the middle of it, they stopped. The older woman was saying, "That man that is the medicine man is my lover." The medicine man upon hearing that turned all red and quickly started singing as if nothing happened.[190]

❖   A traditional ceremony was taking place. A lot of men and women were present. They sat in a circle inside the hogan. When a medicine man chants songs during a ceremony, it's common for the attenders to sing along (even the women). During this ceremony the medicine man noticed two ladies sitting by the door. They would whisper into one another's ears as he sang. He became curious of what they were saying, so he whispered to people on each side of him to stop in the middle of a song when he gave the signal. So they continued to sing until he gave them the signal to stop. When they stopped, one lady whispered into the other lady's ear, "The medicine man is my lover." He was so embarrassed that he cleared his throat and started singing again.[191]

❖   There was to be a wedding, and the groom was sitting in the hogan with his parents and relatives waiting for the bride. A few moments later the bride came in with her parents and relatives behind her. She had a blanket wrapped around her and carried a basket full of corn mush. She sat down next to the groom. Lots of presents were placed in front of them.

The ceremony was going very beautifully until the bride moved to get a pinch of the corn mush. She farted so loudly that everyone in the hogan heard her. The groom couldn't help but laugh so hard that mucus fell out of his nose into the basket of corn mush. They were so ashamed that they just stopped the wedding. Everybody just went home carrying their presents with them. The bride and groom never saw each other again.[192]

❖   There was a man whose girlfriend was going to get married. Of course he didn't want her to get married, so on the day of the wedding he went over there. He was very desperate to get her back, so he put red ants in the blanket of the groom. The groom went in the hogan with his parents and relatives, and he sat on the blanket without spreading it all out. By the time the bride came in, the red ants had come out of the blanket into the groom's clothes. Nobody noticed it. When the eating of the corn mush came about, the ants began to bite him, and he couldn't resist tearing off his clothes in front of everyone else. The bride's parents thought the groom was crazy. They grabbed the bride and rushed out of the hogan. So the man's wishes were granted.[193]

❖   At one time during a Navajo ritual chant, there was a man name of Hosteen [Mr.] Nez who was a very tall man. These group of Navajos were sitting in a circular position with backs to the wall. Hosteen Nez sat on the south side of the hogan. This particular night [ceremony] takes hours and requires two kerosene lamps to be placed in the center of the hogan. Usually a medicine man conducts such a chant as the one [that in] fact is being performed. While the elderly men were chanting, Hosteen Nez noticed his boots were on the wrong feet, and actually he had his legs crisscross. And then he asked the medicine man if he could go outside. The medicine man acknowledged, and he went outside of the hogan and changed his boots. He the entered the hogan and sat in his proper place. This time while he was sitting with his legs straight forward, he noticed that his boots were actually on the wrong feet, and members of the group noticed and began to laugh.[194]

Some Navajo jokes derive humor from double confusion. The Maturation Race, for example, is both inappropriate behavior at a ceremony and a visual pun:

❖   A ceremony was held for a young girl who had her first sign of maturity. As a part of the ceremony, she had to run to the east twice a day for three days. On the fourth day, the major ceremony takes place. Several relatives and neighbors were attending the ceremony. Some of them participate in the running.
        On one of these days, she was running with several men down the road when a policeman stopped them. The policeman was a white man. Not knowing what was going on, he put the men in the panel and took them to jail. They were charged with attempted rape.
        At their hearing, the men explained the whole thing to the judge. They told him that they were having a ceremony. The charges were dropped, and they went home. When they came home, the ceremony was over.[195]

I was visiting with Clyde at his wife's home at Zuni one day when two members of the Ko'yemshi cult came by in their traditional costumes to bless the homes and to receive the gifts that are traditionally offered to them. I had come to Zuni to see Clyde because he stayed in the village when he was not in his sheep camp or staying with his mother. Suddenly I heard the sound of rattles and saw two masked figures going by the front window of the house to the door.

Clyde called to his wife and said, "Looks like we've got some more company." He and I sat in silence. The Ko'yemshi are called in Zuni mythology "old dance men" and are thought to be misshapen supernatural beings. Their personators function through their organization during the long cycle of the Zuni ceremonial year as sacred clowns who accompany the Ko-ko and Shalako dances and dancers and burlesque the onlookers. The Ko'yemshi visit Zuni homes to bless the houses and to accept gifts offered as symbolic tokens of appreciation for service of the organization to the community.

Clyde's wife came out from the back of the house in response to his call. She arranged two dining room chairs facing the front door, and she said to us, "These are Ko'yemshi. Please take off your hats and be quiet."

Clyde took off his hat, and I took off my hat. Clyde's wife ushered the two Ko'yemshi in and seated them in the two chairs with their backs turned toward us. She, her son, and the two Ko'yemshi figures spoke in Zuni. She and her son took sacred cornmeal from the family's traditional terraced bowl and added a liberal sprinkling to the meal which already coated the figures' masks and shoulders. Then they and the Ko'yemshi offered prayers and blessings. She and her son placed cans of corn, tomatoes, and green peas against the Ko'yemshi's backs inside the blankets they had wrapped about them. Then the Ko'yemshi rose and, employing the strangely graceful, ungainly gait typical of their dancing, shuffled off. As the sound of the tortoise shell rattles receded into the distance, Clyde turned to me and said, "Sure a good thing we weren't home alone cause neither one of us would have known what we were supposed to do."

Clyde put his hat back on; I put my hat back on. Thus is Navajo humor shared and created. I had been Clyde's translator at his performance; Clyde had been my translator during my interviews; now we had no translator, and so we smiled together. Navajo humor today includes unplanned, spontaneous expressions of irony and allusions to moments shared in ceremony and in everyday life. It also is replete with manufactured jokes, as Clyde showed me. Navajo jokes in the 1990s are a major genre of Navajo oral tradition, recognized as such by audiences and performers. Indeed, they represent a major verbal art form, and the people prize their skilled performance.

Jokes in Navajo culture undoubtedly serve different functions. Benedict noted that cultures are patterned and that traditional stories may reflect the *opposite* of cultural practice and values as well as directly echoing them. Kluckhohn developed and refined Benedict's patterns-of-culture theory by noting that culture occurs on three levels: pattern, configuration, and integration. He explained, for example, that when he asked Navajos questions about witchcraft, they invariably replied, "Who told you that I knew about witchcraft?" This response he termed "pattern," and he explained that it was governed by a basic Navajo configuration "fear of the malevolent intentions of other persons," which was in turn subsumed under the Navajo integrating concept of *hozho* or wholeness and beauty. Following Kluckhohn's example, jokes in Navajo culture can be described by a three-level formula as follows: pattern = the jokes themselves, configuration = distrust and fear of confusion, and integration = *hozho*.

Navajo humor generally focuses on things at variance with what is culturally expected and accepted. For the Navajo, what is culturally expected is an ultimate value subsumed under the root *hozho*, meaning "happiness," "health," "beautiful," "peaceful," "harmonious," and (most generally) "nice." Navajo belief stresses that people are responsible for establishing this harmony and beauty by ritual and by daily life. Laughter, like ceremony, may well be one way of reversing what should not be and of re-establishing *hozho*.

The opposite of *hozho* is *hoochxo*, or disharmony, manifested in everything from dust devils to interpersonal relationships. Clyde told a story of the time he was the most frightened he had ever been, and his account illustrates *hozho* and *hoochxo* in one of the ways they are experienced by Navajos in their daily lives:

❖   I visited my uncle behind a mountain. I started back late. And then there was no road, so I was walking in a one-lane trail there, and I saw somebody coming. Then we met, and I noticed it was a burro—a donkey—and it stepped to the side there and let me through. I looked at it standing over here; I just took a look at it, and I noticed it was a burro or a donkey. I just didn't think anything of it right then or there. I just saw it and kept walking. I went a mile or two before I got home, and then when I got home I just felt all this cold chills coming down my back. I went in and they said, "Have you seen a ghost?" So that was another time when I met with this. And to come to think of it, there was not a donkey or nobody owned a donkey around there. And later on my aunt tried to scare me that it was a skinwalker. She said, "We don't want you boys out there after dark." So that's one experience I had, but at that time I didn't think it was a skinwalker or anything.[196]

Clyde's story was understandable only in light of the Navajo belief system it reflected about "this" and "that." According to traditional Navajo belief, *yee naaldlooshii* (called "skinwalkers" in English) climb on top of a hogan when a family is asleep and drop corpse powder made from the ground bones of the dead (particularly infants) down the smoke hole of the house causing great harm and misfortune to befall the inhabitants. This corpse powder used by witches represents a reversal of the life force associated with the corn pollen used in healing rituals, and thus symbolizes death and disharmony rather than life and harmony.

Many scholars have noted that Navajo witches in general, and skin-walkers in particular, represent the world turned upside down. They are "inverted" Navajos, or creatures embodying and glorifying all the characteristics opposite of the cooperative, social individuals that are the Navajo ideal—reverse images of what tradition teaches good Navajos should seek to be. *Yee naaldlooshii* are widely recognized and feared by the Navajo as an extreme manifestations of ultimate disharmony, and, like *ch'iidii* (called "ghosts" in English), they often assume animal form. Indeed, disharmony is manifested in *yee naaldlooshii* (as in *ch'iidii*) by the fact that they appear to be something other than what they are. Anything unknown is potentially dangerous because it might be confused with something known, and—by the same token—confusion is a threat.

In some significant and informative field-collected Navajo stories, a *yee naaldlooshii* laughs and returns to human form or dies:

❖   There was a young Navajo lady who was staying by herself with a newborn baby. Everyone else who lived there had gone to a Squaw Dance. That night the moon was full.

     Sometime during the night her baby started crying 'cause he needed his diaper changed. She got up and was changing his diaper when she heard a noise on top of the hogan by the smoke hole. She looked up and seen some ears, she picked up the dirty diaper and threw it at the smoke hole. Then she heard a chuckle, and it sounded as though someone had fell down.

     She woke up early the next morning and looked around and found a dead woman outside who was dressed in skinwalker clothes.

     When a person is a skinwalker, they are not to laugh when they are dressed like that; if they laugh, they will die. Apparently, the skinwalker laughed and that's what killed her.[197]

❖   A Navajo lady was alone in their hogan with her seven-months baby girl. The mother heard a terrible, horrifying noise outside. Pretty soon there appeared a man clothed in a bear skin in the chimney hole. The lady was terribly frightened. She didn't know what to do. At the time the mother was in the process of changing her baby's diaper. She happened to throw up the dirty, soiled diaper into the face of the object. The wolf man laughed and laughed and was never again seen at any time thereafter.[198]

❖   A young boy was learning from his grandfather the evil ways of witchcraft among the Navajo tribe. He learned the chants on how to cast spells. Finally, it was time to learn how to wear the werewolf costume. He and his father put their costumes on and went on their way to seek the houses.

     The young boy was running after his father when he noticed that his long tail was wagging back and forth. It was so funny that he laughed about it. To his surprise, the costume came off. His father warned him not to laugh again because every time he laughs, the suit will come off.[199]

One way of dealing with shapechangers in many cultures that share such a tradition is to make *them* return to human form. The Navajo believe that if *yee naaldlooshii* laugh, they assert the humanity they seek to deny and can have their dark power defeated.

Yee naaldlooshii reveal disharmony at the deepest, most dangerous level, but Navajos also see evidence of it in apparently trivial confusion. The story of Hosteen Nez achieves part of its humor from a widespread belief that putting one's boots on the wrong feet is an extremely bad omen. Disharmony of language and situation is a source of humor in Navajo jokes—and it actually is controlled by laughter. In fact, Navajo jokes are funny largely because they acknowledge confusion but also assert the power of *hozho,* or harmony. They center on disharmony within the Navajo language, within the English language, or where the two meet— disharmony revealed or created by verbal and visual confusion. In the end, though, these very jokes assert people's world view and deal with the tensions disharmony brings.

As is typical of Navajo language and thought, Clyde explained his earlier story of the old man and the coyote in terms of space and movement. "Coyote" he said, "is the one supposed to be ahead of everybody, but he really got caught from behind there."

Coyote, "the spirit of disorder"; coyote, linked with *yee naaldlooshii;* coyote, the trickster cousin who is always surprising the Navajo, is surprised by a Navajo—and he just falls over dead.

Now, that's funny!

CHAPTER SIX

Going Back and Forth Between Cultures

THE PEOPLE ARE STILL THE PEOPLE. The dance continues. Births and deaths, dances and dreams, certainties and fears, and—most of all—stories shared by Zuni and Ramah Navajo individuals and families revealed for us the strength, resilience, and functional beauty of Zuni and Ramah Navajo cultures and their ideals. The concluding phase of our funded research project, however, was to be very different from our early look at the ever-unfolding continuity and power of cultures. Almost all these first interviews were conducted with friends—or friends of friends—in homes as a part of ongoing, evolving relationships with co-researchers. The final project called for interviews of a different nature based upon different relationships.

One hot September day Helen, Kathy, and I were coming back into Zuni, and Helen suggested we stop at Halona Plaza Grocery Store and get some cold pop to drink. We were laughing and talking together as we got out of the car and walked into the store. The check-out clerks and other shoppers in the store turned and looked at us in surprise. At first I could not understand why they were staring at the three of us, and then it dawned on me that to them we didn't fit together. They were asking themselves, "What is that Zuni woman doing with those *melika* (white people)?" or perhaps, "What are those *melika* doing with that Zuni woman?"

We quickly and quietly bought our cold pop and went back to the car. Helen's first comment was, "They sure seemed surprised in there, didn't they?" We agreed and opened our pop. After awhile she said, "Have you guys ever been to Santa Fe?" We said we hadn't, and she said, "You should go. There's lots of things to see. I'd love to show you around." We jumped at the opportunity of having her be our Indian guide again, and we started making plans to go to Santa Fe between fall and spring semesters.

At about the same time, we started to think of another tribe or group of American Indians we could interview to continue our study of views of disability and rehabilitation. We discussed with Helen some of the various groups in the Southwest and asked her for her ideas on others we should contact. She told us about a girl who had been her roommate in school at Santa Fe and who was still her friend. "She would be a good person to work with," Helen said. "She and I are a lot alike, and I think she would enjoy helping as much as I have."

We were pleased at Helen's enthusiasm and told her that the plan sounded great. Then Helen advised us her friend was from a pueblo with a reputation for being closed to research, and we agreed that we had always heard outsiders could not get permission to do interviews there. Helen laughed and said she had heard you always got followed if you drove around the pueblo, but she thought that if she went with us to talk to the governor and tribal council there—and if her friend knew we were also her friends—it could be arranged. We decided to make a presentation at that pueblo on our way up to Santa Fe.

A few days after New Year's we picked Helen up at Zuni and started out for Santa Fe. Helen's father had written out a message for her to give the governor and tribal council, and we discussed our plans. Helen said, "Let's drive around through the pueblo before we go to the tribal building and see if we do get followed." That sounded like a good idea to us, too, and so we did.

We drove past the tribal headquarters building, past the mission, down a long straight narrow street. Before long Helen said, "There's a blue Toyota behind us. Quick, turn and see if they turn."

We did. They did. By now we were at the north end of the pueblo and headed away from the tribal building. I decided to take the next right so that we could turn back toward the middle of the pueblo. At this point Helen said there was a white Ford truck several streets behind the Toyota also following us. I made a third right turn so we were headed south again, and the Ford and Toyota almost ran into each other at the intersection behind us. We three gasped. Helen said later she was sure the driver of the second truck was wearing a neck brace and commented, "I bet they've met there before."

We drove back to the tribal building, went in, and told the secretary who we were and why we were there. She told us we could talk to the tribal officials in about twenty minutes.

We three sat very quietly while we waited. Helen read and reread the message her father had given her, and Kathy and I rethought what we wanted to say. Time slowed down. Every check of the watch indicated the twenty minutes had not gone by, but we felt we had been sitting there for hours. Occasionally someone came by and asked Helen how her parents were. The secretary asked if we wanted coffee, but it still was not time to make our presentation. Finally Helen folded and put away her piece of paper.

"Does it always feel like this?" she whispered.

"Yes," we whispered back.

"Whew!" she said. "This is really hard work sitting here, and you guys do this all the time."

We grinned back.

At last we were ushered into the governor's office. Helen gave her message: "My parents send their regards to the governor and to his family. Good wishes to the Tribal Council for the New Year." The governor's assistant translated her message to the governor, and he nodded gravely.

Next I explained the grant and the work we had been doing at Zuni. My explanation was all carefully translated by the governor's assistant to the governor and the council, and everyone nodded again. Then we explained that we wanted to do the same research at their pueblo. Again the governor's assistant translated our message to the governor and the council. They discussed the matter at some length in their native language. Then the governor responded in his language, and the assistant translated his response for us: "Thank you, but we were just going to do such a project ourselves here."

After his response was translated to us, the governor asked Helen in English how her parents were. Then he asked if they were still making jewelry and described a piece he particularly liked that her dad had made years before. We thanked them for their time. Helen exchanged hugs with all of them, we shook hands all around, and we left.

When we were safely back in the car, we all three sighed huge sighs. Then Helen said, "Boy, they never look up, do they? They all were looking down the whole time." We started driving up the road to Santa Fe. "Oh, gosh," she said. "Is this going to cause problems on your grant?"

"No," we assured her. "We'll just work somewhere else."

The visit to Santa Fe was as good as we had hoped for and better. We had two adjoining rooms with corner fireplaces. Each morning the maids made the beds, cleaned out the fireplaces, and brought in logs and the day's newspapers. When we weren't out windowshopping, we stayed in our rooms and talked. I stretched out on the bed propped up with pillows, and Kathy and Helen sat on the floor near the fireplace and kept the fire going.

Out in the town Helen showed us all her favorite stores, which ran from crystal shops to furriers to a strange furniture place with Mexican and Mexican-American artifacts such as tiles, piñatas, trees of life, huge wardrobes, and what was obviously an old confessional booth. In one shop Helen and I stopped and looked at a glass case displaying some Zuni pottery miniatures. Helen herself is known for exquisite pottery animals, so we were very interested in comparing hers to the ones for sale here. While we were looking at them, Kathy wandered over to another case across the store where a clerk showed her some Navajo rings. While Kathy and the clerk were talking, the clerk looked up at Helen and me and said, "Oh, look! Their auras are just the same color of light! With their heads together that close you can't see where one ends and the other begins."

We wandered through the Plaza of the Governors, talked to people who had jewelry displayed there, and stopped and enjoyed fresh coffee and bread at a bakery on the corner of the plaza. We saw our first tourists of the trip at the bakery. We three were leaning back in our leather chairs enjoying the coffee and the comfortable silence between us when we noticed a *melika* family watching us with the same curious stares we had received at the grocery store at Halona Plaza in Zuni. No one else in all of Santa Fe had acted surprised or puzzled at seeing two Anglos and one American Indian together.

We three turned and smiled at each other.

But where was the someplace else we were going to do research? Conducting the Ramah Navajo interviews with Clyde, we had shared shining moments—surprising, exciting interviews; good stories; unforgettable times. Across the great gulf separating people and cultures there had been deep communication—most often through stories—of our speakers' own sense of being. Encouraged by the successes of this blind sampling technique, Kathy and I planned a series of unassisted initial interviews with urban American Indian health-care professionals representing a wide range of tribal backgrounds in the Phoenix, Arizona, metropolitan area.

We had to find someplace else, and we remained curious about something else. One fact of American Indians' lives is the scarcity of opportunities for gainful employment on most of America's reservations. Unemployment at both Zuni and across the Navajo Reservation is reliably estimated at thirty to sixty percent, and most of the available jobs are such that underemployment probably is even higher. Agriculture at both Zuni and Navajo was always marginal at best; now changing market conditions and expectations have made it less than marginal. Making and selling traditional craft items (rugs and jewelry, for instance) and tourism provide some subsistence income, but very few families can manage comfortable livings from their arts or from service industries.

Opportunities for American Indians, by and large, lie outside their reservations, and people like Norman who have managed successful careers at home are unusual. For most American Indians from reservation tribes, economic progress demands going somewhere away from home to seek training or education and then getting a job somewhere away from their homelands. This dilemma, of course, is not unique to American Indian peoples (there aren't many job opportunities in my hometown either), but it is particularly acute because so many American Indian groups have such strong ties to their tribal lands.

Could the people, would the people, still be the people if they were separated from their cultures, removed from their homes, medicine men, beliefs, and ceremonies? And would contemporary legends, personal-experience stories, and kitchen-table stories—anything matching the depth, power, and revelatory art of the Zuni and Ramah Navajo stories and serving equally to tell lives, to entertain, to teach, to bring together—be called forth by formal interviews across desks in offices with strangers? This chapter begins to answer such questions with fifty-five stories told by the thirteen urban Hopi, Zuni, Apache, Osage, Pima, San Juan, Shoshoni, Ute, Sioux, and Cherokee Indians we interviewed. They are presented in the order in which they occurred and are accompanied by descriptions, interpretations, and more stories.

STAYING CONNECTED

The first interview of the urban American Indian study was conducted with a remarkable Hopi narrator.

The Hopi live the furtherest west of the Pueblo Indian tribes in eleven villages on or near high mesas surrounded by the Navajo Big Reservation of northeastern Arizona. Like the Zuni, thay have a rich, complex ceremonial life.

This Hopi was a professional counselor concerned personally and professionally that American Indians from vital, active tribal societies and cultures not only survive but prosper in the urban white man's world. Her interview was the longest of the entire urban group, and her thirteen stories the most that anyone told. She began by telling two stories that reflect her professional life in the urban setting—ones of the sort often employed for counseling or speechmaking:

❖   Somehow, people coming from the reservation feel like they have to be like everybody here. They feel like they have to completely forget about that. They can't do the same things. (Well, of course, they can't do the same things there as they can here. They can't walk out and see a dance or something like that, but they can do other things that are just as entertaining for their families here as they can there, you know). I mean, somehow the personality just changes. The families start falling apart. The kids—they lose control of the kids—and they just don't continue on the same pattern where you *know* your family, your kids, your realities! It would seem to me that you would be able to follow that pattern because it has worked for so long in terms of your stability. It's kinda been there, so you'd think you'd have to make a few minor adjustments here and there; but basically, you'd go on.

A classic example of that is not too long ago, we had a family of four (two younger children, the wife, and the husband) move down. There were no jobs on the reservation; neither one of them could find jobs. They were living with their relatives, and it just got to be too crowded, so they figured—they were a young couple—they'd come down look for a job—they were both going to get jobs—and really do something with their lives. And they came down, and he couldn't find a job. And she found a job right off the bat—wasn't anything big, but it was a job—and so he was getting real frustrated with the job search process. And what happened was that he ended up taking out a lot of his frustrations on her, and ended up killing her! They hadn't been here more than six months. And so now here he is in prison, the wife's dead, and the children are separated.[200]

Her second story described proprietary schools in the Phoenix area which she had seen adversely affect American Indian students:

❖   We have real problems with recruiters. They are headhunters. They get paid by how many they sign up. Two years ago we had a lady from a Phoenix school go out to the reservation and give, you know, this story about there are no Indian actors or Indian models or whatever, and you'll make it big; you're the only ones. About seventy or eighty percent of those all dropped out, and the tribe paid for the scholarships.[201]

After her thoroughly acculturated professional stories, she told two much more personal stories concerning health care and health. The first described a recent unsatisfactory experience she had when she took her niece to a hospital:

❖   I was just there at the hospital last week with a niece. I went in at ten o'clock that night. She developed a rash, and it just started spreading, and I couldn't figure out what it was, so I called the doctor. And I said, "This is what's happening. What do you want me to do? What do you *think* that I should do?"
    And he said, "Well, bring her right in." We got there at ten o'clock, and we sat in the doctor's office from ten o'clock till one o'clock in the morning. I looked—several times I walked outside the door— I saw the doctor sitting in the emergency room with two other paramedics that had brought in a patient, and they were sitting there drinking a Coke and talking, and I got so frustrated and so upset that I just took the baby and I went home. I figured well, maybe if we come in—if it gets worse and we come in in an ambulance—maybe we'll get the attention right away. But as it worked out I just used the old home remedy of warm salt water; I put it all over her back, and everything cleared up the next day.[202]

Her second story about health was of a much more personal and revelatory nature and described her own experiences of moving between her own and Western health-care systems and beliefs:

❖   I know about four years ago I had a seizure, and I went to the hospital immediately, which is like phenobarbital, valium, anything that will slow you down, and I'm not a person that takes drugs very well, even aspirin [or] Anacin. I get light-headed when I use them. I'll never make it as a drug addict. [*laughs*] I just can't—and they put me on phenobarbital, and I said, "This is too strong." I mean, I take it and an hour or half an hour later I'm asleep for four hours, and I have no control over it. My boss, she told me, "You just can't come to work and sleep," 'cause they just could never wake me up.

Finally I just went off it. We went through all the tests: CAT scans, everything. They couldn't find anything, and I said, "Yeah, but if you don't know what's wrong with me, then why should I continue? This doesn't make sense. If there is nothing you know that is wrong with me, my whole system was off." So I just said, "I'm not going to take these anymore."

And he said, "Well, you know you are going to have a seizure."

That was four years ago, and I haven't had one. I'm not saying that I'll never have one, but I'm just saying that phenobarbital—See, even after I got off it, I couldn't sleep. I mean, I'd stay up all night, and then I would fall asleep from just being tired—from being up—and my system went through the shakes. It's like an addict will come off drugs. I mean it wasn't good!

My grandmother is a medicine woman at Hopi, and she does a lot of the physical things. If you had a broken bone or dislocated knee, you know, she can fix things like that, and if you have an upset stomach, she is able to do those type of things. But any type of preventative medicine or preventative health is just not available. All my grandmother gave me was just the Hopi tea: boil that and drink that at night, you know, just straight, and I, I could relax at that, and I could go to sleep. But it took me almost six months after taking it for a year to feel like I was back to normal. It's a scary thing when you don't have any control over your body. You've got to drive, and you're out in public, and you don't know what's going to happen. [*laughs*] You get so stressed out you don't want to even leave your home—which is not good either. Well—[203]

This account of illness serves to introduce her and her Hopi world—with ceremonial *kiva* rooms, *Kachina* dancers, and supernaturals—as they exist separate from urban Phoenix. Her next four stories move ever deeper into describing and revealing that self and world. The first, in fact, is so thoroughly grounded in her American Indian beliefs that it is largely unintelligible to outsiders who would not recognize that the *"they"* of the story refers to witches or other traditionally conceived forces of evil:

❖   Gosh, how long ago was this? This was about two years ago. There was a guy—when they were having all that dispute about the museum or the artifacts that were up near Flagstaff. There was a dig or something going on—either someone was digging there or someone was grave robbing, and I can't recall whether it was grave robbing or there were people out there actually digging—and one of the researchers saw [a hitchhiker]. He was either going back into town or going out of town—and they never saw or heard from him again. The only reason why I know about that is 'cause when we were out home, at the time there were things missing from our home, and they suspected that a person from there—Tradition among all the beliefs they have was that, you know, *they* can transfer into a different form or into a different being, and that's what he did. That's how they're saying it happened, you know, but that was a long time ago; that was two years ago.[204]

❖   Usually at the time when these things happen, it's usually during our bean dance time, and some of the Kachinas that came around to dance inside the kivas, they were all—well, some of them had come in and were inside the kiva dancing and some of them either got too tired or whatever, and they were just kind of looking in and watching. And they were all kinda laying on top of the kiva like this [*uses hands by face to show their position*], and they all had blankets over them 'cause it was really cold. You know, they didn't notice people around them; they were just laying there kind of looking in, and then they noticed this one figure laying next to them, and he had a blanket over his head, and they were all looking in, so they were kinda—they start talking among themselves, and somebody turned around and to say something to this other guy, and he wouldn't answer. They looked around and they asked him, they said, "Who *are* you?" And whoever or whatever it was, I guess, when he turned and looked at them—whatever expression or whatever facial features he has was not one of them, and then he got up and just took off running, and they started chasing him. See, this was at Walpi, and if you look at Walpi, there's a trail that goes all the way to the end, and then there's rock steps that go down, and that's where the Kachinas go. And he took off running towards that way, and they start chasing him, and all of a sudden he just disappeared. You know, there was nothing. They just couldn't see him or find him or anything. So they all got, you know, really worked up, and they came back, and they started passing the word, and that kind of upset a lot of people. It's usually—you know—if people don't live their lives right, they say that it comes back and reminds them, you know, that they're straying away from what—the way that they're supposed to be. And—[205]

❖   I know my oldest sister—a—on two occasions she's said she's actually seen it. She knows that people don't—she says she *knows* that, "People don't believe me," she said, "but I saw it." See, when we—they were younger, they used to play hide and go seek, but they would play hide and go seek with a drum, and everybody else had to try to find the drummer, so the drummer would run, and then he'd beat the drum, and then they'd all take off towards the sound, and they were doing this up there, and this person that they were chasing was not the person that they were playing with, and then, they chased him all the way to the end, and when they finally caught up, she said it was just—it wasn't a very tall man, but he had like a deerskin, a buckskin, the white ones that are already tan, tied here like this [*puts her hands on her shoulder*], and it just hung down and nothing on underneath it, just this deerskin tied like that—was barefoot and had something on its head—and he just kind of stood there and kind of humped [*leans forward*] over at them and kind of jumped his feet real fast like this [*prances in place with her feet while slapping her knees with her hands quickly*], beat the drum and took off, and they all stood there looking at him like that, and he just—they never saw it after that. And that was during ceremonial time, too, so—

I think—a lot of times—I don't think he's really hurt—I don't think he really hurts anybody, but he's not someone that you want to deal with. You hope you never see him is how you should think about it. My sister was real bad at that time, too.[206]

❖ Owls are really bad symbols for us. Usually somebody is going to die when you get owls around your house. I know with my great-grandmother and another grandfather—grandfather on my dad's side and great-grandmother on my mother's side—it happened like that both times. She was pretty sick, and so she was old and bedridden; but then this owl came and was outside her house, and we all were kinda wondering, and sure enough she died that same, that same week, and grandfather the same way. It's interesting.[207]

All four of these stories are interesting; in fact, the accounts of the "bean dance time" and her oldest sister are such remarkable stories that we will return to them in the final chapter. After this set of four stories embodying and describing Hopi belief and reality, the narrator moved easily into another series of five stories describing Hopi everyday life as it reflects people's sense of their society and their world:

❖ We think of our mates as not heads of the household, but they are providers, and you owe them a certain amount of respect. You want to— whatever they bring home, say, whatever groceries or, back then, whatever meat or whatever food that they brought home, you would thank them for it and then prepare it for them and feed them what they brought home, and the man in the end will say, "Thank you," in Hopi to you for the food, and it's just mutual respect for each other. We still do that now and even in our homes here in Phoenix. The female always provides for the male, but the male doesn't have any say-so in discipline or big decisions or anything like that. Like when my grandmother died in April, the oldest brother sat down and said, "Well"—and all the women were there—"what do you guys want to do? You're the heads of the household, and the men are here to help you do the physical stuff and whatever, but whatever you decide and however you want to hold the funeral, it's up to you."

So we all set down, all the four girls in our family, plus our in-laws 'cause they hold just about the same status as we do, and we discussed what we were going to do, and when, and what kind of clothes and all this. It's still done the same way, and even though my grandmother's gone, the second oldest daughter has assumed all that responsibility now, so it's still through the chain of command.[208]

❖   My oldest brother has a farm in the south, and that belongs entirely to his wife; and if she were ever to get to the point where she didn't want him around, she just puts his clothes outside, and he's got to come live with one of his sisters. I have another brother who just bought a home here on the east side, and it's the same thing. He says, "Well, the house is yours, you know," and another sister and my brother have a home in Paradise Valley, and it's the same way. They are all run pretty much the same way.[209]

❖   Even the little girls in the family are a lot more aggressive than the boys. I have a son, and sometimes I think he lets his nieces bully him a little bit too much, and he gets frustrated. But I tell him, "You know, you're developing a lot of patience, and you're learning how to deal with their personalities, and—once you get used to that—it won't upset you anymore." You have to sit, and you have to explain it to him, you know, "That's just, you know, that's how the girls are." But, see, in return they do a lot for him, too, because I have two nieces—one from southern Arizona, and the one from Paradise Valley. Now the one from Paradise Valley is too young to work yet, but she baby-sits for another sister, so she lives with me and walks over and baby-sits for her. The other one couldn't find a job where her family lives, but she's got two jobs here in Phoenix that she works, so she stays with me. I mean, they rub his back; they fix him breakfast, you know. They do a lot for him, and he knows that. They do what they are supposed to do, *and so,* in return, he tries to—When they need to blow off steam, he's usually the one that gets it, [*laughs*] so—[*voice trails off*][210]

❖   It's like, when we talk to my grandfather, we don't say, "This is what I am going to do." All you do is just say, "Well, I'm going to go to the store now." And you just leave it, because for him to ask you for a favor or something that is going to make him feel like you have got to go out of your way to do this for him, he's not going to do it, and he'll do without it.
He's got arthritis, so if he wants Anacin, he's not going to say, "Can you take me to the store to get some Anacin for my hand?" He'll do subtle things like he'll leave the Anacin bottle out there, and it's empty, so you pick up on that, and you say, "I'm going to go to the store now."
And he'll say, "Well, let me go with you."[211]

❖   My grandmother was eighty when she died, and it's a tradition among the Hopi that when the grandmother is dying, she tells the family things, tells them what to do. But there are members of my family who live all over, and so my oldest brother and her got together and decided they were going to do this. She made a videotape; yeah, she had my brother who had a camera come and film her.

And one thing, see, there was a lot of physical abuse between my parents. I mean that's all we grew up with. Every other day they were always beating each other up and kicking somebody out of the house, and so we always said that we didn't want that in our families. In the video she told my brothers, "If you ever raise a hand to the women of the family, you are cutting the line of the family." And, you know, it was like we all just kind of sat there, and so what she was saying was that even though your mother never divorced, and she stayed in the family, what happened to the children that came from that type of background—you all went through a real, real hard time, but you can learn from that. If you don't do that in your families, your kids are one step ahead of themselves, and they'll have a better chance, a better opportunity.

She spoke in Hopi, and my brother, he translated for her 'cause a lot of the kids still don't know Hopi, so—

You know, it was something we all saw, and it's just like she knew she was dying, and about a month before she died she made the tape. But when she was in the hospital, she stayed alive till she saw everyone in our entire family; then she just went to sleep. And a lot of the things that she'd told us, they're still coming back in bits and pieces. And then when we remember it, we'll call each other up and say, "I remember! I remember what she was saying, and I know what she was saying! It's just as clear as day!" [*laughs*]

The majority of the white people I talk to don't know where they have come from, and that's too bad 'cause we can trace back twelve hundred years, and we are still living in the same homes. It's just one of those things, I guess. We want to continue that videotaping tradition. Next Christmas we want to do it again, any new babies or additions to our family. We want, you know, to try to continue so that everyone remembers where they're from.

It's the tradition, you know; it's the family stories and tradition and all of that. It's still going. Sometimes we don't see it that way; we see—kinda see—ourselves as leading our own lives, but it's really not like that. We're all really connected to each other; we just haven't realized it yet. It's interesting.[212]

Experienced and examined in the order in which she told them, her stories are a coherent, carefully ordered revelation of her self and her culture—a spiritual autobiography and a personal ethnography. Her final story, in particular, is a summation of her Hopi sense of place and what it means to her to be Hopi, and the sequence of her stories is overall so logical and effective that it is amazing. Having this masterful narrator as the subject of our first interview was a totally unexpected pleasure.

ALIVE AGAIN

The next interview was with a Zuni who was a professional counselor. We met Denny at a Native American Rehabilitation Conference. We prepared and presented a paper discussing Zuni culture; and Denny came up to us after the paper, introduced himself, gave us a business card, and told us that he would be willing and pleased to assist us with our research. We filed away his card, called him when we were planning our urban American Indian interviews, and made arrangements to interview him. He kindly suggested other American Indian health-care professionals for us to meet with, and also made arrangements for us to interview his wife at their home. He and his wife were both very intelligent, well-educated, informative interviewees whom we have continued to visit and consult. She told no stories as part of her interview, and he told only one:

❖   I go back to Zuni for Shalako. That's one thing I have learned through growing up there is that it's a once-in-a-lifetime activity and, one way or another, I am going to be going back. In fact, my family is sponsoring a dance this year and having a Shalako house, so we're going back every month or every two weeks, and I enjoy it because I—it *helps* me. The word I always use when I go home is that it regenerates my battery—meaning that it makes me alive again, makes me feel at home. It helps me with my emotional and physical well-being.[213]

Our third interviewee of the morning was a San Carlos Apache. His tribe, located in Arizona, is one of the largest in the Apache language family, which in turn is closely related to the Navajo language. Through guerilla warfare, the Apache earned their reputation for fierce resistance to United States' attempts to keep them on reservations in the 1870s and 1880s.

Like Denny, our San Carlos Apache interviewee told one story:

❖   I heard a story from my grandmother back home at the San Carlos Apache Reservation, actually. She said that the story was from a long time ago: "A man had escaped from jail" (that is the way she put it), [*laughs*] "and he had an iron hand, and he was out to get everybody else that was in sight." That's about it. She told me when I was about fifteen or twelve, in between there. She was actually telling my uncles who were older than I was, and I just happened to pass by, and I just briefly heard it.[214]

Osage tribal history is filled with irony. The Osage once controlled vast areas of what are now the states of Arkansas, Kansas, Missouri, and Oklahoma. After a series of disastrous treaties made under duress from 1808 to 1870, they lost their land and were forced to move to a small reservation in Oklahoma and take up farming. Then, in the late 1880s, a massive pool of oil was discovered under their reservation! In an early attempt at applied anthropology, the government assigned the oil lease rights to the women of the tribe, and the oil made the Osage extremely wealthy. The Osage counselor we interviewed told eight stories, her first explaining and expressing a sense of her cultural identity:

❖   I consider myself a somewhat traditional Osage. My mother for twen-ty-five years had her own store called "The Redman's Store," and she made traditional Osage men and women's clothes and sold them to people that didn't sew. I have always danced at my dances. My children all have their Osage names, and they have gone through their naming ceremony. My oldest boy has danced and had his roach; he received his roach in the traditional way. My youngest son is four and will receive his roach next summer. I have always tried to maintain my ties to my tribe, and my tribe in some ways is not as traditional as a lot of tribes due to the fact that in the late teens or early twenties they came into money, and it provided them an opportunity to do a lot of things that other tribal people couldn't do. I mean, my mom was sent to a boarding school; she went to St. Louis to go to college and a lot of different things, so in many ways my tribe is not as traditional. But when it comes to our dances, we are definitely traditional, and certain things *can* go on and certain things *can't* go on, and so they are trying to maintain that. I think that within my tribe I am very traditional.[215]

Her next two stories both dealt with belief and perceptions of reality. The first of them was, quite possibly, closely related to Anglo-American contemporary legend:

❖   I've heard of a phantom—a car without a driver. A person was driving (and this was a friend of my mom's who told the story, and she said it happened to her). She was driving, and it was late and very dark, and she was on a country intersection, and there was a car. She thought it was real unusual this car was behind her, but she lived in the country, and it didn't dawn on her, so she turned down her road to go home, and the car went straight on. So [she] didn't think anything of it, and she came to the next intersection, and the car *crossed her path* without a person in the driver's seat. So—you know—[216]

The second of her stories about belief was as surely Osage as the first was possibly Anglo-American:

❖   Well, my tribe and several other tribes in the area where I am believe in the deer women; and the story goes that there'd be people dancing; and the dancing gets fast; and the people really get with it; and all of a sudden, they'll see a person; and her feet, they don't have feet, but they have hooves; and then when someone draws attention to it, that person disappears into the woods. The person is dressed in a blanket. You know, a lot of the Osage women around there, they'll wear a Pendleton, and of course it goes all the way to the ground so you don't see their feet.

I really don't know what it means. I've always just heard it said, people say, "Oh, there's the deer women," kind of like that, and I've never really asked. I've never seen it, but, you know, I've heard people say that. The way I perceive it is that to a certain extent the deer woman must be partially evil, or why would people be afraid of her? And yet I am a member of the deer clan in my tribe, so I have a hard time identifying with—unless the person is evil, and they just use different forms.[217]

Her other five stories move in and out of Osage traditional culture and storytelling traditions and Anglo-American culture and storytelling to reveal a confident, secure human being at peace with herself and the various roles she plays in her worlds. Her first story—fifth-grade humor, we used to call it—is one almost all Anglo-American parents have heard from their young children:

❖   My uncle is a great storyteller. You know, he tells it with a twinkle in his eye and a smile on his face. He doesn't heehaw like someone else does, but it's funny. I can't think of one right off the top of my head. The only jokes I can think of are the corny ones my children are now telling me. [*laughs*] Like what my youngest one is always saying, "You want to hear a dirty story?"

And I'll say, "Yeah."

And he'll say, "A boy fell in the mud." That's my four-year-old, so that's all the jokes I can think of now is those kinds of things.[218]

Her second is a personal reminiscence:

❖   Osage ladies' moccasin[s] are real plain. They are rounded on the toe, and there's a slit up the back. That slit opens up so there's like a bead down across your instep, and that part that's open lays down and makes a lapel. Well, my cousin always used to laugh because her foot was so wide that she always used to say that it made the moccasin look like a meat pie, and so she referred to them as "meat pie shoes."

She was just being smart, and one lady came in one day and wanted to order things and said, "What are those?"

Jennie told her, "Those are meat pie shoes," and she just kept a real straight face, and she went in the back and started laughing.

When my mom came out, [the lady] said to my mom, "Well, could you make me a pair of those meat pie shoes in my size?" And my mom had to go back in and scold my cousin.[219]

Her next story is a joke that is widespread in Anglo-American and American Indian cultures, as she notes:

❖   I know another one they used to say, "Well, a traditional Osage family is made up of one mother, one father, two boys, two girls, and an anthropologist," [*laughs*] and I am sure a lot of tribes would say that kind of thing.[220]

Her final two stories are rooted directly in Osage history, Osage ceremony, and others' views of them:

❖   Oh, my tribe has oil headrights and had at one time been very wealthy, you know, and people are always making jokes about the Osages and their money, "Well, where's your Cadillac?" without even understanding that you can't vote, and you can't own a part of a headright until someone dies and gives you that. See, I have been able to vote for a year and a half, and I now have a portion of a headright. And all that time I was half Osage and on the rolls and should have been entitled to all those kinds of things, but (because that's the way our tribe decided to write it) my mother had to die before I had an opportunity to do any of those things.[221]

❖   We kinda make jokes about our giveaways, 'cause on giveaway day, you know, they go on [*drawn out*], and on [*drawn out*], and on [*drawn out*]. Somebody gets up and talks in Osage for fifteen minutes, and the standing joke is then: "Now, let me translate for you." You're tired, and you *know* what he's saying because you hear certain words. One of them is, "I'm a poor, pitiful human being." That's a good phrase Osages like to use, and so we'll laugh and say, "Now, let me translate for you"—which means you go fifteen more minutes before the giveaway even starts.[222]

These stories of the Osage, like those of the first storyteller, provide a wealth of ethnographic detail as experienced and related by a member of a culture who is also at home in the Anglo-American world.

Next we interviewed a Pima woman. The Pima are an agricultural people living on two major reservations near Phoenix, Arizona. They call themselves, in their language, "river people" and have built and utilized extensive irrigation canals from their prehistory to the present.

The Pima we interviewed first told a version of a well-known, widely distributed Anglo-American contemporary legend:

❖   The one I remember was something about a poodle. As a matter of fact, somebody even brought in an article (who knows from where) about this lady who gave her poodle a bath and decided to dry it in a microwave, and there went the poodle! Heavenly days, it's got to be about six years ago I heard it. I think it was from another Indian staff person.[223]

She also told a story based upon her personal experience—a story about storytelling and audience reactions:

❖   It was one of those things. We were out camping in the White Mountains and were all setting around a camp fire, and someone decided to tell
stories, so they pulled this out about a hitchhiker: a girl who had drowned
or whatever or an old woman, and, by the time you get to your destination,
they are no longer there. And at about the high point of the story (you know,
when she is going to vanish) one of our fellow campers had gone to use the
facilities down the hill and came back up and timed it just right and jumped
out of the darkness right in the middle, and I mean everybody went flying
and screaming. His timing was just right. It was a mixed group of Indians
who work here and other friends. The guy telling the story was an Indian,
and it was something that happened on his reservation way, way back—a
very old story. I think he was a Sioux.[224]

The final story she told was one that she identified as closely associated
with her Pima tradition, and, as with her previous story, she included a
good deal of valuable information about context and performance. Indeed,
this Pima narrator consistently demonstrated a greater personal interest in
describing storytelling situations than in telling stories:

❖   There is a story from the Pima in regard to the hoof man. Way, way
back he was supposed to appear to a a young girl—a young Pima girl. He
was a very good-looking Pima man, and it was at some of the dances, and
he would spirit her. And I believe she died. The next morning all they would
find were hoof prints of, like, a deer or an antelope, and supposedly it was
this hoof man. And the parents would always warn their daughters to beware
a handsome stranger. It was kinda a way to keep the girls in line, I'm sure.
That's just an old Pima thing, but I didn't hear it [till] I was in high
school—about the age I needed to be warned, I guess. [*laughs*][225]

The urban Hopi who was our next interviewee told a story of cultural
identity and followed it with a version of "Hoof Man" (she also identified
the figure with Pima culture) and, finally, told a dramatic version of the
Anglo-American "Vanishing Hitchhiker":

❖   I would say I am borderline traditional and urbanized, kind of on the
edge, because I have lived in the city for so many years. But I do participate
in our religious ceremonies, and I do believe in my ways as a Hopi. It is
sometimes hard because I'm not around my own people, the Hopi people.
I'm around mostly different tribes, and they don't speak my language, and
it's kind of hard, but when I do meet up with somebody—that's when I
really talk, and I enjoy talking like that.[226]

❖   This person who told me this was out in the Young area (it was my
girlfriend). She said that they were at a dance at that old school out there,
and this person came in, and he had like hooves on his feet [*points to her feet*]
and here, too. [*places her right hand around her left wrist*] And that person

just disappeared later on, I guess. They called it "Hoofie!" [*laughs*] I guess a lot of people seen this person, too.[227]

This narrator also enjoyed performing stories from other cultural groups. The hitchhiker legend she told next was clearly related to Navajo traditional stories (Dilkon is one of the areas of the Navajo world most frequently associated in traditional stories with witches and *ch'iidii* activity). It evokes Navajo tradition as surely as her "Hoofie" evokes Pima legend:

❖   The story about a hitchhiker just came to my mind more clear. It happened near that one reservation—the Navajo Reservation—Dilkon. Along the road coming from Winslow to the Hopi Reservation, there was this hitchhiker on the road, and this man was driving late at night back home to his reservation just on the Navajo Reservation, and he picked up this hitchhiker. It was a lady, and he was kinda curious as to why she was out late at night, and he asked the lady where she lived. And [she] said, "Just right over here. There's a hogan over here. That's where I live."

     He picked her up and took her to that hogan, and they didn't get real close to the hogan. He just kind of left her off (she said that would be fine—just leaving her off by the side of the road). She had a jacket with her, and when he dropped her off at that hogan (or at the side of the road near that hogan), she left her jacket in the car. He tried to get her attention, but she just kept walking, so he said, "Oh well, I'll just bring it back the next day." So, he went back the next day to that place over there, to that hogan, and it was a *graveyard*. And that's where that person went.[228]

We made another field trip to Phoenix exactly a month later. Our first interviewee was a San Juan Pueblo Indian otitis media therapist. San Juan is one of the six Tewa-language Pueblo Indian villages located north of Santa Fe, New Mexico, in the Espanala Valley. The therapist told three stories of cultural identity as the first part of his interview:

❖   I feel that although I am an urban Indian, I do follow the traditional ways and beliefs of the San Juan tribes. I always feel that I can always go home and participate in the ceremonies that we have there. In a way it's kinda like going back and doing our part—sorta like doing our civic duty to our community.[229]

❖   Twenty years ago I sought the help of my medicine man at my village. It was more like maybe a problem of the spirit—something that—You could say that maybe I had witchcraft directed at me, and I needed their help.[230]

❖   I still—I *still*—believe in my traditional medicine, and I *still* carry safeguards. It's like a pouch with sacred Indian salt and some roots—herbs—

and charcoal. These three items or ingredients are supposed to be used to ward off any kind of evil spirits so I carry them, you know, in my vehicle because, well, there are people out there that have knowledge about witchcraft, and they can turn those things—you call it *power*—against you. Here, a long ways from the reservation, we don't think about it all the time; but they *could* still do something to you, those people that are practitioners of this belief. They have powers; they can do things to you even if you are in the city.[231]

The San Juan man's final three stories included insightful analyses of well-known Anglo-American, Mexican-American, and American Indian contemporary legends and their cultural provenances:

❖ I heard of a lady in Taos, New Mexico, who at a [fried-chicken restaurant] had a deep-fried rat in her food, and also about another place where a person's finger was in a pop bottle or something that was canned. I heard those when I was in the military. Stories about nasty things in food could be both Indian or Anglo, and they would have the same meaning.[232]

❖ There was a story where—in the South somewhere—this person was picked up. (Some of these are real fashionable stories I have heard secondhand, so let me say that this really happened to some people out there; it's not like reading it in a book.) Something happened in, let's see, the southeastern part of the United States around Alabama, northern Georgia, or somewhere around there. There was a young lady that was hitchhiking, I think, and was picked up by—was it a truck driver or a?—somebody picked her up (maybe it was a truck driver). [She] got in the seat beside them or maybe in the back, and they rode along, and then they turned around, and that person was gone—yeah! I think that story is more related with the Caucasian culture.[233]

❖ Being from north-central New Mexico, we have the Spanish people. We have a large Spanish-speaking population, and around April—around Lent right before Easter time—supposedly they see this person dressed in white—white clothes or a nice white suit, but he'll have hooves. And they'll see him there, and that's the story associated with northern New Mexico. The people there are very, very superstitious—the Spanish people—and he is supposed to represent the devil—evil.[234]

Like the Pima narrator who contributed stories, this San Juan man was interested in noting and describing the stories of other groups; like the Hopi narrator who told stories ultimately dependent upon Pima and Navajo tradition, he also was interested in performing them.

The Shoshoni American Indians are the most northerly located of the Shoshonean tribes who once occupied vast portions of Wyoming, Utah, Nevada, and Idaho in small, isolated family groups of eight to ten people.

Widely known for Lewis and Clark's helper, the woman Sacajawea, they now live as farmers and ranchers in Wyoming, Nevada, and Idaho.

The inability of Euro-American *and* tribal medicines to deal with some illnesses is the plot of the first story told by the Shoshoni Indian we interviewed next:

❖   I am Shoshoni, and I had a brother who had cancer of the throat. I guess he was like me; he didn't really believe in the medicine men. But after he had been treated by the doctors and everything, he wanted to try everything, you know, and he went to the medicine man, but the medicine man told him he couldn't do anything. He was too late.[235]

Her final story was a very brief performance of a version of the Anglo-American contemporary legend "The Pet in the Microwave," which appeared very amusing to her:

❖   When they first came out with the microwave, they said that this lady washed her little dog, I guess it was, and dried it [*laughs*] in the microwave![236]

During her interview the Shoshoni health-care professional told us there were two of her clients that she wished to have us interview because she felt they would add to our understanding of the problems facing urban American Indians.

The same pattern the Shoshoni woman had followed—performing a story of cultural identity, followed by a version of the Anglo-American contemporary legend "The Pet in the Microwave"—was repeated by a Hopi lady we interviewed the next day:

❖   I live here in Phoenix just like anybody else, but I can go home and live like my family does. I speak the language. I know the culture, and so I can go back and forth.[237]

❖   I read a story in the paper—I'm not too sure—I think it was in Philadelphia. This lady washed her cat and put it in the microwave. I'm not too sure. It might of been a dog.[238]

The Ute Indians once lived in the mountains and plains of Colorado, Utah, and northern New Mexico, carrying on an active trade with the Pueblo tribes. They now live on reservations in Utah and Colorado—or in cities like Phoenix, where our interviewee opened with two stories of cultural identity:

❖   I am a somewhat traditional Ute. When the Fourth of July comes around, there is a yearly powwow going on back home, and everybody is usually back there if they can. They go back there for vacations, and I do that. That's about the only time I really go back is when something like that is going on, so I can participate. I have also after having a baby kind of stuck to the old ways.[239]

❖　　　This year my son—I have a son—was getting all kinds of sickness. People said it was from the day-care, and I had to take him home for the Fourth of July. They do ceremonies for, you know, something like that, and I had to take him back because my grandmother and I are kind of close, and she says, "Bring him back, and we'll do a prayer for him." He's been better since, too. He had been catching a lot of—He had chicken pox twice, he's had pneumonia, he's had a lot of fevers in between, and he's only six months![240]

She followed her stories of cultural identity with a version of a well-known Anglo-American contemporary legend, which was set in Salt Lake City near her home reservation, and concluded with an acculturated version of "The Vanishing Hitchhiker" localized in her world:

❖　　　There is one incident that happened back home. Someone had gone to a [fried-chicken] place and found a rat in the barrel under the chicken. It wasn't fried; it was just a rat. This happened in Salt Lake. It was a cousin of ours that went, and she told us. They ordered it, but they didn't think the people put it in there. It must of just been set aside, and someways it got in—[241]

❖　　　I have friends that live down in Sacaton area, and I used to go visit them, and we'd set around and talk, and they'd tell me things like, "Don't be in the area when the night falls in this particular area" (it's by the side of a mountain) 'cause they'd heard other people telling them that this couple was down there one time, and this man was walking—no, it was a lady, in fact—and she was riding in the back, and the lady of the family had fallen asleep. The man was driving. He didn't know they had a hitchhiker.
　　　The lady goes, "Where did you pick her up?"
　　　And he goes, "Who?"
　　　They look, and she's setting back there, and they said, "Well, let's get someplace where we can get help." But when they got to where they were going, that person was gone! She was—A lot of people say she used to live on the reservation there, and something had happened. The people didn't like her or something, and a couple of guys had taken her out and raped her right in that spot where she keeps coming out. Recently we went there, and they told us it's still happening.[242]

Sacaton is like Dilkon in one very basic way: it is one of the places cited in traditional American Indian stories as a home of evil.

A HEAD FULL OF STORIES

The nineteen-year-old Standing Rock Sioux we interviewed next was employed as a maintenance worker at an American Indian health-service facility. The Sioux once lived throughout the northern plains and controlled this vast area by their military prowess. They are most famous among Anglo-Americans for defeating George Custer, and popular culture has based many of its stereotypes of American Indians upon the Sioux. Today, most of the Sioux live on reservations.

The Sioux storyteller began his interview by saying, "My head is full of stories," and he proceeded to prove his statement. The first two he told were stories of perceived cultural identity:

❖ I belong to the Standing Rock Sioux tribe. My father is traditional, and I have been through a period where—the best way I can explain it is this is my life. [*holds hands about two feet apart*] This much is traditional. [*moves hands closer together*] What it means to be traditional is to have all of the values of bravery, wisdom, and that sort of thing. Traditional values are for the four stages of life. You go through the learning process, bravery, wisdom, and finally I think is death—and then you pass on.[243]

❖ I have been treated for a growth on the back of my neck. We went through a ceremony which was—you know, I was fourteen years old, and it was incredible. It was a feeling I will never forget. The medicine man actually described what was wrong with me, and how this thing grew, and why it grew, and what the problem was, and when I went to the hospital to get it operated on to get it taken off (which wasn't really necessary but for cosmetic reasons), the doctors said the same thing. Which is one reason why I tend to sway toward the traditional. I've seen—I've seen things which make your hair stand up on the back of your neck.[244]

The next three stories he told reflected his Sioux world and beliefs even more directly:

❖ This story has surfaced and resurfaced through the generations in our tribe, and it is about a man that is hooved. There is this town—it says that he reappears because the town is being punished—and this little town is on the reservation on the Lewis and Clark Trail just a little ways off the highway. I'd say it is infamous for alcoholics, people that go by and stab each other—you know, things like that. Two years, three years ago when I was a sophomore in high school, this story resurfaced where this guy is a real good-looking Indian guy—wears a leather coat—and he hitchhikes, and you pick him up. You can hear him walk up to the car with his hooves, and you think he had boots on, and you give him a ride, or you get into an area where they say they have actually seen the hooves, and they say that he can like walk into people's homes. Was on the national news. I think Dan Rather said something about it. We have a town on the reservation called Little Eagle that got national[ly] famous for it due to the sightings. It's Satan.[245]

❖   Another one is a little man that lives in the ground near the town where I lived. This happened last year where he stole blankets off clotheslines and the place where all the teenagers go to park to have fun. He was said to live around the area, and we had been out looking for just an adventure type of thing, going looking for him, and they said it was bad luck to see such a thing. And my dad [*pauses for five seconds*], near where my dad is born there is a place whose name means "Bad Hollow." It looks like a piece of the Bad Hills stuck on the plain. It's a real beautiful place with a nice clear stream that goes through it. You can actually drink the water, and he says that there is a tribe of Indians about that high [*holds right index finger and thumb apart*], and it's real bad luck to see them.[246]

❖   In the 1930s local farmers and the mayor of a town took all the peace pipes from the Indians and burned them because the Indians were *seen* flying due to the power of the pipe. They seen people *fly* like thirty feet above the ground.[247]

In the early 1800s the Cherokee Indians were widely considered one of the most prosperous and progressive tribes in America; nonetheless, the tribe was forced to undergo the infamous forced march, The Trail of Tears, to the Indian Territory during the winter of 1838-39. Nearly a thousand members of the tribe—fewer by far than the number who died on the march—escaped to the Smoky Mountains in western North Carolina. The rest re-established the Cherokee Nation in Oklahoma and set up a successful society with its own schools and churches. In the late 1800s the federal government abolished the tribal government of the Oklahoma Cherokee and opened most of this land, as well, to white settlement.

The elderly Cherokee lady we interviewed in her home was a client of an Indian health-service organization rather than a health-care professional, and she was one person the insightful Shoshoni interviewee said we should meet. We were glad we had taken the advice. She told a poignant story of cultural identity lost and regained as the first story of her interview:

❖   I am Cherokee. My father was full blood, so that makes me half. I came to Phoenix in '42, and living the way I was, I had little to do with Indian affairs. I have never been to a medicine man. My husband passed away four years ago (he was white), but I'm getting in the Indian Senior Citizens Center here, and I feel like there's something to live for. I'm glad I am Indian. I just got lost. When I went out to the center, they said, "Where have you been all these years?" I wish I knew; I just got lost.[248]

Her second story illustrated a widespread American Indian belief about the eagle. It is interesting that some tribes view this bird as a harbinger of death while many more cast the owl in the same role:

❖   My daughter lives in Mesa, my oldest daughter, and her next-door neighbor was dying, was very ill and dying, and they sat up at night. They had a porch swing outside, and that night before he died a *big* [*drawn out*] eagle came and flew down. My daughter said, "Oh, that's a sign of death," and it wasn't two minutes till that man's wife come and said he was dead. An eagle is always the sign of death.[249]

Her third story further developed the themes of alienation and return:

❖   All through high school and all through Arizona till I came to Phoenix, I went by my Indian name. It's Cherokee, means "hummingbird." Then when I went to work down here for the state, people says, "Don't you have another name?" They thought my Indian name was so hard. So that's when I started going by Mary, but down at the Indian center there's this girl who knew me before I ever married (she's one of the volunteers down at the center now). She told them my real name and said, "I've known her before she ever married, and her sister and I was the very best of friends." (She is an Arizona Indian; she's Pima.) And years ago I don't remember, but I used to be a very thin person, and she sat down there and told them (now, there's no truth in them, but this is what she told them). She said, "The town where we used to live was a very small town, and she was the prettiest girl up there." And she said, "She was slender," and she turned to me, "Do you have any pictures?" I could have crowned her![250]

The story is a complicated story within a story made particularly meaningful by the widespread Indian emphasis upon the sanctity and power of names. According to many American Indian cultures, to take away people's names is to degrade and enslave them.

Her final story was a classic death story of the sort people cross-culturally tell in the face of loss:

❖   The Lord took the good away early. He died right here. My diabetes was acting up. I was awfully tired. We always set up and watched the news together, but I told him, "Honey, I'm so tired I'm going to bed."

He said, "That's all right."

I can't use this arm. I fell, and I had to have surgery on this arm. So I said, "I need help to get this blouse off."

He helped me, and he said, "I'm going to watch the news, and I'll be right to bed."

I went in, and I guess I really was tired, 'cause that was ten o'clock, and at twenty-five till two I woke up. Being a diabetic, I had to go to the bathroom, and there he lay on the floor dead.[251]

The young Pima girl who was our last interviewee was also a client suggested by the Shoshoni counselor rather than a health professional, and we also visited her at a home. She began with a clear, though only loosely narrative, statement of her sense of tradition:

❖   I have two weeks in the ninth grade, and then quit because I didn't like school. I am Pima, but I have lived in Phoenix all my life. I don't know much of anything about Pima tradition; I've never taken much interest in it.[252]

Next she told the story of her personal tragedy—her baby's injury and the dire legal consequences:

❖   About a year and a half ago, I was at work, and my son was home with my husband (my son was only about five months old) and was getting to a stage to where he would climb up on things. He was in his crib, and he climbed up on the rail and wasn't quite able to stand very good; and he let go and fell back, and he had a *solid* oak crib and hit his head, and that's what caused it to, to bleed inside. He was in the hospital for about a month, and then a couple weeks after that happened the state, they said we were abusive parents, you know, that we didn't take care of him and all of that—
        Well, I was only sixteen when he was born, and I didn't know much about babies, and so they decided that he would be better off in state custody, and so they've had him ever since. He's been going to therapy and everything, and when they used to bring him to visit me, the therapist used to come over, and I'd do some of the things she taught me to do with him. I guess I haven't seen him in about three months, and that's about it really. [*sobs*] They told me he was going to be mentally retarded, but there's no signs of it. He lives with a foster family in another town, as far as I know, but I don't get to see him.
        I have another son; he's a year old.[253]

The account was as compelling as the Cherokee lady's story of her husband's death and was clearly motivated by a similar sense of loss, sorrow, and need to narrate. Her final story was a performance of the traditional Pima account of the man with hooves, which she remembered only vaguely and could no longer experience traditionally:

❖   My mom, she always told me about this story. On your way to the reservation, there's a mountain (they call it Devil Mountain), and they said there is a man with hooves, and he is supposed to be the devil. They say there was a man that went there over fifty years ago. (It was when mom and dad were young.) He went in there and sold his soul to the Devil, and after he made a deal with him or something. They didn't see him after that. It is really strange![254]

We attempted to contact the Pima lady again a few weeks later, and she had vanished. She had been baby-sitting for a neighbor the night we interviewed her, and the neighbor said she had left the housing complex, and no one had any idea where she had gone.

She was our final interviewee as a part of our funded research project. Thirteen interviewees, ten tribes, fifty-five stories, and she was the only one who presented herself by her conversation and her stories in a less than positive way. Of the two interviewees who were clients rather than professionals, one who was lost has been found; but the other remains lost somewhere in the gap between the worlds—and, in some way at some level, it is destroying her. She is fulfilling the awful stereotype of urban American Indians deeply ingrained in Anglo-American folklore and popular culture: people who—like the urban Pima deprived of her son—have lost their way and live spiritually and physically bankrupt existences on the fringes of Anglo-American society, or—as is in the first story we were told—are crushed emotionally or physically by moving away from their families and cultures.

Yet the vast majority of the men and women we interviewed are highly trained health-care professionals and counselors living in upper-middle-class Anglo-American culture in terms of education, income, and social status. They have succeeded in the white man's world in the white man's way, and they have done so by retaining their tribal identities, awareness, and respect for traditional ways and beliefs. The vast majority (in the words of one) "go back and forth" from Anglo-American culture to their tribal worlds, ceremonies, and stories. As a group, they are unusually intelligent, open people with a highly polished ability to communicate cross-culturally (many do so professionally) and an interest in sharing their cultures and their lives with others who are interested. The main tool they employ to communicate cross-culturally is *storytelling*. Many of them have an analytical interest in the stories of other cultures—including Anglo-American contemporary legends. Some also have an interest in performing these stories of other cultures, but they often set or interpret them—including Anglo-American contemporary legends—within the cultural or geographic context of their own cultures.

These are the stories we collected in formal interviews with urban American Indians—initially strangers to us. Some are complete and polished by tellings. Some are fragmentary. Many have great depth and power. And all provide their narrators a way to present themselves and their concerns, to entertain, to instruct, to communicate the dangers of the gap between the worlds, to proclaim that tradition is the way which leads safely back and forth across this gap.

Such is the power of communication by storytelling.

CHAPTER SEVEN

The Untranslatable

IT *IS* INTERESTING! The nature of culture, stories, and storytelling shines forth through and from the 250 American Indians' stories re-created thus far in the book and the one which is to follow in this chapter. Walt Disney Technicolor Mickey Mouse sand paintings, grandfather horned toad jokes, satellite television, Catholic and Protestant Christianity, New Age crystals, the continuing dance, the people who are still the people, tradition leading safely back and forth between worlds. From all these: the nature of performance.

These 251 stories told by American Indians in conversations or interviews include contemporary legends, jokes, and personal-experience stories, and they demonstrate that each culture has its own *unspoken* traditions as to what kinds of conversational stories are accepted and preferred.

Most of the conversational stories Kuiceyetsa, Helen, and other Zunis told were personal-experience stories—direct, personal accounts of what it means to be Zuni.

The Ramah Navajo are expert in telling jokes and legends, and Clyde was the most studied and successful of all the Ramah Navajo storytellers we interviewed. He was a master: his culture offered him storytelling as a desirable skill, and he excelled at it. He loved telling stories to an appreciative audience, and he told Ramah Navajo legends and jokes extremely well—indirect, fictive accounts of what it means to be Ramah Navajo.

Other traditions govern what kinds of conversational stories are appropriate and desirable among other American Indian groups because cross-culturally, conversational stories—always traditional in performance and often traditional in content—are a major means of communication in small groups.

All these American Indians' stories—direct and indirect accounts of realities, conversational stories, kitchen-table stories—include, involve, and are that which is told, how it is told, and the cultures evinced by their telling.

The actual telling—the performance—of conversational stories is a complex, unspoken, ongoing dialogue between audience and storyteller marked by false starts, silences, connections, understandings, communication. Conversational stories of the the nonhuman, in particular, are powerful, difficult, even dangerous dialogues precisely because they evoke the nonhuman and timeless—what Jung termed *the Other.* Tellers of such stories call forth, in the poet Yeats's words, "a World where Time is not."

Carl Jung came from Vienna to Taos, New Mexico, and spent some time experiencing what it meant to be a Taos American Indian. The experience profoundly affected his view of reality and suggested the challenge of fully grasping it. "Such a consciousness," Jung wrote, "would see the becoming and the passing away of things simultaneously with their momentary existence in the present, and not only that, it would also see what [the Other] was before their becoming and will be after their passing hence."

The Other defines the human. And for Southwestern Indians, conversational stories frequently are told to involve the audience in affirming, experiencing, and—perhaps to some extent—in controlling the Other.

One of the first American Indian stories of the Other we recorded was told by a Navajo lady who powerfully and chillingly evinced her culture. She said that she considered herself to be a very traditional Navajo; I consider her story to be a very traditional Navajo contemporary legend:

❖   There's the lady who was noticed among the singers at a Squaw Dance singing, so this man went over and asked her if, you know, could take her some place, and so she went, and when they got there where they were going, she disappeared.
    She didn't talk.
    Her tracks were the tracks of a coyote along side the man's tracks.[255]

The telling of this Navajo contemporary legend involves a three-part structure, plus silence. "There's the lady" is one of the introductory formulas frequently employed to indicate (or key) Navajo storytelling.

Soon there develops a sense of movement within the narration—much like the sense of motion in Navajo speech and ceremony.

The first section of the story begins with an expletive, moves to a passive verb, moves to an active verb, uses four verbs indicating motion in quick succession, and concludes with the story's climax skillfully preceded by a doubled statement of location, "When they got there where they were going, she disappeared."
There is a pause.
Then there is a short section with an active verb.
There is another pause.

The pause is followed by the conclusion using a verb of being but an adverbial indicator of motion.

The dance is a Squaw Dance—a part of the Enemy Way Ceremony designed to restore wholeness, or *hozho,* to the entire audience as well as to the individual for whom it is held. It is also seen as a time of possible danger because so many strangers are brought together at night. *Yee naaldlooshii,* skinwalkers—witches who wear animal skins and travel about at night—and *ch'iidii,* ghosts—the evil part of the spirit of a dead person—are more difficult to avoid at this time because of the large number of strangers who are present at the ceremony.

The Squaw Dance is a major social event of the Navajo summer season, and there are published stories describing it:

❖   The activities for which the ceremony is popularly named has nothing to do with the ritual being performed and is entirely social. The returning of warriors in the past was seen as a good time to announce the readiness of young women for marriage. These young unmarried women, dressed in their best clothing and displaying their wealth in turquoise and silver, appeared each night to select partners to join them in a simple shuffling dance. The primacy of women in Navajo life is again reflected in the etiquette of the dance. No young man, once selected, can refuse to dance with a girl unless he can prove that he is a member of the girl's or some other ineligible clan. Should a man refuse, the girl's mother, aunts, and older sisters may well descend upon him and drag him into the center of the circle of wagons and campfires that forms each night. If a young man does not want to carry the affair further, he must make some small payment at the end of the dance. Should he refuse to pay, he binds the young woman to be his partner through the rest of the dance. If she has second thoughts about her choice, she is trapped unless she can steal his hat, blanket, or some other possession and ransom it, thus receiving the payment necessary to free her.[256]

❖   A few girls, making their first appearance, may be shy and must be encouraged by their mothers; but, watching, one understands fully the independent, not to say dominant, position of the Navajo matron, who is truly a matriarch.

The woman approaches the man, standing resistant among his friends, links her right arm into his so that they face in opposite directions, and pulls him into the circle. Then they dance, up and down and back and forth, to the short staccato beat of the chanting voices. That is all; but it is quite enough to define the position of the lady. Sternly, firmly, relentlessly she holds him. Where she goes, he goes. She may seem to pay no attention to her particular quarry; facing away from him gives her a fine impersonal air. She goes forward while he goes back; when she backs up, he goes forward; but always when she goes, he follows. There is no escape. It is lady's night, and no mistake.[257]

These published stories show the considerable power of women in Navajo culture at its zenith—and this was the point of Clyde's traditional Navajo jest that someone who has moved to an area from far away "must have met his wife at a Squaw Dance." A Navajo man is expected to assist his wife's family in many ways. He, in turn, expects to be assisted by his family and *is*—unless his family lives far away. The jest reflects the fact that Squaw Dances are a time when men may be entrapped and risk having to move away from their families and outfits to a situation with more culturally mandated responsibilities and fewer privileges.

But beyond that, the Ramah Navajo lady's powerful story uses the Squaw Dance for a crucial purpose. By naming it as the setting, she calls into play a rich complex of cultural beliefs against which the story moves. The Squaw Dance, as her Navajo listeners would know, is a time the Other walks among the people.

There is a pause.

A line follows: "She didn't speak." This calls into play another cluster of cultural beliefs. Neither *yee naaldlooshii* nor *ch'iidii* speak because to do so would assert their humanity and cause them to reveal their true forms.

There is another pause. Tension builds.

The narrator adds the final shock: "Her tracks were the tracks of a coyote along side the man's tracks."

Coyote is, among other things, the animal figure in Navajo stories most often assumed by *yee naaldlooshii* and *ch'iidii,* and this poor person has "gone with" coyote. Now, that's contamination!

Then there is silence. The story has successfully invoked the Navajo Other in the shadows of the room; chills run up and down the spines of the narrator and the audience.

And that takes us back to a conversational legend performance of two Hopi stories about the appearance of strangers who are found not to be human at a dance. The dramatic storyteller characterized herself as a traditional Hopi and explained, "Even though I live in Phoenix, I follow [Hopi] traditions and chains of command." Her telling of the stories was both more animated and interactive than the text itself can convey:

❖   Usually at the time when these things happen, it's usually during our bean dance time, and some of the Kachinas that came around to dance inside the kivas, they were all—well, some of them had come in and were inside the kiva dancing and some of them either got too tired or whatever, and they were just kind of looking in and watching. And they were all kinda laying on top of the kiva like this [*uses hands by face to show their position*] they and all had blankets over them 'cause it was really cold. You know, they didn't notice people around them; they were just laying there kind of looking in, and then they noticed this one figure laying next to them, and he had a blanket over his head, and they were all looking in, so they were kinda—they start talking among themselves and somebody turned around and to say something to this other guy, and he wouldn't answer. They looked around and they asked him, they said, "Who *are* you?" And whoever or whatever it was, I guess, when he turned and looked at them—whatever expression or whatever facial features he has was not one of them, and then he got up and just took off running, and they started chasing him. See, this was at Walpi, and if you look at Walpi, there's a trail that goes all the way to the end, and then there's rock steps that go down, and that's where the Kachinas go. And he took off running towards that way, and they start chasing him and all of a sudden he just disappeared. You know, there was nothing. They just couldn't see him or find him or anything. So they all got, you know, really worked up, and they came back, and they started passing the word, and that kind of upset a lot of people. It's usually—you know—if people don't live their lives right, they say that It comes back and reminds them, you know, that they're straying away from what—the way that they're supposed to be. And—[258]

❖   I know my oldest sister—a—on two occasions she's said she's actually seen it. She knows that people don't—she says she *knows* that, "People don't believe me," she said, "but I saw it." See, when we—they were younger, they used to play hide and go seek, but they would play hide and go seek with a drum, and everybody else had to try to find the drummer, so the drummer would run, and then he'd beat the drum, and then they'd all take off towards the sound, and they were doing this up there, and this person that they were chasing was not the person that they were playing with, and then they chased him all the way to the end, and when they finally caught up, she said it was just—it wasn't a very tall man, but he had like a deerskin, a buckskin, the white ones that are already tan, tied here like this [*puts her hands on her shoulder*], and it just hung down and nothing on underneath it, just this deerskin tied like that—was barefoot and had something on its head—and he just kind of stood there and kind of humped [*leans forward*] over at them and kind of jumped his feet real fast like this [*prances in place with her feet while slapping her knees with her hands quickly*], beat the drum and took off, and they all stood there looking at him like that, and he just—they never saw it after that. And that was during ceremonial time, too, so—
        I think a lot of times—I don't think he's really hurt—I don't think he really hurts anybody, but he's not someone that you want to deal with. You hope you never see him is how you should think about it. My sister was real bad at that time, too![259]

The performance includes two stories. The first tells of dancers dis-covering a stranger watching a ceremony with them. The dancers chase the figure to the end of a protrusion on the mesa, and he disappears. They "pass the word"; a lot of people are upset.

The second story tells of children playing Hopi hide-and-seek and discovering that they were following an "it"—a figure dressed only in a buckskin and carrying a drum. They all stand looking at him, and he jumps his feet at them and runs away.

The telling of these stories is marked by the skillful employment of many linguistic and paralinguistic features. The performer not only varies the pitch, dynamics, tempo, and stress; she also makes extensive use of gestures and replicates the sound of the man "jumping his feet at them" by prancing in place and slapping her hands on her knees. There is a sort of breathless urgency and rapid overall tempo to the performance resulting from the unusually high percentage of one- and two-syllable words and the long compound units between major pauses. The next to the last concluding unit in the first plot, for example, contains thirty-five words, and only three of them have more than two syllables.

The storytelling invokes "bean dance" time—one of the many multi-faceted Hopi dances characteristic of her complex culture. Although it does involve bean-seed-planting, the bean dance actually is an eight-day ceremony with many visitations of supernatural figures bringing many warnings and messages urging fidelity to the Hopi way. Witch figures threaten and punish children who have been "bad." Every fourth year, an initiation takes place as children are whipped by the "flogger" Kachina and then see that he and the other Kachinas are masked people.

In general, the bean dance is a time of demands from the Other for "living right." In distinct contrast with the impersonal Other of the Navajo contemporary legend, the Hopi Other is a recognizable individual who has a name. He is *Maasaw*, a major figure of Hopi contemporary legends and religion, as complex and multifaceted as Hopi culture itself. Maasaw is the God of Death and the Giver of Life and is portrayed in contemporary Hopi stories as both ridiculous and sublime. He is believed to have given the Earth to the Hopi to care for until he reclaims it, and their Hopi premillennial eschatology and sense of stewardship influences their relationships with themselves, with Maasaw, and with other people.

The Hopi woman's contemporary legend begins with a dazzling linguistic and paralinguistic performance that transports the audience immediately to a story world. Then follows the gradual unfolding of a general, nonspecific plot with a general, nonspecific warning.

The storyteller pauses expectantly.

Silence clusters around the word *and.*

The performer judges the listeners' reactions and decides that they have passed the test. Then the story continues its breathless headlong rush by beginning a second plot with a personal story highlighting family and friends.

There is another silence clustering after *so,* and the audience must mentally supply the missing fact that the appearance was a warning. This dialogue between storyteller and audience also leads listeners to identify the Other as Maasaw, and thus brings into play the complex belief system concerning this complex figure.

A sense of the need for repentance and right living fills the room.

WHEN THERE WAS A DANCE

Because we thought these stories offered such fascinating dialogues, Kathy called Kuiceyetsa to ask if *she* had ever heard a story of a dancer who disappeared. Kuiceyetsa said that she had heard the story when she was a child and would try to recall it for us. Several months later when we were visiting with her, two of her daughters, and six of her grandchildren, Kuiceyetsa told us the story she had remembered:

❖ Oh, Oh. How shall I start it?

I was told long time ago that um—the people from the Zuni heaven, the ones that died, the spirits, they used to come to the Village of Zuni when there was a dance—to join in with the group that was dancing the ceremonial dance. And a—and then there were some ladies, young ladies, who fell in love with dancers, and when they left—they followed them, one of them followed—a—this one dancer, and he was not—a—he was a, had been dead, but—a— he went back to Zuni heaven, and, and the girl followed—and— they told her that they could not accept her there, to let her—a—stay there with them, but they instructed her to come to Zuni—and tell her relatives, her brothers, to prepare prayer sticks, and then in four days if she still cared to come—that—a—they could receive her then, but she had to go back to Zuni and—get herself ready and and tell her—relatives—what to do—and her relatives asked her if she, if that's what she really wanted to do, and she said she wanted to. —So they prepared prayer sticks and—a—and on the fourth day in the morning, they found her dead. —So they planted the prayer sticks asking for—a—a flight, a safe flight, to where she was going, that she was not to bother—them with her—a——sigh—or anything that—a—she used to do when she was still alive, when she was still alive,—so—that's the way I heard it—told, and then this day our parents used to tell us when the dancers go home,—to where they are—a—staying, a—we are never to follow behind them because if we wanted a longer life, we would refrain from doing this thing.

I am sure—I think that is how it was told to me.[260]

The plot of Kuiceyetsa's story is that a young lady fell in love with a dancer at a Zuni dance, followed him, discovered he was a spirit, and was instructed to return to Zuni and have her relatives perform certain rites if she wished to live with the dancer. She and her relatives followed their instructions, and she died and went to live with the spirit. The story ends with the statement that *that* is why people are not to follow the dancers, and Kuiceyetsa explained later that the story also tells why spirits can no longer be seen as they participate in the Zuni dances.

Kuiceyetsa's telling of her conversational story is marked by a straightforward delivery. She makes special use of pauses, formulas, and appeals to tradition—all in all a very carefully measured performance.

As Zuni storytellers reveal in their stories, Zuni dance is yearlong and lifelong. All Zunis are expected to participate as sponsors, dancers, helpers, or audience members. Almost all Zunis believe that the spirits of the dead and the supernaturals participate in the dances, though only mediums will be able to see them. Zunis, by and large, take quiet pleasure in their culture and ceremonies. This feeling of one mind when the people come together at dances is highly cherished.

Kuiceyetsa begins her story with a question: "Oh, Oh. How shall I start it?" echoing the traditional narrative framing employed in formal Zuni-language storytelling.

There is a pause during which the audience acknowledges the transition into the Zuni story world.

The storytelling continues with another formulaic meta-narrative ascription making doubly sure that a transition has been made into a Zuni story world of spirits and dances.

Her mention of a dance without specifying *which* dance also serves to involve the imagination of the listeners. People are called to remember the many Zuni dances they have attended with Kuiceyetsa and to recollect the dance images of power and beauty that have been most meaningful to them.

The story proceeds at a slow, measured pace with many pauses—particularly long ones as the narrator seems to search for English equivalents for Zuni ethnocentric concepts. These pauses serve to involve the audience ever deeper in the narrative, and the story moves forward with a calm unfolding of its plot through the many references to cultural details and the authority of the past. (Cushing even wrote in the late nineteenth century that the main purpose of Zuni storytelling was to present ethnographic detail and ethnographic etiologies.)

The performance ends with two more meta-narrative assertions which emphasize that the story and the storytelling have been true to Zuni culture.

There is a pause. Audience and performer feel their hearts strangely warmed. The Zuni conversational story has taught a rule of behavior at ceremonial activities and has explained the sweet reasonableness of the rule by calling forth a Zuni Other that is not frightening but familiar and kindly and exists among and in the service of the living.

Kuiceyetsa's story is a prayer and a parable. The Ko-ko are the Ko-ko, the Zuni Other; Maasaw is Maasaw, the Hopi Other; and the nameless Navajo Other is that that it is. All these Others are evinced in American Indians' conversational stories, but they are not translated because they cannot be translated.

Although the Other cannot be translated, it can be shared, can be experienced. Telling stories of a world re-creates and empowers that world anew. American Indians' conversational stories are told precisely because they are that which they tell, how they tell it, and the cultures they evince. To know and understand something of American Indians' conversational stories, no matter how imperfect the knowledge, is to know and understand something of what it means to be Apache, Cherokee, Hopi, Ramah Navajo, Osage, Pima, San Juan, Shoshoni, Sioux, Ute, Zuni.

To know …

To dream …

On one of our many unsuccessful trips to see the Ramah Navajo medicine man, Clyde told Kathy and me about a psychoanalytic theorist from Germany whom he had assisted with his inquiries. The man had come to Ramah area—much as Jung had earlier gone to Taos—to see other realities. He asked Clyde to tell him what he had dreamed, and he wrote Clyde's dreams all down in a little book. Clyde commented, "That professor sure was interested in dreams."

I don't know who that professor was or whether he ever published anything about Ramah (others in the area tell stories about his visit, too, by the way), but I think of him whenever I have this one dream every month or two weeks.

The place is different from dream to dream. Sometimes Kathy and I are walking along the rock paintings of the Zuni dance figures on the cliffs. Sometimes Kathy and I are seated at a very large, circular table in a boundless Kuiceyetsa's kitchen.

The people in the dream differ from version to version. Kuiceyetsa, and Helen, Clyde, and Mrs. Flores are almost always in the dream—together or separately. Mr. Lopez and his chickens are often in the dream—by themselves, or with the American Indians we came to know in Phoenix.

The predominant sound is not the same in all the dreams. Sometimes I feel the high-pitched, non-human chanting of the Yeii dancers in my bones. Sometimes the sounds of Mid-summer Dance permeate my being.

The actions which occur in the dream are different, too. Sometimes someone is telling stories in Navajo or some kind of language and Clyde is translating. Most often, however, all of us are living stories together, and talking together—and eating together—and laughing together.

The setting, characters, predominant sound, and actions differ from dream to dream, but it is *one* dream for always there is a feeling of joy and peace; there is a sense of the interconnectedness of all things; there is an ongoing, pulsating, endlessly rushing, whirring sound; and—there is the light: always we are all surrounded by a softly glowing circle of iridescent golden light growing ever wider, glowing ever brighter as it spirals counterclockwise around us.

Notes

These notes are designed to give further information about the stories in the book, their collection, and their storytellers. The first sentence of each indicates the age, gender, and tribal affiliation of the person who told the story and when and where it was collected. Following that is more information or a discussion of the story.

If the story contains folktale motifs included in Ernest W. Baughman's *Type and Motif-Index of the Folktales of England and America* or Stith Thompson's *Motif-Index of Folk Literature*—the standard indexes of narrative elements in folk literature used by folklorists to annotate folktales in order to demonstrate their existence and distribution within tradition—their numbers are cited at the conclusion of the note.

Baughman's numbers are cited first, and Thompson's numbers are given if Baughman does not list parallel material. Since American Indians' stories in general—and the conversational stories which constitute the bulk of the stories in this book in particular—are very much underrepresented in these indexes, numbers cited do not fully indicate historical or spatial relationships.

Four Anglo-American contemporary legends included in chapter 3 and forty-six Navajo jokes in chapter 5 were collected and recorded by Northern Arizona University students (these are indicated by the letters "SC" after the place and date collected). Two descriptions of Navajo Squaw Dances included in chapter 7 were written by previous researchers and are so noted. The remaining 198 American Indians' stories in the book were recorded and transcribed by Keith and/or Kathryn Cunningham.

A number of interview texts have been shortened for this book by the publisher. Any additions—annotations and words not actually spoken by the storytellers—appear in brackets. Among the stories presented and analyzed exactly as transcribed are several performance texts, numbered 81 (255), 205 (258), 206 (259), and 260. Complete interview transcriptions for all stories are available from the author.

CHAPTER 1
1. Thirty-year-old Zuni woman interviewed at Zuni, New Mexico, September 29, 1984.

As noted in the introduction, the heart and soul of this book is a series of 251 American Indian stories—including this one—collected and transcribed to allow the storytellers to speak for themselves in their own voices. We conducted a series of tape-recorded interviews with American Indians over a five-year period, identified the stories on the field tapes by close listening in terms of their performance and unity, transcribed them word for word as they were told, and then attempted to interpret and explain them in such a way that they could be experienced by a non-American Indian audience.

This first note is an ideal place to discuss the very important question of naming. All storytellers, as required by the funding agencies which supported the basic research and collecting, are either not named at all or are identified by pseudonyms. The general name "American Indian" is used in the book rather than any of the many alternatives which have been suggested because the vast majority of the people interviewed indicated that it was the term they preferred.

This story is interesting in that Helen began with a discussion of "health problems" in very general terms and then moved to a story of her "uncle's wife." It is also interesting to note that in this story and in real life—as contrasted to motif indexes—paralysis is not seen as a punishment for breaking a taboo.

2. Thirty-year-old Zuni woman interviewed at Zuni, New Mexico, September 29, 1984.

Dennis Tedlock, whose research concerning the performance of Zuni language formal stories is highly regarded by narrative scholars, identified four kinds or types of Zuni stories: parts of the origin story which can be told at any time of day or in any season, tales which are told only at night and during winter, less formal accounts of recent history, and stories of personal experiences (*Spoken Word*, 159-60). Most of the English-language Zuni stories included in this book are informal stories of recent history and personal experience.

3. Thirty-year-old Zuni woman interviewed at Zuni, New Mexico, September 29, 1984.

Helen's second story about Angel's health is much more fully developed than the two brief, almost elliptical stories in her first answer because it is a response to a direct, specific question about a member of her family.

This story shows a major difference between the formal Zuni language stories Tedlock collected and informal English-language Zuni stories. Tedlock noted his stories tended to use extensive "keying"—a term used in recent narrative research to describe the ways conversation is transformed into storytelling—involving extremely elaborate tags and audience response. He stated that the need for framing may well be proportional to the extent to which the enclosed narration departs from what the audience accepts as reality (*Spoken Word*, 160–64). The fact that these stories do not depart from what the teller accepts as reality may, in turn, explain the fact that they so seldom use formal keys of any kind.

One of the questions with which folklore research has long struggled is traditionality. It is my contention that this story—and all the stories in this book—are traditional in performance and often in form. Helen's mother-in-law had told us the story of the time Angel had pneumonia and had carefully ascribed the story to Helen. Helen, in turn, responded with the story instantly and easily when Kathy asked her to tell it to us. The story is one which Helen has clearly told often enough that it has become one of the stories which she traditionally tells and has assumed a standard form. Furthermore, the Zuni traditional, cultural, narrative-performance aesthetic is implicit in this story, governing its telling and reflecting traditional Zuni beliefs and values.

The belief that certain illnesses are caused by witches magically inducing foreign objects into the human body has been widespread in the history of the world. Helen's concern that her children may have been witched reflects an observation Matilda Coxe Stevenson made a century ago that "Young mothers especially are solicitous for their infants, since these are the targets for the venom of diabolical beings" (*The Zuni Indians,* 392).

The motif numbers applicable to this story are G263.4, "Witch causes sickness"; D700, "Person disenchanted."

4. Thirty-year-old Zuni woman interviewed at Zuni, New Mexico, September 29, 1984.

Worldwide belief among those cultures which acknowledge witchcraft often includes ways of preventing being witched, and this story shows that the Zuni are no exception.

Motif number G272, "Protection against witches," seems to apply to this story, but the specific protections mentioned in the motif index do not include either arrowheads or crystals.

5. Thirty-year-old Zuni woman interviewed at Zuni, New Mexico, September 29, 1984.

Once a subject has been raised in communication in small groups, stories often lead to more stories on the same or related topics.

6. Thirty-year-old Zuni woman interviewed at Zuni, New Mexico, September 29, 1984.

The description of a witch as a longhaired young man is common at Zuni and is in marked contrast with the familiar Anglo-American Halloween figure.

Motif numbers are G263.4, "Witch causes sickness"; G219.4, "Witch with very long hair"; D700, "Person disenchanted."

7. Thirty-year-old Zuni woman interviewed at Zuni, New Mexico, September 29, 1984.

It is particularly interesting that the motif indexes do not include either a white face as a characteristic of a witch or witches causing illness by touching their victim; both are certainly common in Zuni stories. Parsons wrote in her article "Notes on Zuni" that a man was accused of witchcraft in the 1890s because his face was painted gray with ashes (270).

Motif number is G263.4, "Witch causes sickness."

8. Thirty-year-old Zuni woman interviewed at Zuni, New Mexico, September 29, 1984.

This story provides a rather complete description of how a Zuni medicine man cures witch-induced illnesses.

Motif numbers are G263.4, "Witch causes sickness"; D700, "Person disenchanted."

9. Thirty-year-old Zuni woman interviewed at Zuni, New Mexico, September 29, 1984.

This story gives further information about what Zunis believe is in the bundles witches use to cause illness.

Motif numbers are G263.4, "Witch causes sickness"; G262.4, "Witch kills with aid of witch-ball (hair rolled in beeswax)"; D991.3, "Magic ball of hair"; D2070.1, "Magic hair-ball used for witching"; D1274.1, "Magic conjuring bag. Filled with nail pairings, human hair, feet of toads, and the like"; D700, "Person disenchanted."

10. Thirty-year-old Zuni woman interviewed at Zuni, New Mexico, September 29, 1984.

When Kathy asked Franklin to describe the sickness he had when he was witched by the horse, he told her, "When my mom would tell me to clean up, I would get real mad and be rude and stuff like that."

Motif numbers are G263.4, "Witch causes sickness"; G211.1.1, "Witch in form of horse"; D700, "Person disenchanted."

CHAPTER 2

Portions of the materials included in chapter 2 originally were a part of an article we published in *The World & I.* This article appeared in the December 1990 issue and is reprinted with permission from *The World & I,* a publication of *The Washington Times Corporation,* copyright (c) 1990.

11. Seventy-two-year-old Zuni woman interviewed April 19, 1990.

If infant diarrhea is not controlled, it can rather quickly lead to severe dehydration and death. The syndrome is one of the leading causes of infant morality in many parts of the world and once was so at Zuni. The teller of this story is Kuiceyetsa, Helen's mother.

12. Thirty-year-old Zuni woman interviewed at Zuni, New Mexico, May 17, 1985.

Helen attributes her use of Jello water to treat infant diarrhea to her mother and describes another home remedy she learned from her grandmother. It is interesting, however, that she reports using the Jello water alone rather than in conjunction with the Hopi medicine her mother used.

13. Thirty-five-year-old Zuni woman interviewed at Zuni, New Mexico, May 31, 1985.

There are illnesses which are culturally specific—Mexican-American *susto,* or fright, for instance—and can only be treated by culturally specific therapies. Zuni fright is another example of such a culturally defined illness and cure.

Motif number is W121.8, "Illness from fear." There are motifs listed for burning cut hair to prevent witchcraft (D2176.5.) and to lay a ghost to rest (E446.2.1.), but there is no motif number for burning cut hair to cure fright.

14. Thirty-year-old Zuni woman interviewed at Zuni, New Mexico, May 17, 1985.

This finely crafted story is much more dramatic and complete than the one on the same theme which proceeds it, but it is intelligible to a non-Zuni audience only because of the more complete explanation contained in the first story.

Motif number is W121.8, "Illness from fear."

15. Seventy-five-year-old Hopi-Tewa woman interviewed at Zuni, New Mexico, May 16, 1985.

The first line of this story is—as is typical of many performed Zuni conversational stories—its major point. The topic and meaning of Zuni conversational stories are often announced at the beginning of a performance.

16. Fifty-one-year-old Zuni man interviewed at Zuni, New Mexico September 29, 1984.

17. Thirty-year-old Zuni woman interviewed at Zuni, New Mexico, May 17, 1985.

Helen's story of the little white girl whose broken arm was cared for by a Zuni bone presser supports the value of the native therapy and is a narrative she has obviously polished by frequent tellings.

18. Thirty-year-old Zuni woman interviewed at Zuni, New Mexico, May 17, 1985.

Helen's story about being treated by her bone presser is loaded with ethnographic details (researchers from Cushing to Tedlock have noted that a major function of Zuni narrative is to explain the Zuni way) and also—viewed with the wisdom of hindsight—served to raise the idea that bone pressing is of use in treating back problems.

19. Thirty-year-old Zuni woman interviewed at Zuni, New Mexico, May 17, 1985.

20. Seventy-four-year-old Zuni man interviewed at Zuni, New Mexico, December 14, 1986.

Just two short sentences are enough for the bone presser to tell *his* story which establishes his professional credentials.

21. Seventy-four old Zuni man interviewed at Zuni, New Mexico, December 14, 1986.

The story of the arrowhead told—and the arrowhead shown—further demonstrates and validates the credentials of the bone presser.

Motif number is D849.8, "Magic object found on ground."

22. Thirty-year-old Zuni woman interviewed at Zuni, New Mexico, May 17, 1985.

Cats have often been associated with witches at Zuni not as familiars but as one of the animal forms witches are most likely to assume.

Motif number is G211.1.7, "Witch in form of cat."

23. Thirty-year-old Zuni woman interviewed at Zuni, New Mexico, May 17, 1985.

Stevenson reported a number of incidences of suspected witchcraft and witchcraft trials which she witnessed or was told about when she was living at Zuni (*The Zuni Indians*, 392-406). Her general description was that witches were executed by being suspended by their elbows from a beam in the ruin of the old mission church but were often clubbed to death to relieve prolonged suffering. Helen's description tallies very closely with Stevenson's. In his article "The Witches Were Saved," Tedlock quoted a Zuni who described similar witch trials of the past and added the important fact that suspected witches who confessed were felt to have lost their supernatural powers by speaking about them and were most often not killed but released and allowed to leave the village or even—in some cases at least—to rejoin the community. The United States Army forceably ended witch trials—and executions—around the turn of the century.

Motif number is G291, "Witch executed for engaging in witchcraft."

24. Thirty-year-old Zuni woman interviewed at Zuni, New Mexico, May 17, 1985.
The idea that shapeshifters can be killed while they are in animal form has been widely reported around the world wherever shapeshifting is acknowledged. The most interesting feature of Helen's performance of her story was that she pointed out the window toward the place when this most recent case was said to have occurred.

Motif number is G275.12, "Witch in the form of an animal is injured or killed as a result of the injury to the animal."

25. Thirty-year-old Zuni woman interviewed at Zuni, New Mexico, May 17, 1985.
The idea that persons suspected of witchcraft should be treated with special politeness is typical of Zuni manners today. Once when the village was in the midst of a hotly contested election, one of our co-researchers told us that we could identify members of the different factions by how they greeted each other in public—the warmer the greeting, the greater the degree of political disagreement.

Motif number is D1819.1, "Magic knowledge of another's thoughts."

26. Twenty-eight-year-old man and twenty-six-year-old woman interviewed at Zuni, New Mexico, May 17, 1985.

It was fascinating to hear and see this couple tell their story together, and the story is a reminder of the fact that folk medicine usually involves veterinary as well as human ailments and treatments.

Motif numbers are D1819.1, "Magic knowledge of another's thoughts"; D2161, "Magic healing power"; G265.4, "Witches cause disease or death of animals"; T584.0.1, "Childbirth assisted by magic."

27. Thirty-year-old Zuni woman interviewed at Zuni, New Mexico, May 17, 1985.
As this story indicates, the Zuni concept of witchcraft is such that anyone can be suspected; but in actual practice this description of a witch as an adolescent or preadolescent male seems to be the most common—perhaps because this gender-age group is the most nearly powerless one in Zuni society.

Motif number is G219.4, "Witch with very long hair."

28. Thirty-year-old Zuni woman interviewed at Zuni, New Mexico, May 17, 1985.
The language used to summon a medicine man is a special archaic, formal Zuni which must be used correctly.

29. Thirty-year-old Zuni woman interviewed at Zuni, New Mexico, May 17, 1985.
One of the questions of great interest to us was how a Zuni decided to call a Western doctor or a Zuni medicine man, and Helen's explanation that "you just get to know" is the most complete explanation anyone offered.

30. Twenty-six-year-old Zuni man interviewed at Zuni, New Mexico, August 25, 1985.

In a recent convention presentation James G. Chadney reported his analysis of male/female power in world societies based upon a highly sophisticated computer analysis of data included in the Human Relations Area File and concluded that women had more control at Zuni than in any other society. I couldn't follow his computer analysis, but his conclusion is certainly supported by the stories and people I have known. The Chinese anthropologist Li An-Che did research at Zuni in the 1930s and wrote:

It is not correct to say that woman rules man in Zuni, but what is true and important is the fact that woman is not ruled by man at all.... The realization of the carefree atmosphere surrounding Zuni womanhood carries significance.... It is the husband who must make the necessary adjustment. And this makes all the difference in the world. She ... and her sisters ... have only themselves to care about ... while her husband has to be considerate and calculating. ("Some Observations and Queries," 75)

The Indian anthropologist Triloki Pandey wrote, "I was fascinated by the ease and freedom women enjoyed at Zuni" ("India Man," 194). This storyteller is a young Zuni man—and his hesitation when telling his story—as well as his problems with alcohol—may well reflect his sense of powerlessness.

Motif numbers are G263.4, "Witch causes sickness"; D700, "Person disenchanted."

31. Thirty-year-old Zuni woman interviewed at Zuni, New Mexico, May 17, 1985.

32. Seventy-five-year-old Hopi-Tewa woman interviewed at Zuni, New Mexico, May 16, 1985.

This story is an excellent, clear-cut example of what—thanks to the seminal research of Sandra Stahl—has only recently been recognized by folklorists as a narrative genre—the personal-experience story. It is also interesting to note that the reason Stahl noted for the neglect of the form (folklorists "have considered the standard narrative genres more important or at least more interesting than such minor genres as the personal narrative" and therefore "not really folklore or at least not a folklore genre") applies as well to most of the stories in this book, and her defense of personal-experience stories as folklore applies equally well to other Zuni conversational stories ("The Personal Narrative," 3).

33. Thirty-five-year-old Zuni woman interviewed at Zuni, New Mexico, May 31, 1985.

Zuni has an extremely complex set of unspoken narrative rules governing who tells conversational stories to whom and when. One of the most basic expectations is that the teller should have been a witness to his story or, at a minimum, have a personal, clan, or family relationship with the people who are the characters of the story. Thus, to some extent, *all* Zuni conversational stories are personal experience stories or personal experience stories once removed. One time when we were talking with Helen (unfortunately not a time when we were recording her), she had a great story she wanted to tell us but got completely bogged down in how she was related to the principal character and finally had to settle for saying, "Oh, you know," so she could finish it.

34. Fifty-six-year-old Zuni woman interviewed at Zuni, New Mexico, May 31, 1985.

This story of a severely physically handicapped child shows the tragedy of life, the ability of people to deal with the tragedy, and the place of conversational narratives in communicating both.

35. Thirty-eight-year-old Zuni woman interviewed at Zuni, New Mexico, August 24, 1985.

36. Thirty-eight-year-old Zuni woman interviewed at Zuni, New Mexico, August 24, 1985.

37. Thirty-year-old Zuni woman interviewed at Zuni, New Mexico, May 17, 1985.

38. Thirty-year-old Zuni woman interviewed at Zuni, New Mexico, May 17, 1985. Most Zunis would probably agree with the idea of this story that Zuni and Western medicines are not in opposition but are complementary. Motif numbers are G263.4, "Witch causes sickness"; D700, "Person disenchanted"; M369.7.3, "Prophecy: sex of unborn child."

39. Fifty-one-year-old Zuni man interviewed at Zuni, New Mexico, September 29, 1984. There is a movement from the general to the personal in this story as in others, but in this case the movement is almost overwhelming. Belief is one thing—experience yet another. Motif number is C152, "Tabus during pregnancy."

40. Thirty-eight-year-old Zuni man interviewed at Zuni, New Mexico, July 16, 1985. This detailed personal-experience story is a fitting end to this chapter on Zuni medicine. The young man who was paralyzed by a car accident has had to modify his life and reality, and so have the Zuni medicine men who regularly treat him.

CHAPTER 3

41. Twenty-four-year-old Anglo-American man interviewed at Flagstaff, Arizona, February 5, 1987. SC. This student-collected, Anglo-American contemporary legend—included so that it can be compared with American Indians' stories—is not counted in the total of 251 American Indians' stories in the book. Jan Brunvand reported the story of a pet placed in a microwave oven in his 1978 edition of his book *The Study of American Folklore* (111), and I published a version in 1979 and offered the interpretation that the story illustrated an Anglo-American distrust of modern technology ("Hot Dog! Another Urban Belief Tale," 27-28). The legend was for some years the most frequently reported contemporary legend in my folklore classes at Northern Arizona University.

42. Twenty-four-year-old Anglo-American man interviewed at Flagstaff, Arizona, August 12, 1984. SC. The legend of "The Kentucky Fried Rat" was included by Brunvand in his 1981 book *The Vanishing Hitchhiker* and is another of the most frequently reported Anglo-American contemporary legends (81-84, 88-100, 154, 168, 177-78, 188, 201). It is also included for comparison and is not counted in the total of 251 American Indians' stories in the book.

43. Twenty-four-year-old Anglo-American woman interviewed at Flagstaff, Arizona, April 1, 1984. SC. "The Mouse in the Coke" is another widespread Anglo-American legend—Brunvand called it "the all-time favorite story about food contamination"—included for comparison (*Vanishing Hitchhiker*, 84). Gary Alan Fine has thoroughly investigated

published accounts of mice in Coke; the earliest he found traced back to the second decade of this century ("Cokelore and Coke Law"). "The Mouse in the Coke," like "The Kentucky Fried Rat," seemed an ideal legend to ask Navajos about because it seemed, at first glance anyway, to fit the widely documented Navajo concern with contamination.

44. Twenty-two-year-old Anglo-American woman interviewed at Flagstaff, Arizona, May 9, 1986. SC.

"The Vanishing Hitchhiker," one of the granddaddies of Anglo-American contemporary legends, was also included for purposes of comparison. The story was the subject of a seminal, early article in *California Folklore Quarterly* by Beardsley and Hankey (1943). Brunvand, who used the title of the story as the title of his first book on contemporary legend, reported that the basic story was well known in both the United States and Europe by the end of the nineteenth century. Folklorist Lydia Fish—talk about one-upmanship—traced it back to the New Testament accounts of the post-Resurrection appearances of Jesus!

Motif number is E332.3.3.1, "The Vanishing Hitchhiker."

45. Fifty-two-year-old Navajo man interviewed near Fence Lake, New Mexico, May 29, 1986.

This story is an introduction to Navajo jokes (the subject of chapter 5), to their performance, and to our chief Navajo co-researcher Clyde.

Motif number is C401, "Tabu: speaking during certain time."

46. Eighty-two-year-old Navajo man interviewed near Ramah, New Mexico, December 7, 1985.

Over a two-year period Kathy and I interviewed seven Ramah Navajo men and eighteen Ramah Navajo women ranging in ages from nineteen to ninety-five and in formal education from none to post-graduate. Rereading this first story gathered by interviewing, I am impressed anew by how hard these kind Navajos tried to help these strange *bilagaana*—Navajo for white people—who came knocking at their doors, and how conscientiously they tried to answer the strange questions they were asked. I am also impressed anew by the fact that the difference between a full-fledged contemporary legend and a story which is not a full-fledged contemporary legend is much more a matter of distribution—which, in turn, depends upon function—than it is a matter of theme.

47. Twenty-eight-year-old Navajo woman interviewed near Ramah, New Mexico, December 7, 1985.

This story is the result of another attempt by another Navajo informant to be helpful and is, as well, another example of the differences between a full-fledged, oft-told, thoroughly traditionalized contemporary legend and a recollection of things past.

48. Ninety-five-year-old Navajo woman interviewed near Mountain View, New Mexico, May 29, 1986.

49. Eighty-two-year-old Navajo man interviewed near Ramah, New Mexico, December 7, 1985.

The bear is accorded a special place in traditional Navajo thought, and eating bear meat is absolutely taboo. It is widely believed than any Navajo unfortunate enough to accidentally eat bear meat will become seriously ill and will require a special ceremony to recover.

Motif number is C221.1, *"Tabu: eating flesh of certain animal."*

50. Twenty-nine-year-old Navajo man interviewed near Ramah, New Mexico, December 7, 1985.

Sheila Douglas presented a paper at the 1985 Contemporary Legend Conference demonstrating that some legends recount practical jokes. This man's story demonstrates that some practical jokes re-create legends.

51. Thirty-three-year-old Navajo woman interviewed near Ramah, New Mexico, December 7, 1985.

52. Twenty-eight-year-old Navajo woman interviewed near Ramah, New Mexico, December 7, 1985.

53. Twenty-eight-year-old Navajo woman interviewed near Ramah, New Mexico, December 7, 1985.

Brunvand noted that in the versions of "The Kentucky Fried Rat" Anglo-American teenagers usually tell, the characters are usually sharing a romantic evening before a fireplace so that the dim light allows one of them (almost always the woman) to eat a few bites before discovering what she has eaten (*Vanishing Hitchhiker*, 83). Gary Alan Fine theorized that the stories hinge upon a kind of dramatic irony which punished the woman for not preparing her family's food ("Kentucky Fried Rat"). The fried rat of this story was found by a person whose gender is not identified, and in these Ramah Navajo stories in general a man was as apt to find—or bite—the rat as a woman. The fact is a reminder that the same story may well have different functions in different cultures. The story is almost a summary of "The Kentucky Fried Rat" story, but it lacks the details and emotional thrust of the typical, more fully developed, Anglo-American story.

54. Twenty-one-year-old Navajo woman interviewed near Ramah, New Mexico, December 7, 1985.

55. Thirty-three-year-old Navajo woman interviewed near Ramah, New Mexico, December 7, 1985.

56. Fifty-three-year-old Navajo woman interviewed at Ramah, New Mexico, May 28, 1986.

"There was a man" is an opening ascription frequently used in Navajo narration to indicate a fictive story. "This one woman" is more specific and indicates a "true" story.

57. Fifty-three-year-old Navajo woman interviewed at Ramah, New Mexico, May 28, 1986.

"Her mother" is more specific that "this one woman" and even more unequivocally indicates a "true" story.

58. Sixty-three-year-old Navajo man interviewed near Mountain View, New Mexico, May 29, 1986.

59. Sixty-nine-year-old Navajo woman interviewed near Ramah, New Mexico, May 30, 1986.

This story is another about the ill effects of eating bear (see the note to story 49), and in addition is a reminder of a time when the federal government attempted to force the Navajo to assimilate into Anglo-American culture by rounding up Navajo children, taking them away from their families, sending them to boarding schools, and—according to legend—feeding them bear meat.

Motif number is C221.1, "Tabu: eating flesh of certain animal."

60. Forty-six-year-old Navajo woman interviewed near Ramah, New Mexico, June 13, 1986.

The emphasis on place and firsthand experience is typical of Navajo storytelling of "true" stories.

61. Seventy-six-year-old Navajo woman interviewed near Fence Lake, New Mexico, June 13, 1986.

62. Thirty-five-year-old Navajo-Zuni woman interviewed at Zuni, New Mexico, November 8, 1985.

This story—like the other Ramah Navajo stories concerning vanishing and appearing hitchhikers which follow—is a more fully developed and dramatically told legend than the food contamination stories which proceed it.

Baughman motif number is E581.8, "Ghost rides in automobile."

Thompson motif numbers are E332.3.3, "Ghost asks for ride in automobile"; E545.0.2, "The dead are silent"; F517.1.1, "Person without feet." A number of motifs refer to feet, but the ghost without feet seems to be culturally specific and is not included in any of the major indices.

63. Thirty-three-year-old Navajo woman interviewed near Ramah, New Mexico, December 7, 1985.

The emphasis on the *who* of this story is typical of Navajo storytelling. Though the Ramah Navajo share the British/Anglo-American expectation that storytellers will clearly indicate story by its performance, the expected and accepted ways of giving this information are different. The carefully presented "friend-of-a-friend" ascription so common in British and Anglo-American contemporary legend performance, for example, is rare in the Ramah Navajo legends, which are most often told with firsthand immediacy and ascription. Several of the people we interviewed, in fact, said that they had heard a story similar to the one we were asking about but could not tell it because they could not remember to whom it had happened. Kluckhohn noted that the Navajos he interviewed were very careful to distinguish between things they knew and things they had heard. They still are.

Baughman motif number is E581.8, "Ghost rides in automobile."

Thompson motif numbers are E332.3.3.1(b), "Ghostly rider leaves token in automobile when he leaves"; E422.4.4(h), "Female revenant in old-fashioned garb." A major feature of this story and several which follow is that they most often are set within a "real rainy, rainy day"; the indexes accord similar weather linked with "The Wild Hunt" a special number, but have nothing similar for "ghostly rider" stormy weather.

64. Twenty-eight-year-old Navajo woman interviewed near Ramah, New Mexico, December 7, 1985.

The emphasis on the *where* of this story is also typical of Navajo telling of stories which are to be viewed as "true"; the list of Southwestern place names in the story— "Artesia south of Albuquerque between Carrizozo and Tularosa"—rings like a litany.

The motif number E411.0.1, "Spirit travels with extraordinary speed," comes close to describing this story, but for the fact that the teller says, "I don't know if it was a lady or a guy or what was sitting on a motorcycle with a helmet" and the fact that the motif usually doesn't refer to a motorcycle!

65. Thirty-three-year-old Navajo woman interviewed near Ramah, New Mexico, December 7, 1985.

The fact that the story indicates the central character "was cruising by some *graveyard*" is particularly significant in terms of Navajo traditional culture and thought. Freud defined religion (by which he seemed to have meant primarily a belief in immortality) as the universal obsessive-compulsive neurosis of mankind; Marx damned it as the opiate of the people; Niebuhr praised it as a citadel of hope built on the edge of despair. In their traditional way the Navajo build no citadels, take no opiates, nor believe in the future of illusions. The Navajo, in short, are unusual in the long recorded history of human thought in that they have no concept of personal immortality. Their eschatology affirms the mortality of man and the immortality of evil. In traditional Navajo thought it is believed that the evil which was within individuals lives after them, while the good is, at best, set free to journey to the North to a vaguely defined land of ancestral shades. Evil is particularly apt to make itself known at or near a place of burial. For this reason the Navajo traditionally avoided the dead and the places where they were buried; marked graves with high mounds, a slashed saddle, a solitary pole, or broken vessels; and indicated hogans in which a death had occurred by boarding up windows and doors and making an opening in the north wall so that all were warned and could avoid going near and placing themselves in danger.

Baughman motif number is E581.8, "Ghost rides in automobile."

Thompson motif number is E334.2, "Ghost haunts burial spot."

66. Thirty-three-year-old Navajo woman interviewed at Pine Hill, New Mexico, May 28, 1986.

The ascription of the story to a councilman speaks volumes about Navajo acceptance of their relatively new political system; a councilman is obviously an important, believable witness—and it was raining!

Baughman motif number is E581.8, "Ghost rides in automobile."

Thompson motif number is E332.3.3.1, "The Vanishing Hitchhiker."

67. Thirty-three-year-old Navajo woman interviewed at Pine Hill, New Mexico, May 28, 1986.

Motif numbers are E421.1.2(a), "Ghost scares horse"; E221, "Dead spouse's malevolent return"; E581.2.1, "Ghost jumps on horse behind man"; E272.2, "Ghost rides behind rider on horse"; E439.5, "Revenant forced away by fire"; E439.7, "Ghost will not approach a light left burning."

68. Fifty-four-year-old Navajo woman interviewed at Pine Hill, New Mexico, May 28, 1986.

In Navajo traditional thought a grandmother is equal to—or perhaps even outranks—a councilman in social status and reliability.

Baughman motif number is E581.8, "Ghost rides in automobile."

Thompson motif number is E545.0.2, "The dead are silent."

69. Sixty-three-year-old Navajo man interviewed near Mountain View, New Mexico, May 29, 1986.

Until recently Navajo burials were solitary and isolated; the Veterans' Cemetery was one of the first to put an awful lot of dead Navajos in one place and is, therefore, seen as particularly dangerous and an ideal setting for ghost stories.

Baughman motif number is E581.8, "Ghost rides in automobile."

Thompson motif numbers are E332.3, "Ghost on road asks traveler for ride"; E334.2, "Ghost haunts burial spot."

70. Fifty-eight-year-old Navajo woman interviewed near Ramah, New Mexico, May 29, 1986.

The account is unusual in that the supernatural figure is recognized as the ghost of a specific dead person known to the central character in the story.

Baughman motif number is E581.8, "Ghost rides in automobile."

Thompson motif number is E334.2, "Ghost haunts burial spot."

71. Thirty-eight-year-old Navajo man interviewed near Ramah, New Mexico, May 29, 1986.

Baughman motif number is E581.8, "Ghost rides in automobile."

Thompson motif numbers are E442.4.4(h), "Female revenant in old-fashioned garb"; E332.3.3.1, "The Vanishing Hitchhiker."

72. Twenty-seven-year-old Navajo man interviewed near Ramah, New Mexico, May 30, 1986.

Baughman motif number is E581.8, "Ghost rides in automobile."

Thompson motif number is E332.3.3.1, "The Vanishing Hitchhiker."

73. Ninety-year-old Navajo woman interviewed near Ramah, New Mexico, June 13, 1986.

In this story, as in many others told by Navajos, there is a certain degree of uncertainty about the nature of the supernatural figure.

Baughman motif number is E581.8, "Ghost rides in automobile."

Thompson motif number is E332.3.3.1, "The Vanishing Hitchhiker."

74. Forty-six-year-old Navajo woman interviewed near Ramah, New Mexico, June 13, 1986.

The attribution of this story to a preacher, like the attribution of story number 64 to a councilman, shows the ever-changing nature of Navajo culture.

Baughman motif number is E581.8, "Ghost rides in automobile."

Thompson motif numbers are E332.3.3.1, "The Vanishing Hitchhiker"; E272, "Road-ghosts. (Ghosts which haunt road.)"

75. Forty-six-year-old Navajo woman interviewed near Ramah, New Mexico, June 13, 1986.

Except for the gender, motif number E422.4.4(e), "Female revenant in black dress," fits this story. Other motifs are: E585.1.2, "Dead person rides horse"; E545.0.2, "The dead are silent"; E411.0.1, "Spirit travels with extraordinary speed." The problem in assigning specific motif numbers to this story is that they depend on the nature of the supernatural figure while the woman telling it does not identify it beyond the fact that it was not "a regular person."

76. Twenty-eight-year-old Navajo man interviewed near Fence Lake, New Mexico, June 13, 1986.

In this story, as in story number 68, the ghostly behavior described includes the fact that a ghost does not look directly at the living. This behavior is so frequently reported among the Navajo that it probably would have been assigned a motif number of its own if more extensive collections of Navajo stories had been available to the people who compiled the indexes.

Baughman motif number is E581.8, "Ghost rides in automobile."

Thompson motif numbers are E332.3, "Ghost on road asks traveler for ride"; E545.0.2, "The dead are silent"; E334.2, "Ghost haunts burial spot"; E421.2.1, "Ghost leaves no footprints."

77. Seventy-six-year-old Navajo woman interviewed near Fence Lake, New Mexico, June 13, 1986.

This is an interesting and somewhat unusual story both in the fact that it mentions an "old style hogan" and in the fact that it features a hitchhiking couple. The old style hogan presumably is more likely to be an abandoned burial hogan; and two old style hogans presumably indicates two burials as well as two vanishing hitchhikers.

Baughman motif number is E581.8, "Ghost rides in automobile."

Thompson motif numbers are E334.2, "Ghost haunts burial spot"; E421.2.1, "Ghost leaves no footprints."

78. Fifty-two-year-old Navajo man interviewed near Ramah, New Mexico, June 14, 1986.

Baughman motif number is E581.8, "Ghost rides in automobile."

Thompson motif numbers are E422.4.4(a), "Female revenant in white clothing"; E332.3.3.1, "The Vanishing Hitchhiker."

79. Thirty-five-year-old Navajo-Zuni woman interviewed at Zuni, New Mexico, November 8, 1985.

The storyteller expresses surprise at having discovered that basically the same story is told in two different locations with two different settings.

Motif number is G303.4.5, "The devil's feet and legs." G303.4.5.3.1, "Devil detected by his hoofs," seems to fit this story except for the fact that the teller says she doesn't know what the devil's feet look like and the fact that the number specifically refers to the story—well known in Ireland and elsewhere—of the devil discovered when he drops a card at a card game.

80. Ninety-five-year-old Navajo woman interviewed near Mountain View, New Mexico, May 29, 1986.

Baughman motif numbers are E493(f), "Ghost dances with mortal"; E599.8(a), "Person meets girl at dance, dances with her, often drinks with her, takes her home. He goes to see her next day, finds she has been dead several years. Often a coat he has lent her is found on her grave." This motif is not exactly the same as this story or the ones which follow, but it is very similar.

Thompson motif numbers are E334.2, "Ghost haunts burial spot"; E545.0.2, "The dead are silent"; E425.1, "Revenant as woman"; E423.2, "Revenant as wild animal"; E544, "Ghost leaves evidence of his appearance"; J1117.2, "Coyote as trickster," may all apply to this story as it would be heard and understood by a knowledgeable audience.

81. Fifty-eight-year-old Navajo woman interviewed near Ramah, New Mexico, May 29, 1986.

This story is such a perfect example of the interaction between performer and audience essential for communication in small groups that its cross-cultural performance is analyzed at length in the final chapter (see number 255).

Motif numbers are E545.0.2, "The dead are silent"; E425.1, "Revenant as woman"; E423.2, "Revenant as wild animal"; E544, "Ghost leaves evidence of his appearance"; J1117.2, "Coyote as trickster," may all apply to this story as well.

82. Twenty-two-year-old Navajo woman interviewed near Ramah, New Mexico, May 29, 1986.

Baughman motif numbers are E493(f), "Ghost dances with mortal"; E599.8(a), "Person meets girl at dance, dances with her, often drinks with her, takes her home. He goes to see her next day, finds she has been dead several years. Often a coat he has lent her is found on her grave."

Thompson motif numbers are E425.1, "Revenant as woman"; E423.2, "Revenant as wild animal"; E544, "Ghost leaves evidence of his appearance"; J1117.2, "Coyote as trickster," may all apply to this story as well, and E474, "Cohabitation of living person and ghost," is perhaps more evident to an Anglo-American audience in this story than in some of the other similar ones because the teller uses the Anglo-American euphemism "they slept" to suggest intercourse while other storytellers employ Navajo euphemisms of movement—"they went"—for the same purpose.

83. Thirty-eight-year-old Navajo man interviewed near Ramah, New Mexico, May 29, 1986.

"This man came to dance ..." seems to indicate that perhaps it is not good form to be too eager to participate in the social activities of the Squaw Dance.

Baughman motif numbers are E493(f), "Ghost dances with mortal"; E599.8(a), Person meets girl at dance, dances with her, often drinks with her, takes her home. He goes to see her next day, finds she has been dead several years. Often a coat he has lent her is found on her grave.

Thompson motif number is E422.4.4(e), "Female revenant in black dress."

84. Seventy-six-year-old Navajo woman interviewed near Fence Lake, New Mexico, June 13, 1986.

This story seems to strongly suggest cohabitation of living person and ghost, but she disappeared before they "got down"—another Navajo euphemism of motion suggesting sexual intercourse. In light of the facts of the story, it is understandable that he didn't "bother to check for tracks."

Baughman motif numbers are E493(f), "Ghost dances with mortal"; E599.8(a), Person meets girl at dance, dances with her, often drinks with her, takes her home. He goes to see her next day, finds she has been dead several years. Often a coat he has lent her is found on her grave.

Thompson motif number is E474, "Cohabitation of living person and ghost."

85. Fifty-two-year-old Navajo man interviewed near Ramah, New Mexico, June 14, 1986.

Clyde's story is only intelligible because of the earlier versions we collected together. It is also interesting that he left the motif about the footprints out of his version because he felt it was illogical.

Baughman motif numbers are E493(f), "Ghost dances with mortal"; E599.8(a), "Person meets girl at dance, dances with her, often drinks with her, takes her home. He goes to see her next day, finds she has been dead several years. Often a coat he has lent her is found on her grave."

86. Eighty-two-year-old Navajo man interviewed near Ramah, New Mexico, December 7, 1985.

Baughman motif number is E581.8, "Ghost rides in automobile."

Thompson motif numbers are E425.1, "Revenant as woman"; E434.9, "Candlelight protection against ghost"; E439.5, "Revenant forced away by fire"; and E439.7, "Ghost will not approach a light left burning," are all related to this story, but there is no specific number in any of the major indexes referring to a car dome light.

87. Fifty-four-year-old Navajo woman interviewed at Pine Hill, New Mexico, May 28, 1986.

The majority of the telling of this story functions to distance the storyteller from it.

Baughman motif number is E581.8, "Ghost rides in automobile."

Thompson motif numbers are E425.1, "Revenant as woman;" E545.0.2, "The dead are silent."

88. Fifty-two-year-old Navajo man interviewed near Ramah, New Mexico, June 14, 1986.

Clyde's performance of his hitchhiker story is unusual in that he speaks directly to the figure and assures it that it is "welcome to ride."

Baughman motif number is E581.8, "Ghost rides in automobile."

Thompson motif number is E545.0.2, "The dead are silent."

CHAPTER 4

89. Zuni man interviewed at Zuni, New Mexico, October 21, 1988.

Stories of unidentified flying objects have been reported frequently in Anglo-American folklore for at least forty years—and infrequently for much longer than that. In fact, in an article published in the April 1981 issue of *Current Anthropology*, the Russian anthropologist Valerii I. Sanarov traced stories of airship sightings back to the ninth century and noted a number of similarities between UFO stories—he called them "non-fairy-tale prose"—and other traditional stories of unusual phenomena in the sky such as "World-Tree Tales" and "Rope Trick" tales. Such stories have been found in many cultures in many times, and Zunis, too, tell stories of personal sightings and encounters with UFOs.

90. Zuni man interviewed at Zuni, New Mexico, October 21, 1988.

From Zuni to Vietnam—join the army and see this world and maybe even others! The technical trappings and jargon of this story somehow seem very appropriate.

91. Zuni man interviewed at Zuni, New Mexico, October 21, 1988.

Thomas E. Bullard's article "UFO Abduction Reports: The Supernatural Kidnap Narrative Returns in Technological Guise" traced the history of first-person accounts of capture by alien beings as Anglo-American traditional narrative to 1961 and convincingly demonstrated their folkloric character. Among the early accounts he claimed caused the prominence of the abduction story in public awareness in America was a famous abduction incident reported within Arizona a few years ago, and Norman's story echoes some of the details of the incident as it was reported by the man who claimed to have been taken into a UFO.

The basic story, as reported by the media of the time, was that on November 5, 1975, six members of an Arizona work crew watched in horror as a bluish or greenish-blue ray of light came out from the bottom of a UFO and knocked their companion Travis Walton to the ground. They fled.

When they returned to the scene fifteen minutes later, they could not find Walton or the hovering object they had seen earlier. They notified authorities of the disappearance of their friend, and search and rescue teams on foot, horseback, and helicopter combed the area unsuccessfully for five days. Travis was located only after he called his brother-in-law from a roadside phone booth near Heber, Arizona. His brother-in-law notified his brother who was among the original witnesses to the abduction. When his brother found Walton, he was crumpled on the floor of the phone booth. He reported that he had been held captive for five days within a spaceship, which then dropped him off beside the road. Authorities—and lie detector tests—were never able to disprove the story, and it was widely believed.

Norman's half-joking reference in his story ("Watch. A green light'll come out and transport us up there") probably refers to the Walton case and shows how a story may be used as an allusion in other stories.

Motif number is F178.2, "Green as otherworld color."

92. Zuni man interviewed at Zuni, New Mexico, October 21, 1988.

Bullard documented that stories of UFO crashes have circulated among Anglo-Americans since at least the early 1950s and noted that the stories often include the facts that the aliens aboard the doomed craft survived and made a secret treaty with the United States government allowing them to carry out abductions for scientific purposes. The Southwest in general—and New Mexico in particular—is the area of America most associated in these stories with UFO crashes and government cover-ups, and it is also the area most frequently mentioned in the stories as the location of the aliens' base. Norman's story of the explosion of the large ship and the escape of several smaller ones fits in well with these widely distributed Anglo-American stories.

Bullard concluded that in Anglo-American folklore the alien abduction stories in particular—and UFO stories in general—fill a vacancy caused when science evicted ghosts and witches from popular belief. They serve the same functions as the stories of "creatures lurking in the dark" that had been abandoned. At Zuni UFO stories may well have been added to the stories of supernatural danger, but they have certainly not supplanted stories of witchcraft.

93. Seventy-one-year-old Zuni woman interviewed at Zuni, New Mexico, October 21, 1988.

Kuiceyetsa's mention of Heber, where Travis Walton claimed the spaceship had abducted him, and Taylor, where his family lived, suggests that she, like her son before her, may have been referring to this well-publicized story.

94. Zuni man interviewed at Zuni, New Mexico, October 21, 1988.

The Thompson motif index has a number (D1408.1, "Magic sphere burns up country") referring to a similar—but much more widespread—phenomenon attributed to magic.

95. Zuni man interviewed at Zuni, New Mexico, October 21, 1988.

The story of the "Coming of the Witches" was collected and reported by Stevenson, Parsons, Bunzel, and Tedlock. All these versions included an explanation of the origin of life after death as a part of the story. It is interesting to compare Stevenson's version with Norman's much more recent version which does not include this motif:

While the A'shiwi were at A'wisho the Divine Ones organized four esoteric fraternities. The A'shiwi were happy here. Day after day they were followed by those who had failed to come to this world with them, for many, becoming tired had fallen back. Every time the A'shiwi heard a rumbling of the earth (earthquake) they knew that others were coming out. They would say "My younger brother comes;" or, "Some of my people come." The exodus from the underworlds continued four years. The last observed to come forth were two witches, a man and a wife, who were all-powerful for good or evil. Kow'wituma and Wats'usi, hearing a rumbling of the earth, looked to see who had arrived, and met the two witches, whose heads were covered with loose hoods of coarse fiber blowing in the breeze. Kow'wituma inquired of the witches: "Whither are you going?" They replied: "We wish to go with your people to the Middle place of the world." Kow'wituma said: "We do not want you with us." The witches, holding seeds in their closed hands under their arms, said: "If we do not go we will destroy the land. We have all seeds here." When the Divine Ones again told the witches they were not wanted, they declared that it would not be well if they were not allowed to go, saying: "We have all things precious for your people." The man, extending his closed hand over the seeds, said: "See, I wish to give this to the Kia'kwemosi; and I wish him to give us two of his children, a son and a daughter. When we have the children the corn shall be his." "Why do you wish the children?" asked Kow'wituma. "We wish to kill the children that the rains may come." The Divine Ones hastened to repeat what they had seen and heard to the Kia'kwemosi, who replied: "It is well." When the witches appeared before the Kia'kwemosi and claimed two of this children, he said: "I have no infant children; I have a youth and a maiden; what do you wish to do with them?" "We wish to destroy them." "Why do you wish to destroy my children?" "We wish to destroy them that there may be much rain. We have things of great value to you, but we must first have much rain." "It is well," said the Kia'kwemosi; and when the youth and maiden slept the two witches shot their medicine into their hearts by touching the children with their hands, causing their deaths. Their remains were buried in the earth, and the rains fell four days. On the fifth morning a rumbling noise was heard, and Kow'wituma saw the youth appearing from his grave. Again there were four days of heavy rains, and on the fifth morning after the resurrection of the youth a rumbling was heard, and Kow'wituma saw the girl coming from the earth. The same night the two witches planted all the seeds in the wet earth, and the following morning the corn was a foot high and the other things were of good size. (*The Zuni Indians*, 29-30)

Motif number is G203.2, "Witches come forth at emergence of mankind."

96. Seventy-one-year-old Zuni woman interviewed at Zuni, New Mexico, October 21, 1988.
Loud, rowdy behavior does not fit the Zuni sense of form.

97. Seventy-one-year-old Zuni woman interviewed at Zuni, New Mexico, October 21, 1988.
Nicknames based upon physical appearance or traits are very much a part of Zuni naming practices.

98. Seventy-one-year-old Zuni woman interviewed at Zuni, New Mexico, October 21, 1988.
For as long as there is any information about Zuni—the archaeological record begins somewhere around A. D. 600—they have been noted as traders. By the time the Spanish arrived on the scene, Zuni was one of the major trade centers of the West with well-marked, well-worn trails leading out in all directions like the spokes of a giant wheel. Then—as now—the Zunis were widely known and respected as sharp but honest traders.

Tejja:na:qe is the Zuni word for "outlaw, cattle rustler." According to Stanley Newman's Zuni dictionary, the Zuni word *tejja:na:qe* is from the Spanish word *tejano* which means "Texan." Kuiceyetsa had translated from Zuni through Spanish to English, which quite possibly explains why she hesitated before giving us a definition for *tejja:na:qe*.

99. Seventy-one-year-old Zuni woman interviewed at Zuni, New Mexico, October 21, 1988.
This is a story Kuiceyetsa tells frequently, and another of her tellings ended with Franklin saying, "Who cares? These people are all wet anyway."

100. Seventy-one-year-old Zuni woman interviewed at Zuni, New Mexico, October 21, 1988.
"Keening" is the word used to describe Irish ritual wailing for the dead; Zuni at one time had a similar custom.

101. Seventy-one-year-old Zuni woman interviewed at Zuni, New Mexico, October 21, 1988.

102. Seventy-one-year-old Zuni woman interviewed at Zuni, New Mexico, October 21, 1988.
The story emphasizes that it is possible for outsiders to get to know the Zunis.

212 American Indians' Kitchen-Table Stories

Motif number is F1041.1.1, "Death from broken heart."

103. Seventy-one-year-old Zuni woman interviewed at Zuni, New Mexico, October 21, 1988.

Ouija Boards are a copyrighted device used in Anglo-American culture either as a game or as a part of serious efforts to communicate with the spirits of the dead. The board "game" was invented by William Fuld of Baltimore about 1890 to facilitate the "automatic writing" used by many spiritualists to communicate with the dead at the seances popular during the period. The small board has the letters of the alphabet, the numbers 0 through 9, and the words "yes" and "no" printed on it. A small, three-legged piece serves as a pointer. Two or more people hold the board on their laps and rest their fingers lightly on the pointer, which supposedly answers questions by moving to a word or number, or by spelling out words. The device quickly gained popularity on both sides of the Atlantic and is still widely used today.

104. Seventy-one-year-old Zuni woman interviewed at Zuni, New Mexico, October 21, 1988.

One of my County Donegal Irish co-researchers told me a very similar story of young Irish students accidentally making contact with evil spirits by experimenting with an Ouija Board and being terrified as a result.

Motif numbers are G303.16, "How the devil's power can be escaped or avoided"; J21.50, "Idleness begets woe; work brings happiness."

105. Seventy-one-year-old Zuni woman interviewed at Zuni, New Mexico, October 21, 1988.

See the note to story 95.

106. Seventy-one-year-old Zuni woman interviewed at Zuni, New Mexico, October 21, 1988.

Stories of sensing a beneficent presence are discussed by David Hufford in *The World Was Flooded with Light*, a book he co-wrote with a woman who described having had such an experience. Kuiceyetsa's story is an important addition to the examples collected. Kuiceyetsa several times in several ways—and several stories—had previously indicated that she was extremely close to her grandfather.

107. Seventy-one-year-old Zuni woman interviewed at Zuni, New Mexico, October 21, 1988.

Walnut Canyon is a prehistoric cliff dwelling located near Flagstaff, Arizona, and many archaeologists and many Zunis believe that it was one of the places the people who were to become the Zuni lived for a time as they wandered looking for the middle place which was destined to be their home for all time.

108. Seventy-one-year-old Zuni woman interviewed at Zuni, New Mexico, October 21, 1988.

109. Seventy-one-year-old Zuni woman interviewed at Zuni, New Mexico, October 21, 1988.

Kuiceyetsa's story is particularly poignant in light of the fact that she now is diabetic.

110. Seventy-one-year-old Zuni woman interviewed at Zuni, New Mexico, October 21, 1988.

111. Seventy-one-year-old Zuni woman interviewed at Zuni, New Mexico, October 21, 1988.
Kuiceyetsa's careful avoidance of blame in her story is typical of Zuni ideals.

112. Seventy-one-year-old Zuni woman interviewed at Zuni, New Mexico, October 21, 1988.

113. Seventy-one-year-old Zuni woman interviewed at Zuni, New Mexico, October 21, 1988.

114. Seventy-one-year-old Zuni woman interviewed at Zuni, New Mexico, October 21, 1988.
Even as a child Kuiceyetsa was very observant and interested in other languages, other cultures.

115. Seventy-one-year-old Zuni woman interviewed at Zuni, New Mexico, October 21, 1988.
Kuiceyetsa's joy and laughter at her recollection of her round brother in his hand-me-down fur coat which made him look like a bear and made them a sled was wondrous to share.

116. Seventy-one-year-old Zuni woman interviewed at Zuni, New Mexico, March 15, 1989.
Although it is not clear who "she" is in the text, it is in the telling. Kuiceyetsa follows the Zuni practice of not using the name of a dead person and regularly refers to her children's grandmother as "she."
Motif number is C762.2, "Tabu: too much weeping for dead."

117. Seventy-one-year-old Zuni woman interviewed at Zuni, New Mexico, March 15, 1989.
This story and the two that follow are examples of a fascinating kind of story: stories about people who collect stories told by the people from whom they have collected them. People who have studied people have always collected stories; some of them in some of their writings—Kluckhohn's *Navaho Witchcraft*, for example—retold the stories they had collected; many of them based their writings upon analyses of the stories. People whose stories are collected and studied tell stories about the people who collected them—and so do their descendants unto at least the third generation.
These stories about collectors are an integral, though seldom published, part of Anglo-American folklore. Everyone who has collected folksongs has been told stories about Alan Lomax or, more recently, Les Blank—and they also were frequently encountered but rarely published by cross-cultural fieldworkers until Triloki Pandey's seminal 1972 article "Anthropologists at Zuni" presented a number of stories told by Kuiceyetsa's parents' generation.
Kuiceyetsa begins by giving a list of anthropologists who have stayed with her family while they were doing research at Zuni and then tells her story about Cushing.
Frank Hamilton Cushing arrived at Zuni in 1879 and lived with the people in the village until 1884 and was the first professional anthropologist to actually reside for a

relatively long period of time with the people he wished to study. So involved was his participant-observer method that he became the only person in history who could—and did—sign his letters, "1st War Chief of Zuni, U. S. Ass't Ethnologist."

Pandey collected and published two stories about Cushing at Zuni told by Zunis; they offer a fascinating comparison with Kuiceyetsa's:

> Palowahtiwa [Petricio Pino] was Cushing's best friend in Zuni and he lived with him in his house right in the village. Cushing took our headmen to the East for bringing sacred water from the Ocean. He was a good friend of the Indians and that's why he was made a Bow Priest. My father was a good friend of Cushing. He used to visit with him every day. Cushing had a living antelope and my father used to take me to his house in order to show me his antelope.

> Several of other older informants remembered the white man who had been made a Bow Priest. An old woman who was born while Cushing was in Zuni and was named after his wife told me that he was a weak man when he came but was made strong by the Zuni. When I read these statements to my hostess, who was considered an important member of the tribe, she said, "Yes, my mother told me about Cushing. She told me that her folks were responsible for making him a Bow Priest. But just a few years after making him a Bow Priest three high priests were killed in the Ramah area and the people said that because those priests made that white man a high priest, they were killed." ("Anthropologists," 323)

118. Seventy-one-year-old Zuni woman interviewed at Zuni, New Mexico, March 15, 1989.

Elsie Clews Parsons began her field research at Zuni in 1915, returned as often as she could for the rest of her life, and published a truly monumental series of monographs and articles about the people she had come to love.

Pandey's hostess gave him a rather full, personal description of Mrs. Parsons:

> She was a very rich lady, but you could not guess it from the way she lived. She always dressed in sloppy dresses. One summer she brought white shoes with her. I thought it was funny and I told her so. She became mad, so I explained that when the rains come she would realize her mistake. I told her that anyone who comes to Zuni should know that it is not New York City. The roads are muddy here. After a while she was all right.

> She was a real friend of my husband and me. We always wrote to each other. She had four children, as I have, and they were born at the same times when mine were. We joked about it. Although she was very talkative, we enjoyed having her with us and she was very glad for that. She used to pay us well and we did whatever she wanted us to do. You see, she did not have many friends at Zuni. We were her best friends and we worked hard for her. I am not a Zuni and I don't know everything about the Zunis. So if there was something Mrs. Parsons wanted to know about them and I didn't know, I asked the people and they told me everything. My husband was an important Zuni and he helped me a lot. One year she asked me to maintain a diary of whatever took place in Zuni and I did that. I guess she got that published as a book.

Mrs. Parsons brought her friends to meet me. One year an artist—whose name I don't remember now—came with her. He wanted to sketch the Zuni dances, but they wouldn't let him. I guess he drew some natural scenes and went back.

One thing which always makes me sore when I remember Mrs. Parsons is that she invited me to visit her in New York City and I promised her to do so, but never went there. One day I got a letter from her secretary telling me about her death. She knew that we were great friends and that I would appreciate her giving me that news. ("Anthropologists," 329)

119. Seventy-one-year-old Zuni woman interviewed at Zuni, New Mexico, March 15, 1989.

Matilda Coxe Stevenson, who accompanied her husband to Zuni in 1879, was the first woman ethnographer to do research in the Southwest, and her emphasis on women and children was unique in her time. Her studies are one of the foundations of Pueblo research, and she is the person perhaps most responsible for negotiating the purchase of Zuni ethnographic and religious items for the Smithsonian collection.

Pandey also collected a story at Zuni told about Stevenson:

She was disliked by many Zunis. She lived in a camp which was guarded by two Zuni men whom she paid every day. Some of the Zunis wanted to get rid of her. You cannot believe how arrogant she was. She entered the Kivas (ceremonial chambers) without asking permission of the high priests. She took pictures because the Zunis did not know what she was doing. Old people told me that Fewkes was the same way. But, you see, then the Zunis were not educated and did not know what these people were doing.

Those days, life was real hard here. There was terrible poverty in the pueblo. There was a smallpox epidemic just two years before I came to teach school here in 1899. That was the year when Christian Reformed missionaries, old man [Andrew] Vanderwagen and his wife, who was a trained nurse, came to Zuni. They helped Zunis and won their confidence, but Mrs. Stevenson did nothing for them. She bought their religious objects and took them to the museum in Washington. She took advantage of the Zuni poverty. ("Anthropologists," 326-27)

Kuiceyetsa's stories are all more personal, human interest accounts of anthropologists at Zuni than those previously collected, but they are clearly within a tradition.

120. Seventy-one-year-old Zuni woman interviewed at Zuni, New Mexico, March 15, 1989.

Goldman noted in the 1930s that the Zuni were beginning to develop the concept of individual, personal property because of the influence of western civilization and predicted that the changing values would lead to violence based upon theft within the community in the near future. Kuiceyetsa's story demonstrates that he was correct.

121. Thirty-four-year-old Zuni woman interviewed at Zuni, New Mexico, March 15, 1989.

It is fascinating—and perhaps more than coincidental—that the social deviants Helen describes in this story and the three which follow it all are young Zuni males, and that it is Navajo crystal gazers, traditional experts in divination, who locate the hidden body.

122. Thirty-four-year-old Zuni woman interviewed at Zuni, New Mexico, March 15, 1989.
Motif number is N255, "Escape from one misfortune into worse."

123. Thirty-four-year-old Zuni woman interviewed at Zuni, New Mexico, March 15, 1989.

124. Thirty-four-year-old Zuni woman interviewed at Zuni, New Mexico, March 15, 1989.
For a Zuni grandchild to behave in such a manner that his Zuni grandmother is afraid of him is unthinkable and deviance of the highest order.

125. Seventy-one-year-old Zuni woman interviewed at Zuni, New Mexico, March 15, 1989.
"I'm not lost; I just couldn't find my way." The resemblance to the well-known story about the traveler or explorer who said he had never been lost but had once been confused for a few weeks (the story is often "told on" Daniel Boone) is striking.

126. Seventy-one-year-old Zuni woman interviewed at Zuni, New Mexico, March 15, 1989.
Zunis traditionally inter a corpse the day after the person dies. There is a traditional all-night ceremony before burial which the Zuni call in English a "wake." The body is ritually cleansed and laid out in a home (most often that of the deceased), and family and clan members remain with it during the night. Ritually prepared food is brought by traditionally designated individuals and given to the dead during the night, and a window is left open in the home to facilitate the spirit's journey to the spirit village to dance for the people for all eternity. Ghosts are not frequently reported at Zuni, but when they are they are most often described as spirits who have become trapped in a house after a death and have not been able to complete their journey to the Zuni spirit village and are, therefore, more to be pitied than feared. Standard Zuni procedures for ridding places of trapped spirits include "smoking" the house and, most important of all, leaving windows and doors open so that the spirit can be freed.
Baughman motif numbers are E338.6, "Ghost haunts hotel"; X1280, "Lies about insects."

CHAPTER 5

127. Fifty-two-year-old Navajo man interviewed near Ramah, New Mexico, June 13, 1986.
Motif number is N384, "Death from fright."

128. Thirty-seven-year-old Navajo man interviewed at Chinle, Arizona, July 24, 1974. SC.
Motif number is N384, "Death from fright."

129. Nineteen-year-old Navajo woman interviewed at Chinle, Arizona, July 24, 1974. SC.
Motif number is N384, "Death from fright."

130. Fifty-two-year-old Navajo man interviewed near Ramah, New Mexico, June 14, 1986.

It is interesting to note that there is a well-known Anglo-American contemporary legend about the horrible death of "Little Mikey," the central character of the Life commercial upon which Clyde's story and performance were based, from eating Pop Rocks and having them explode in his stomach, and that Clyde was not familiar with this legend.

This is the only version of this story that we have found among American Indians—or any other group, for that matter. More field research might well uncover others, but it suffices to say that the text was traditional to Clyde and his *performance* of the text was guided by Navajo narrative traditions and is similar to a long international line of humor or frustration based upon the difficulties of herding or capturing animals—rabbits, for example—which are not used to being herded or are difficult to capture.

Motif numbers are H1154, "Task: capturing animals"; B845, "Wild animals herded"; K346.2, "Herdsman slaughters animals entrusted to him."

131. Forty-year-old Navajo man interviewed in Flagstaff, Arizona, October 9, 1982. SC.

This story is the most frequently reported Navajo joke, and I have included a full sixteen versions of it (131 through 146) to demonstrate the basic nature of traditional stories—how they are always the same yet always different.

132. Nineteen-year-old Navajo woman interviewed in Chinle, Arizona, June 30, 1973. SC.

133. Fifty-eight-year-old Navajo woman interviewed in Tuba City, Arizona, July 17, 1981. SC.

134. Nineteen-year-old Navajo man interviewed in Flagstaff, Arizona, October 5, 1982. SC.

135. Twenty-nine-year-old Navajo man interviewed near Ramah, New Mexico, December 7, 1985.

136. Thirty-three-year-old Navajo woman interviewed near Ramah, New Mexico, December 7, 1985.

137. Fifty-four-year-old Navajo woman interviewed at Pine Hill, New Mexico, May 28, 1986.

Parsons collected and published a story in her article "Navaho Folk Tales" related to this storyteller's explanation of the horned toad stories:

Long ago there was a big giant *(Ye'itso)* who killed people. Giant was very tall, as tall as that. (The narrator indicated the stove-pipe which ran through the ceiling). Giant told an Indian *(tinee')* to build a fire. He dug a little hole. Giant was going to kill that man and cook him in a hot fire. But Turtle had given the man a hat and when Giant was about to kill him, he got out that hat, and Giant was afraid of that hat and began to back away from it. Close by there was a big canyon. Giant was walking backwards. Pretty soon as he was walking backwards he fell down into the canyon, and he died. ("Navajo Folk Tales," 373)

Coupled with Parsons' text, this story explains that the horned toad is a sacred animal to the Navajo and is called grandfather or grandpa within the culture because of his role in their myth tradition.

Motif numbers are G11.2, "Cannibal giant"; F828, "Extraordinary crown"; J2611, "Person frightened into falling down a cliff."

138. Thirty-three-year-old Navajo woman interviewed at Pine Hill, New Mexico, May 28, 1986.

139. Sixty-three-year-old Navajo man interviewed near Mountain View, New Mexico, May 29, 1986.

140. Ninety-five-year-old Navajo woman interviewed near Mountain View, New Mexico, May 29, 1986.

141. Fifty-eight-year-old Navajo woman interviewed near Ramah, New Mexico, May 29, 1986.

142. Sixty-nine-year-old Navajo woman interviewed near Ramah, New Mexico, May 30, 1986.

143. Twenty-seven-year-old Navajo man interviewed near Ramah, New Mexico, May 30, 1986.

144. Ninety-year-old Navajo woman interviewed near Ramah, New Mexico, June 13, 1986.

The story is certainly familiar by now, but this version of it is overshadowed by the comments the old woman makes after she tells it. The golden age is a reality for many older people in many cultures, and this woman's poetic contrast of today with "way back" "when the days were right" is a beautiful, powerful statement of her perception of that which is passing away.

145. Forty-six-year-old Navajo woman interviewed near Ramah, New Mexico, June 13, 1986.

146. Twenty-eight-year-old Navajo man interviewed near Fence Lake, New Mexico, June 13, 1986.

147. Seventy-four-year-old Navajo man interviewed in Fence Lake, New Mexico, June 13, 1986.

This story—identified as "not the horny toad story exactly" by its teller—is another example of how one story leads to another.

148. Eighteen-year-old Navajo woman interviewed at Chinle, Arizona, August 3, 1976. SC.

149. Thirty-four-year-old Navajo man interviewed at Flagstaff, Arizona, October 24, 1982. SC.

The hint of bestiality in this story and the two other versions which follow it is a major part of their humor.

150. Thirty-three-year-old Navajo woman interviewed at Chinle, Arizona, July 21, 1984. SC.

151. Eighty-two-year-old Navajo man interviewed near Ramah, New Mexico, December 7, 1985.

152. Sixty-two-year-old Navajo woman interviewed at Ganado, Arizona, July 19, 1980. SC.

153. Twenty-nine-year-old Navajo man interviewed at Flagstaff, Arizona, August 5, 1984. SC.

154. Sixty-five-year-old Navajo man interviewed at Ganado, Arizona, January 21, 1976. SC.
Talking about "the latest news" before asking a specific question is very much in keeping with traditional Navajo conversational practice.

155. Thirty-four-year-old Navajo woman interviewed at Flagstaff, Arizona, July 12, 1984. SC.
Motif number is J1805.1, "Similar sounding words mistaken for each other."

156. Eighty-six-year-old Navajo woman interviewed at Chinle, Arizona, March 25, 1986. SC.
Jokes based upon the pretended obscene are very much enjoyed by the Navajo.
Motif number is J2496.2, "Misunderstanding because of lack of knowledge of a different language than one's own."

157. Twenty-two-year-old Navajo woman interviewed at Flagstaff, Arizona, July 20, 1980. SC.
Motif number is J2496.2, "Misunderstanding because of lack of knowledge of a different language than one's own."

158. Twenty-nine-year-old Navajo man interviewed at Flagstaff, Arizona, August 5, 1984. SC.
Motif number is J2496.2, "Misunderstanding because of lack of knowledge of a different language than one's own."

159. Twenty-two-year-old Navajo woman interviewed at Flagstaff, Arizona, July 20, 1980. SC.
The fact that the English word "bun" refers to either hair or buttocks only adds to the humor of this story.
Motif number is J2496.2, "Misunderstanding because of lack of knowledge of a different language than one's own."

160. Nineteen-year-old Navajo woman interviewed at Flagstaff, Arizona, March 30, 1983. SC.
Motif number is J2496.2, "Misunderstanding because of lack of knowledge of a different language than one's own."

161. Thirty-two-year-old Navajo woman interviewed at Flagstaff, Arizona, July 16, 1983. SC.
The pun on the word "have" is undoubtedly intentional.
Motif number is J2496.2, "Misunderstanding because of lack of knowledge of a different language than one's own."

162. Twenty-seven-year-old Navajo man interviewed at Flagstaff, Arizona, July 17, 1980. SC.

Navajo—as the language is spoken today—includes many English words which have been adopted; "battery" and "generator" are such words.

Motif number is J2496.2, "Misunderstanding because of lack of knowledge of a different language than one's own."

163. Thirty-four-year-old Navajo man interviewed at St. Michaels, Arizona, July 11, 1981. SC.

Motif number is J2496.2, "Misunderstanding because of lack of knowledge of a different language than one's own."

164. Nineteen-year-old Navajo woman interviewed at Flagstaff, Arizona, October 8, 1982. SC.

Folklorist James P. Leary included a version of this story (told by Norwegians about or "on" Swedes) in his book *Midwestern Folk Humor* and noted its publication in a number of joke books from 1909 on (144). This joke, therefore, spans two categories: it may be a Navajo borrowing of an English-language pun, and it may be a Navajo pun based upon similarities of English-language words. It probably is both.

Motif number is J2496.2, "Misunderstanding because of lack of knowledge of a different language than one's own."

165. Twenty-year-old Navajo woman interviewed at Flagstaff, Arizona, November 1, 1982. SC.

This English-language pun has been widely reported across America. A telling of it was included in Tom Davenport's documentary film *The Upperville Show*, and it was so well known that Rex Stout referred to it without explaining it in his Nero Wolfe detective story *The Rubber Band*.

166. Twenty-seven-year-old Navajo man interviewed near Ramah, New Mexico, May 30, 1986.

167. Twenty-eight-year-old Navajo man interviewed near Fence Lake, New Mexico, June 13, 1986.

168. Fifty-two-year-old Navajo man interviewed near Ramah, New Mexico, June 14, 1986.

Welsh folklorist Christie Davies has spent much of his professional life exploring and writing about "ethnic jokes," stories told by one group to make fun of another group. His convention presentations and his book included examples from many world cultures, and there is a bit of the ethnic joke about Clyde's story.

169. Thirty-one-year-old Navajo man interviewed at Flagstaff, Arizona, July 15, 1981. SC.

170. Thirty-three-year-old Navajo woman interviewed at Pine Hill, New Mexico, May 28, 1986.

This story—another example of the pretended obscene—was a delight to hear told. This was indeed a master storyteller who had polished and enjoyed her art.

171. Forty-year-old Navajo man interviewed at Flagstaff, Arizona, September 10, 1982. SC.

James P. Leary included a version of this story told by an Ojiwba American Indian in *Midwestern Folk Humor* and noted that it had also been associated with other ethnic groups (58). In practice, folklore is a comparative science; the problem is that the first reporting of a text is, by definition, incomparable. This text, therefore, gives added meaning to Leary's text, and in turn is more important because of his reporting. The fact that the two texts were collected from two different American Indian tribes, furthermore, suggests something beyond either. These texts are the first documented, cross-culturally field collected versions of a story suggesting that Navajos, too, have ethnic jokes; the Sioux fill the same role in these Navajo narratives as the Irish or "Polacks" fill in stories in other traditions; and these Navajo ethnic jokes are shared by different American Indian tribal groups.

172. Twenty-six-year-old Navajo woman interviewed at Flagstaff, Arizona, October 18, 1982. SC.

Richard Dorson frequently noted that the dialect joke is one of the most typical and widespread forms of Anglo-American humor. In *Midwestern Folk Humor* James P. Leary included a number of Ojiwba jokes hinging upon misunderstanding caused by dialect or confusion between human speech and animal sounds (54-55). This story, the ones which follow it, and the ones he reported, too, are dialect jokes and demonstrate that American Indians share this tradition with Anglo-Americans.

173. Twenty-two-year-old Navajo woman interviewed at Pinon, Arizona, July 10, 1980. SC.

The idea that filling out forms is so important that even information given by the family cat will suffice is perhaps a comment on Navajo attitudes toward social workers.

Motif number is J1811, "Animal cries misunderstood."

174. Twenty-nine-year-old Navajo man interviewed at Flagstaff, Arizona, August 5, 1984. SC.

There is a story well known across America about talking dogs who say that "roof" is the top of a building and "Ruth" was the world's greatest baseball player, but—to the best of my knowledge—only Navajo dogs say "Rough Rock."

Motif number is J1811, "Animal cries misunderstood."

175. Fifty-four-year-old Navajo woman interviewed at Pine Hill, New Mexico, May 28, 1986.

Several motifs refer to stories of the grasshopper and the ant but none is exactly the same as this Navajo joke.

176. Forty-six-year-old Navajo woman interviewed near Ramah, New Mexico, June 13, 1986.

177. Twenty-eight-year-old Navajo man interviewed near Fence Lake, New Mexico, June 13, 1986.

This is the most complete and dramatic of the three texts, and it is the one told by the man who had moved from the big reservation—where the "ant-hill" hogan is still found—to the Ramah area.

178. Fifty-seven-year-old Navajo woman interviewed at Shiprock, New Mexico, July 11, 1980. SC.

This text validates the traditionality of the one which follows, and the two together would justify a motif number if the indexes were truly representative of American Indian oral tradition.

179. Twenty-one-year-old Navajo woman interviewed at Flagstaff, Arizona, June 13, 1986. SC.

The fact that an "Anglo man died of shock sitting on the toilet" indicates that there is at least an element of the ethnic joke in this story, too.

Motif number is N384, "Death from fright."

180. Fifty-one-year-old Navajo man interviewed at Salina Springs Trading Post, Chinle, Arizona, October 9, 1978. SC.

181. Fifty-four-year-old Navajo woman interviewed at Window Rock, Arizona, July 19, 1980. SC.

Clyde told us another version that we were not able to record, adding information that the grandson also had a lamp wick for a belt and had traveled overseas as a part of the United States Army. American Indians were declared a part of the draft beginning with the Second World War. Navajos have served with distinction in all United States wars since, and the return of those who served has frequently been a source of cultural conflict and concern—perhaps making returning veterans natural foci for Navajo humor.

Motif number is J1772, "One object thought to be another."

182. Thirty-year-old Navajo woman interviewed at Red Valley, Arizona, July 21, 1984. SC.

This joke belongs to a whole cycle of American Indian ethnic jokes making fun of tourists. Folklorist Deirdre Evans-Pritchard has presented and written a good deal on this subject and, in fact, consulted my collection and included this text as an example in her 1987 American Folklore Society Convention presentation.

183. Nineteen-year-old Navajo woman interviewed at Salina Springs Trading Post, Chinle, Arizona, October 9, 1978. SC.

184. Twenty-three-year-old Navajo woman interviewed at Salina Springs Trading Post, Chinle, Arizona, October 8, 1978. SC.

The motion of grinding clearly was mistaken for another motion more commonly performed under blankets.

185. Fifty-one-year-old Navajo man interviewed at Salina Springs Trading Post, Chinle, Arizona, October 9, 1978. SC.

Being struck by lighting is an extremely significant and important event in Navajo culture, and not the least of the grandfather's concern may be the fact that it requires hosting a very expensive feast and ceremony.

186. Thirty-three-year-old Navajo woman interviewed at Leupp, Arizona, July 13, 1973. SC.

Many Navajo have ambiguous attitudes toward medicine men, and these mixed feelings may be reflected in this story.

187. Twenty-four-year-old Navajo woman interviewed at Tsaile, Arizona, July 23, 1983. SC.

188. Fifty-four-year-old Navajo woman interviewed at Pine Hill, New Mexico, May 28, 1986.
This story is similar to the story Clyde told about the *Ye'ii* dancer (number 45).

189. Seventy-six-year-old Navajo woman interviewed near Fence Lake, New Mexico, June 13, 1986.
Clyde translated this story, and his statement "so this is where he made his mistake" is yet another of the insider jokes he shared with us.

190. Fifty-one-year-old Navajo man interviewed at Salina Springs, Arizona, October 9, 1982. SC.

191. Forty-eight-year-old Navajo man interviewed at Chinle, Arizona, March 25, 1986. SC.
The fact that the medicine man stopped the ceremony to satisfy his curiosity about what the women were whispering provides a certain justice to the fact that he was embarrassed.

192. Nineteen-year-old Navajo woman interviewed at Salina Springs, Arizona, July 13, 1973. SC.

193. Fifty-one-year-old Navajo man interviewed at Salina Springs, Arizona, October 9, 1982. SC.
Being bitten by the red ant of the Southwest is not a laughing matter, and babies and small children have been known to die from the effects of multiple bites.
Motif number is K2220, "Treacherous rivals."

194. Thirty-six-year-old Navajo woman interviewed in Flagstaff, Arizona, July 18, 1981. SC.

195. Twenty-year-old Navajo woman interviewed at Salina Springs Trading Post, Chinle, Arizona, October 9, 1978. SC.
The maturation ceremony, *kinaashdaah* in Navajo, is one of the major ceremonies in the life of a Navajo girl because it marks her passage to adulthood.

196. Fifty-two-year-old Navajo man interviewed near Ramah, New Mexico, June 14, 1986.
In 1897 Charles Lummis published a book of short stories entitled *The Enchanted Burro*. The title story is said to have been based on a Isleta Pueblo legend he collected, which in turn was based upon the belief—similar to that reflected in this story—that witches turn themselves into burros. Florence R. Kluckhohn reported the same belief from the Spanish-American culture south of Ramah in her 1961 book *Variations in Value-Orientations: A Theory Tested in Five Cultures*.
Motif number is G211.1, "Witch in form of domestic beast."

197. Twenty-four-year-old Navajo woman interviewed in Flagstaff, Arizona, July 17, 1981. SC.
The story is an excellent narrative and an excellent explanation of Navajo belief concerning skinwalkers.

Motif numbers are C460, "Laughing tabu"; D510, "Transformation by breaking tabu"; G275.12, "Witch in the form of an animal is injured or killed as a a result of the injury to the animal."

198. Fifty-five-year-old Navajo woman interviewed at Burnhams, New Mexico, July 16, 1980. SC.

The implication is that wolf man was no longer a wolf man as a result of his laughing.

Motif numbers are C460, "Laughing tabu"; D510, "Transformation by breaking tabu"; G211.2.2, "Witch in form of bear."

199. Eighty-five-year-old Navajo woman interviewed near Chinle, Arizona, October 8, 1982. SC.

Having the werewolf costume come off when the person wearing it laughs is yet another way of saying that skinwalkers must not laugh or they will return to human form.

Motif numbers are C460, "Laughing tabu"; D510, "Transformation by breaking tabu"; G211.2.2, "Witch in form of wolf."

CHAPTER 6

200. Thirty-four-year-old Hopi woman interviewed at Phoenix, Arizona, August 10, 1987.

201. Thirty-four-year-old Hopi woman interviewed at Phoenix, Arizona, August 10, 1987.

Many of the American Indian tribal groups have scholarship programs, and it is a terrible waste of severely limited resources when, as this story recounts, "seventy or eighty percent" of the people receiving them for a specific program drop out.

202. Thirty-four-year-old Hopi woman interviewed at Phoenix, Arizona, August 10, 1987.

One of the most frequently reported complaints about the government operated facilities for American Indians in urban areas is the time spent waiting to receive services, and the story reflects this common frustration.

203. Thirty-four-year-old Hopi woman interviewed at Phoenix, Arizona, August 10, 1987.

The story centers upon the fact that sometimes Euro-American medicine seems almost as undesirable as the illness it is designed to treat and upon the contrast between Euro-American and Native American medicine.

204. Thirty-four-year-old Hopi woman interviewed at Phoenix, Arizona, August 10, 1987.

This story hints at witchcraft, and the fact that a question about "The Vanishing Hitchhiker" called it forth shows how direct questions may be an effective part of non-directive interviewing.

Motif number is D630, "Transformation and disenchantment at will."

205. Thirty-four-year-old Hopi woman interviewed at Phoenix, Arizona, August 10, 1987.

Motif numbers are A120.1, "God as shape-shifter"; K1811, "Gods (saints) in disguise visit mortals"; A125.; "Deity in human form"; D2095, "Magic disappearance."

206. Thirty-four-year-old Hopi woman interviewed at Phoenix, Arizona, August 10, 1987.
Motif numbers are A120.1, "God as shape-shifter"; K1811, "Gods (saints) in disguise visit mortals"; A125.; "Deity in human form"; D2095, "Magic disappearance."

207. Thirty-four-year-old Hopi woman interviewed at Phoenix, Arizona, August 10, 1987.
Motif numbers are B147.2.2.4, "Owl as bird of ill-omen"; B143.0.3, "Owl as prophetic bird"; M341, "Death prophesied."

208. Thirty-four-year-old Hopi woman interviewed at Phoenix, Arizona, August 10, 1987.

209. Thirty-four-year-old Hopi woman interviewed at Phoenix, Arizona, August 10, 1987.
The procedure described for divorce in this story is typical of the practice of many matrilocal American Indian societies. In the past, the woman wishing to terminate a marriage put the man's saddle outside the door of the home, and this modern story says that she puts his clothes outside to achieve the same result. One divorce we knew at Zuni was announced by the wife's putting her husband's stereo and tapes on the porch of her home. He got the message.

210. Thirty-four-year-old Hopi woman interviewed at Phoenix, Arizona, August 10, 1987.
Childhood rearing practices that prepare children for the adult world in which they must live are—by definition—functional and good; a Hopi boy needs to learn "that's just how girls are."

211. Thirty-four-year-old Hopi woman interviewed at Phoenix, Arizona, August 10, 1987.

212. Thirty-four-year-old Hopi woman interviewed at Phoenix, Arizona, August 10, 1987.
In Hopi tradition, the dying matriarch is expected to devote her last thoughts and words to the future of the family because she has special knowledge as a result of her nearness to death; the only thing unusual about this story is the fact that this final speech was videotaped. There is also in this story a sense of sympathy for Anglo-Americans who—unlike the Hopi—"don't know where they have come from."
Motif number is J155, "Wise words of dying woman (queen)."

213. Thirty-one-year-old Zuni man interviewed at Phoenix, Arizona, May 17, 1987.
Denny is as much at home in the urban white world as any urban American Indian we interviewed, and he measures time in terms of the American Indian unit of four rather than in terms of the Anglo-American equally pervasive sets of three—and he participated when his family sponsored a dance at Zuni. We took a twenty-five pound bag of Bluebird flour and a case of Shasta pop to his family's Shalako house, we ate with

them, we saw him and his son sitting in the sponsors' place bedecked with their family's and clan's ceremonial necklaces and bracelets—and it regenerated our batteries, too. Motif number is V4, "Value of religious exercise."

214. Twenty-nine-year-old San Carlos Apache woman interviewed at Phoenix, Arizona, August 10, 1987.

215. Forty-year-old Osage woman interviewed at Phoenix, Arizona, August 11, 1987.
The roach, a roll of hair brushed straight back from the sides of the head (or a ceremonial headdress resembling it), is a mark of maturity which can only be worn after a special ceremony.

216. Forty-year-old Osage woman interviewed at Phoenix, Arizona, August 11, 1987.

217. Forty-year-old Osage woman interviewed at Phoenix, Arizona, August 11, 1987.
Deer Woman is a supernatural figure in Osage stories. She attempted to seduce men, and they died if she succeeded. This storyteller, however, is obviously somewhat removed from the tradition and is only vaguely aware of the details of the stories concerning this figure.
Motif numbers are F517.1, "Person unusual as to his feet"; F551.5, "Animal foot on human being."

218. Forty-year-old Osage woman interviewed at Phoenix, Arizona, August 11, 1987.
His story is probably one of the most frequently told stories all across America and often plays a major role in the development of humor in children. It is so familiar that it has seldom been reported.
Motif number is X700, "Humor concerning sex."

219. Forty-year-old Osage woman interviewed at Phoenix, Arizona, August 11, 1987.

220. Forty-year-old Osage woman interviewed at Phoenix, Arizona, August 11, 1987.
Rightly or wrongly many American Indians share a certain amount of resentment toward anthropologists they feel have exploited them.
Motif number is X460, "Humor concerning other professions."

221. Forty-year-old Osage woman interviewed at Phoenix, Arizona, August 11, 1987.
This story is a joke told by outsiders and is basically directed toward the Osage.

222. Forty-year-old Osage woman interviewed at Phoenix, Arizona, August 11, 1987.
This story is an insiders' joke the Osage tell about themselves.

223. Forty-one-year-old Pima woman interviewed at Phoenix, Arizona, August 11, 1987.

This is more a summary of "The Pet in the Microwave" contemporary legend than it is an actual telling of it.

224. Forty-one-year-old Pima woman interviewed at Phoenix, Arizona, August 11, 1987.

Either Baughman motif number E332.3.3.1 (c), "Ghost of recently drowned girl leaves water spot on automobile seat"; or Baughman E332.3.3.1(d), "Woman or old woman given ride in automobile, makes a prediction or prophecy; she disappears suddenly or gives other evidence of ghostly nature" might apply to the original story; there simply is not enough information to tell. There is also a motif number Z13.1, "Tale-teller frightens listener: yells 'boo' at exciting point," but in this case it was a member of the audience who yelled.

225. Forty-one-year-old Pima woman interviewed at Phoenix, Arizona, August 11, 1987.

Some stories in some cultures function primarily as cautionary tales warning against behavior the culture finds dangerous or unacceptable; this tale is one such story. It is also interesting that this Pima Hoof Man is reported to have deer or antelope feet rather than the chicken feet or cows' or goats' hooves which usually identify the otherwise similar figure in Mexican-American tradition.

Baughman motif number is G303.6.2.1, "Devil appears at dance."

Thompson motif numbers are G303.3.1.2, "Devil as well-dressed man"; F517.1, "Person unusual as to his feet"; F551.5, "Animal foot on human being"; G303.4.5, "The Devil's feet and legs."

226. Thirty-three-year-old Hopi woman interviewed at Phoenix, Arizona, August 11, 1987.

This storyteller indicates that language is an important part—but by no means the only part—of being traditional.

227. Thirty-three-year-old Hopi woman interviewed at Phoenix, Arizona, August 11, 1987.

This is a retelling of a Pima legend by a Hopi and is unusual in that the mysterious stranger is described as having hooves for hands as well as for feet.

Baughman motif number is G303.6.2.1, "Devil appears at dance."

Thompson motif numbers are F517.1, "Person unusual as to his feet"; F551.5, "Animal foot on human being"; G303.4.5, "The Devil's feet and legs."

228. Thirty-three-year-old Hopi woman interviewed at Phoenix, Arizona, August 11, 1987.

Motif number is E332.3.3.1, "The Vanishing Hitchhiker."

229. Forty-three-year-old San Juan Pueblo man interviewed at Phoenix, Arizona, September 11, 1987.

This highly articulate storyteller indicates that his tribal ceremonies' major function for him is to assert his identity.

230. Forty-three-year-old San Juan Pueblo man interviewed at Phoenix, Arizona, September 11, 1987.

Motif numbers are G263.4, "Witch causes sickness"; D2064, "Magic sickness"; D700, "Person disenchanted."

231. Forty-three-year-old San Juan Pueblo man interviewed at Phoenix, Arizona, September 11, 1987.
Motif numbers are G272, "Protection against witches"; G272.16, "Salt protects against witches."

232. Forty-three-year-old San Juan Pueblo man interviewed at Phoenix, Arizona, September 11, 1987.
The storyteller's analysis of the cross-cultural meaning of this contemporary legend is unusual and insightful.

233. Forty-three-year-old San Juan Pueblo man interviewed at Phoenix, Arizona, September 11, 1987.
The San Juan storyteller is careful to assert that this story, a version of "The Vanishing Hitchhiker," is true.
Baughman motif number is E581.8, "Ghost rides in automobile."

234. Forty-three-year-old San Juan Pueblo man interviewed at Phoenix, Arizona, September 11, 1987.
The San Juan storyteller is careful to assert that this story, a Spanish-American version of "The Devil at the Dance," is superstition.
Motif numbers are G303.3.1.2, "Devil as well-dressed man"; F517.1, "Person unusual as to his feet"; F551.5, "Animal foot on human being"; G303.4.5, "The Devil's feet and legs."

235. Forty-one-year-old Shoshoni woman interviewed at Phoenix, Arizona, September 11, 1987.
American Indian and Euro-American medicine are very much alike in one very basic way—there is one illness or accident per patient which they cannot cure.

236. Forty-one-year-old Shoshoni woman interviewed at Phoenix, Arizona, September 11, 1987.

237. Thirty-four-year-old Hopi woman interviewed at Phoenix, Arizona, September 12, 1987.
This Hopi woman implicitly defines traditionality as knowing culture and language.

238. Thirty-four-year-old Hopi woman interviewed at Phoenix, Arizona, September 12, 1987.
Contemporary legends are frequently ascribed to newspapers, and newspapers frequently report contemporary legends.

239. Thirty-three-year-old Ute woman interviewed at Phoenix, Arizona, September 18, 1987.

240. Thirty-three-year-old Ute woman interviewed at Phoenix, Arizona, September 18, 1987.
"Something like that" probably indicates witchcraft.

241. Thirty-three-year-old Ute woman interviewed at Phoenix, Arizona, September 18, 1987.

242. Thirty-three-year-old Ute woman interviewed at Phoenix, Arizona, September 18, 1987.
Baughman motif number is E581.8, "Ghost rides in automobile."

243. Nineteen-year-old Standing Rock Sioux man interviewed at Phoenix, Arizona, September 18, 1987.
There are echoes of American Indian oratory, a highly valued oral performance form, in this assertion of traditionality.

244. Nineteen-year-old Standing Rock Sioux man interviewed at Phoenix, Arizona, September 18, 1987.
After telling of having been treated by a medicine man, this skilled storyteller mentioned the Sioux Sun Dance as one "of the things" he had seen which "make the hair stand up on the back of your neck." In this ceremony—vividly portrayed in the film *A Man Called Horse*—pointed objects are thrust under the skin on a man's chest and attached to ropes; the participant runs and pulls until he rips his skin and breaks loose.
Motif numbers are F1041.2, "Horripilation, hair rises on end in extraordinary fashion from joy, anger, or love"; D2161, "Magic healing power."

245. Nineteen-year-old Standing Rock Sioux man interviewed at Phoenix, Arizona, September 18, 1987.
Motif numbers are G303.3.1.2, "Devil as well-dressed man"; F517.1, "Person unusual as to his feet"; F551.5, "Animal foot on human being"; G303.4.5, "The Devil's feet and legs"; Q220.1, "Devil plagues impious people."

246. Nineteen-year-old Standing Rock Sioux man interviewed at Phoenix, Arizona, September 18, 1987.
The Sioux, as well as several other American Indian tribes, have traditional stories of "the little people."
Motif numbers are F451.4, "Dwarfs live under the ground"; F451.5.2.2, "Dwarfs steal from human beings."

247. Nineteen-year-old Standing Rock Sioux man interviewed at Phoenix, Arizona, September 18, 1987.
The peace pipe has long been and remains a central part of Sioux ceremony, and—at various times, at various places—whites have taken away the pipes and forbidden their use.
Motif number is D1531, "Magic object gives power of flight."

248. Seventy-one-year-old Cherokee woman interviewed at Phoenix, Arizona, September 18, 1987.

249. Seventy-one-year-old Cherokee woman interviewed at Phoenix, Arizona, September 18, 1987.
Motif number is B147.2.2.5, "Eagle as bird of ill-omen."

250. Seventy-one-year-old Cherokee woman interviewed at Phoenix, Arizona, September 18, 1987.

251. Seventy-one-year-old Cherokee woman interviewed at Phoenix, Arizona, September 18, 1987.

252. Nineteen-year-old Pima woman interviewed at Phoenix, Arizona, September 18, 1987.

253. Nineteen-year-old Pima woman interviewed at Phoenix, Arizona, September 18, 1987.

254. Nineteen-year-old Pima woman interviewed at Phoenix, Arizona, September 18, 1987.
Motif numbers are F517.1, "Person unusual as to his feet"; F551.5, "Animal foot on human being"; G303.4.5, "The Devil's feet and legs"; M211, "Man sells soul to Devil."

CHAPTER 7

255. Fifty-eight-year-old Navajo woman interviewed near Ramah, New Mexico, May 29, 1986.
Motif numbers E545.0.2, "The dead are silent"; E425.1, "Revenant a woman"; E423.2, "Revenant as wild animal"; E544, "Ghost leaves evidence of his appearance"; J1117.2, "Coyote as trickster" are all implicit in this story.

256. James F. Downs, *The Navajo* (New York: Holt, Rinehart and Winston, 1972), 104-05.

257. Erna Fergusson, *Dancing Gods* (Albuquerque: University of New Mexico Press, 1931), 207.

258. Thirty-four-year-old Hopi woman interviewed at Phoenix, Arizona, August 10, 1987.
Motif numbers are A120.1, "God as shape-shifter"; K1811, "Gods (saints) in disguise visit mortals"; A125, "Deity in human form"; D2095, "Magic disappearance."

259. Thirty-four-year-old Hopi woman interviewed at Phoenix, Arizona, August 10, 1987.
Motif numbers are A120.1, "God as shape-shifter"; K1811, "Gods (saints) in disguise visit mortals"; A125, "Deity in human form"; D2095, "Magic disappearance."

260. Seventy-year-old Zuni woman interviewed at Zuni, New Mexico, June 10, 1988.
After Kuiceyetsa told the story, she said that Cushing had published it, pulled out a copy of his *Zuni Folk Tales*, and opened it to the lead story in which a man unsuccessfully seeks the return of his wife from the land of the dead. Her sense that the stories are the same indicates that for her the major emphasis of the stories is the journey to Zuni heaven to be united with a spirit spouse or sweetheart. Kuiceyetsa's story is even more similar to the version Parsons published in "Notes on Zuni" (302-07) than it is to Cushing's, for in her account—as in Parsons'—the attempt is successful.
Motif numbers are F6991, "Marvelous dancer"; F80, "Journey to lower world."

Works Cited

Beardsley, Richard K., and Rosalie Hankey. "The Vanishing Hitchhiker." *California Folklore Quarterly* 1 (1943): 303-35.

Benedict, Ruth. *Patterns of Culture.* Boston and New York: Houghton Mifflin, 1934.

———. *Zuni Mythology.* 2 vols. 1939. Reprint. New York: AMS Press, 1969.

Brunvand, Jan H. *The Choking Doberman and Other "New" Urban Legends.* New York: Norton, 1984.

———. *Curses! Broiled Again!* New York: Norton, 1989.

———. *The Mexican Pet: More "New" Urban Legends and Some Old Favorites.* New York: Norton, 1986.

———. *The Study of American Folklore: An Introduction.* 2nd ed. New York: Norton, 1978.

———. *The Vanishing Hitchhiker: American Urban Legends and Their Meanings.* New York: Norton, 1981.

Bullard, Thomas E. "UFO Abduction Reports: The Supernatural Kidnap Narrative Returns in Technological Guise." *Journal of American Folklore* 102 (1989): 147-70.

Bunzel, Ruth. Foreword. *Chichicastenango: A Guatemalan Village.* Locust Valley, New York: J. J. Augustin, 1952.

Chadney, James G. "Male and Female Dominance in Preindustrial Societies: A Reexamination of the Cross-Cultural Codes." Western Social Science Association 32nd Annual Conference, Portland, Oregon. 26 April 1990.

Cunningham, Keith. "Hot Dog! Another Urban Belief Tale." *Southwest Folklore* 3 (1979): 27-28.

Cushing, Frank H. *My Adventures in Zuni.* 1882. Reprint. Santa Fe, NM: The Peripatetic Press, 1941.

———. *Zuni Folk Tales.* 1901. Reprint. Tucson: University of Arizona Press, 1986.

Davies, Christie. *Ethnic Humor Around the World: A Comparative Analysis.* Bloomington: Indiana University Press, 1990.

Dorson, Richard M. *America in Legend: Folklore from the Colonial Period to the Present.* New York: Pantheon Books, 1973.

Douglas, Sheila. "Practical Jokes and the Legends Surrounding Them." In *Monsters with Iron Teeth: Perspectives on Contemporary Legend,* edited by Gillian Bennett and Paul Smith, 241-43. Sheffield, Eng.: Sheffield Academic Press, 1988.

Downs, James F. *The Navajo.* New York: Holt, Rinehart and Winston, 1972.

Evans-Pritchard, Deirdre. "'When the New World Comes, the White People Will Be Indians and the Indians Will Be White People.'" American Folklore Society Annual Meeting, Albuquerque, New Mexico. 24 October 1987.

Fergusson, Erna. *Dancing Gods.* Albuquerque: University of New Mexico Press, 1931.

Fine, Gary Alan. "Cokelore and Coke Law: Urban Belief Tales and the Problem of Multiple Origins." *Journal of American Folklore* 92 (1979): 477-82.

———. "The Kentucky Fried Rat: Legends and Modern Mass Society." *Journal of the Folklore Institute* (1980): 222-43.

Fish, Lydia M. "Jesus on the Thruway: The Vanishing Hitchhiker Strikes Again." *Indiana Folklore* 9 (1976): 5-13.

Goldman, Irving. "The Zuni Indians of New Mexico." *Cooperation and Competition Among Primitive Peoples,* edited by Margaret Mead, 313-53. 1937. Reprint. Boston: Beacon Press, 1961.

Hill, W. W. *Navaho Humor.* Menasha, WI: Banta, 1943.

Hufford, David J., and Genevieve W. Foster. *The World Was Flooded with Light: A Mystical Experience Remembered.* Pittsburgh: University of Pittsburgh Press, 1985.

Jung, Carl G. *Psychological Types, or the Psychology of Individuation.* Trans. H. Godwin Baynes. *Collected Works,* vol. 13. New York: Pantheon Books, 1964.

Kluckhohn, Clyde. *Navaho Witchcraft.* 1944. Reprint. Boston: Beacon Press, 1967.

———. "Patterning as Exemplified in Navaho Culture." In *Language, Culture, and Personality,* edited by L. Spier, A. I. Hallowell, and S. S. Newman, 109-30. Menasha, WI: Sapir Memorial Publication Fund, 1941.

Kluckhohn, Florence R., and Fred L. Strodtbeck. *Variations in Value-Orientations: A Theory Tested in Five Cultures.* Evanston, IL: Row, Peterson and Company, 1961.

Leary, James P. *Midwestern Folk Humor: Jokes on Farming, Logging, Religion and Traditional Ways.* Little Rock: August House, 1991.

Leighton, Dorothea C., and Clyde Kluckhohn. *Children of the People.* Cambridge, MA: Harvard University Press, 1947.

Li An-Che. "Zuni: Some Observations and Queries." *American Anthropologist* 39 (1937): 62-76.

Lummis, Charles F. *The Enchanted Burro: And Other Stories as I Have Known Them from Maine to Chile to California.* Chicago: A. C. McClurg and Company, 1897.

Newman, Stanley. *Zuni Dictionary.* Indiana University Research Center in Anthropology, Folklore, and Linguistics no. 6. Bloomington, 1958.

Pandey, Triloki Nath. "Anthropologists at Zuni." *Proceedings of the American Philosophical Society* 116 (1972): 321-37.

———. "'India Man' Among American Indians." In *Encounter and Experience: Personal Accounts of Fieldwork,* edited by Andre Beteille and T. N. Madan, 194-213. Honolulu: University Press of Hawaii, 1975.

Parsons, Elsie Clews. "Notes on Zuni." In *Memoirs of the American Anthropological Association* 4 (1917): 151-325.

———. "Navaho Folk Tales." *Journal of American Folklore* 36 (1923): 368-75.

Sanarov, Valerii I. "On the Nature and Origin of Flying Saucers and Little Green Men." *Current Anthropology* 22 (1981): 163-67.

Stahl, Sandra Kay Dolby. "The Personal Narrative As a Folklore Genre." Diss. Indiana University, 1975.

Stevenson, Matilda Coxe. *The Zuni Indians: Their Mythology, Esoteric Societies, and Ceremonies.* 1904. Reprint. Glorieta, NM: The Rio Grande Press, 1985.

Tedlock, Dennis. *The Spoken Word and the Work of Interpretation.* Philadelphia: University of Pennsylvania Press, 1983.

———. "The Witches Were Saved: A Zuni Origin Story." *Journal of American Folklore* 101 (1988): 312-20.

Index of Storytellers
(with story numbers)

ANGLO-AMERICAN
1. Twenty-two-year-old woman: 44.
2. Twenty-four-year-old woman: 43.
3. Twenty-four-year-old man: 41.
4. Twenty-four-year-old man: 42.

CHEROKEE
Mary: 248, 249, 250, 251.

HOPI
1. Thirty-three-year-old woman: 226, 227, 228.
2. Thirty-four-year-old woman: 200, 201, 202, 203, 204, 205, 206, 207, 208, 209, 210, 211, 212, 258, 259.
3. Thirty-four-year-old woman: 237, 238.

NAVAJO
1. Cora: 48, 80, 140.
2. Linda: 60, 74, 75, 145, 176.
3. Eighteen-year-old woman: 148.
4. Nineteen-year-old woman: 129, 132.
5. Nineteen-year-old woman: 160.
6. Nineteen-year-old woman: 183, 192.
7. Nineteen-year-old woman: 164.
8. Twenty-year-old woman: 165.
9. Twenty-year-old woman: 195.
10. Twenty-one-year-old woman: 54.
11. Twenty-one-year-old woman: 179.
12. Twenty-two-year-old woman: 82.
13. Twenty-two-year-old woman: 157, 173.
14. Twenty-two-year-old woman: 159.
15. Twenty-three-year-old woman: 184.
16. Twenty-four-year-old woman: 187.

17. Twenty-four-year-old woman: 197.
18. Twenty-six-year-old woman: 172.
19. Twenty-eight-year-old woman: 47, 52, 53.
20. Twenty-eight-year-old woman: 64.
21. Thirty-year-old woman: 182.
22. Thirty-two-year-old woman: 161.
23. Thirty-three-year-old woman: 51, 63, 136.
24. Thirty-three-year-old woman: 55.
25. Thirty-three-year-old woman: 65.
26. Thirty-three-year-old woman: 66, 67, 138, 170.
27. Thirty-three-year-old woman: 150.
28. Thirty-three-year-old woman: 186.
29. Thirty-four-year-old woman: 155.
30. Thirty-six-year-old woman: 194.
31. Fifty-three-year-old woman: 56, 57.
32. Fifty-four-year-old woman: 68, 87, 137, 175, 188.
33. Fifty-four-year-old woman: 181.
34. Fifty-five-year-old woman: 198.
35. Fifty-seven-year-old woman: 178.
36. Fifty-eight-year-old woman: 70, 81, 141, 255.
37. Fifty-eight-year-old woman: 133.
38. Sixty-two-year-old woman: 152.
39. Sixty-nine-year-old woman: 142.
40. Seventy-six-year-old woman: 61, 77, 84, 189.
41. Seventy-nine-year-old woman: 59.
42. Eighty-five-year-old woman: 199.
43. Eighty-six-year-old woman: 156.
44. Ninety-year-old woman: 73, 144.
45. Clyde: 45, 78, 85, 88, 127, 130, 168, 196.
46. Mr. Lopez: 147.
47. Nineteen-year-old man: 134.
48. Twenty-seven-year-old man: 72, 143, 166.
49. Twenty-seven-year-old man: 162.
50. Twenty-eight-year-old man: 76, 146, 167, 177.
51. Twenty-nine-year-old man: 50, 135.
52. Twenty-nine-year-old man: 153, 158, 174.
53. Thirty-one-year-old man: 169.
54. Thirty-four-year-old man: 149.
55. Thirty-four-year-old man: 163.
56. Thirty-seven-year-old man: 128.
57. Thirty-eight-year-old man: 71, 83.

Index of Places Where Stories Were Collected
(with story numbers)

ARIZONA
Chinle: 128, 129, 148, 150, 156, 191, 199.
Flagstaff: 41, 42, 43, 44, 131, 134, 149, 153, 155, 157, 158, 59, 160, 161, 162, 164, 165, 169, 171, 172, 173, 174, 179, 194, 197.
Ganado: 152, 154.
Leupp: 186.
Phoenix: 200, 201, 202, 203, 204, 205, 206, 207, 208, 209, 210, 211, 212, 213, 214, 215, 216, 217, 218, 219, 220, 221, 222, 223, 224, 225, 226, 227, 228, 229, 230, 231, 232, 233, 234, 235, 236, 237, 238, 239, 240, 241, 242, 243, 244, 245, 246, 247, 248, 249, 250, 251, 252, 253, 254, 258, 259.
Red Valley: 182.
Salina Springs Trading Post: 132, 180, 183, 184, 185, 190, 192, 193, 195.
St. Michaels: 163.
Tsaile: 187.
Tuba City: 133.
Window Rock: 181.

NEW MEXICO
Burnhams: 198.
Fence Lake area: 45, 61, 76, 77, 84, 146, 147, 167, 177, 189.
Mountain View area: 48, 58, 69, 80, 139, 140.
Pine Hill: 66, 67, 68, 87, 137, 138, 170, 175, 188.
Ramah area: 46, 47, 49, 50, 51, 52, 53, 54, 55, 59, 60, 63, 64, 65, 70, 71, 72, 73, 74, 75, 78, 81, 82, 83, 85, 86, 88, 127, 130, 135, 136, 141, 142, 143, 144, 145, 151, 166, 168, 176, 196, 255.
Ramah: 56, 57.
Shiprock: 178.
Zuni: 1, 2, 3, 4, 5, 6, 7, 8, 9, 10, 11, 12, 13, 14, 15, 16, 17, 18, 19, 20, 21, 22, 23, 24, 25, 26, 27, 28, 29, 30, 31, 32, 33, 34, 35, 36, 37, 38, 39, 40, 62, 79, 89, 90, 91, 92, 93, 94, 95, 96, 97, 98, 99, 100, 101, 102, 103, 104, 105,